Praise for *Aristotle*

"Hall's new book clears a rare middle way for her reader to pursue happiness. . . . *Aristotle's Way* carefully charts the arc of a virtuous life that springs from youthful talent, grows by way of responsible decisions and self-reflection, finds expression in mature relationships, and comes to rest in joyful retirement and a quietly reverent death. Easier said than done, but Aristotle, Hall explains, is there to help."

—*The New York Times Book Review*

"Hall explains some of the philosopher's most complex ideas in an approachable way, covering his notes on everything from the power of community to understanding your goals and why you should always consult a third party when making a decision. . . . When it comes to happiness, perhaps it's actually time to say out with the new and in with the old." —*Time*

"In clear, patient language, Hall deftly weaves threads pulled from this daunting range of material into lessons that pertain directly to dilemmas of modern life. . . . We are told that Hall 'first encountered Aristotle when she was twenty, and he changed her life forever,' one of the book's strengths is her tone of unmistakable sincerity." —*American Scholar*

"[A] lucid account . . . Nontechnical but deeply grounded . . . Can happiness come from virtue? This lively book makes a good argument in the affirmative." —*Kirkus Reviews*

"Delivers an expansive, practical assessment of Aristotle . . . She handles weighty, difficult topics such as depression and everyday tasks such as preparing for an important meeting or job interview with the same measured, clear prose. . . . Her book is an engaging, thrilling approach to Aristotle's pragmatic thought. It is a useful introduction to the ideas of one of the most important philosophers in world history."

—*Publishers Weekly*

PENGUIN BOOKS

ARISTOTLE'S WAY

Edith Hall first encountered Aristotle when she was twenty, and he changed her life forever. Now one of Britain's foremost classicists and a professor at King's College London, she is the first woman to have won the Erasmus Medal of the European Academy. In 2017 she was awarded an honorary doctorate from Athens University, just a few streets away from Aristotle's own Lyceum. She is the author of several books, including *Introducing the Ancient Greeks*. She lives with her family in Cambridgeshire.

Also by Edith Hall

The Ancient Greeks: Ten Ways They Shaped the Modern World

Aristotle's Way

HOW ANCIENT WISDOM CAN CHANGE YOUR LIFE

EDITH HALL

PENGUIN BOOKS

PENGUIN BOOKS

An imprint of Penguin Random House LLC

penguinrandomhouse.com

First published in Great Britain by The Bodley Head,
an imprint of Penguin Random House UK, 2018
First published in the United States of America by Penguin Press,
an imprint of Penguin Random House LLC, 2019
Published in Penguin Books 2020

Map illustration by Emmy Lopes

LIBRARY OF CONGRESS CATALOGING-IN-PUBLICATION DATA
Names: Hall, Edith, 1959– author.
Title: Aristotle's way : how ancient wisdom can change your life / Edith Hall.
Description: New York : Penguin Books, 2020. | Originally published: London :
The Bodley Head, 2018. | Includes bibliographical references and index.
Identifiers: LCCN 2019026256 (print) | LCCN 2019026257 (ebook) |
ISBN 9780735220829 (paperback) | ISBN 9780735220812 (ebook)
Subjects: LCSH: Aristotle. | Happiness. | Life.
Classification: LCC B491.H36 H35 2020 (print) |
LCC B491.H36 (ebook) | DDC 171/.3—dc23
LC record available at https://lccn.loc.gov/2019026256
LC ebook record available at https://lccn.loc.gov/2019026257

Printed in the United States of America
3 5 7 9 10 8 6 4

This book is dedicated to the memory of
Aristotle the Stageirite, son of Nicomachus and Phaestis

CONTENTS

TIMELINE (ALL DATES BCE)

384   Aristotle is born in Stageira to Nicomachus and Phaestis.

c.372   Aristotle's father dies and he is adopted by Proxenus of Atarneus.

c.367   Aristotle moves to Athens to study at Plato's Academy.

348   Philip II of Macedon destroys Stageira but rebuilds it on Aristotle's request.

347   Aristotle leaves Athens when Plato dies and joins Hermias, ruler of Assos.

345–344 Aristotle conducts zoological research on Lesbos.

343   Philip II invites Aristotle to teach his son Alexander in Macedon.

338–336 Aristotle may have spent time in Epirus and Illyria.

336   Philip II is assassinated and Alexander becomes King Alexander III ("the Great"). Aristotle moves to Athens and founds his Lyceum.

323   Alexander III dies in Babylon.

322   Aristotle is prosecuted for impiety at Athens and moves to Chalkis, where he dies.

The places where Aristotle lived are shown in bold. The dotted areas indicate the Greek-speaking world of the fourth century BCE.

Aristotle's Way

Introduction

⸺⟩⟨⟨⟨⟨⟩⸺

The words "happy" and "happiness" work hard. You can buy a Happy Meal, or drink a cheap cocktail during happy hour. You can pop "happy pills" to improve your mood or post a "happy" emoji on social media. We value happiness highly. Singer Pharrell Williams' song "Happy" was number one and the bestselling song of 2014 in the United States, as well as in twenty-three other countries. Happiness, according to Williams, was a transitory moment of elation, or feeling like a hot-air balloon.

Yet we are confused about happiness. Almost everyone believes that they want to be happy, which usually means a lasting psychological state of contentment (despite what Williams sings). If you tell your children that you "just want them to be happy," you mean permanently. Paradoxically, in our everyday conversations, happiness far more often refers to the trivial and temporary glee of a meal, cocktail, e-mail message. Or, as Lucy in the *Peanuts* comic strip put it after hugging Snoopy, an encounter with "a warm puppy." A "happy birthday" is a few hours of enjoyment to celebrate the anniversary of your birth.

What if happiness were a lifelong state of being? Philosophers are divided into two main camps about what that would actually mean. On one side, happiness is objective, and can be appreciated, even evaluated, by an onlooker or historian. It means having, for example, good health, longevity, a loving family, freedom from financial problems or anxiety.

According to this definition, Queen Victoria, who lived to over eighty, gave birth to nine children who survived into adulthood and was admired around the world, had a clearly "happy" life. But Marie Antoinette was clearly "unhappy": two of her four children died in infancy, she was reviled by her people and executed while still in her thirties.

Most books about happiness refer to this objective "well-being" definition, as do the studies set up by governments to measure the happiness of their citizens on an international scale. Since 2013, on 20 March every year the United Nations has celebrated the International Day of Happiness, which seeks to promote measurable happiness by ending poverty, reducing inequality and protecting the planet.

But on the other side are philosophers who reject this, and instead understand happiness subjectively. To them, happiness is not akin to "well-being" but to "contentment" or "felicity." According to this view, no onlooker can know if someone is happy or not, and it is possible that the most outwardly boisterous person might be suffering from deep melancholy. This subjective happiness can be described, but not measured. We cannot assess whether Marie Antoinette or Queen Victoria was happier for a greater proportion of her time alive. Perhaps Marie Antoinette enjoyed long hours of intense gratification, and Victoria never did, having been widowed early and having lived for years in seclusion.

Aristotle was the first philosopher to inquire into this second kind of subjective happiness. He developed a sophisticated, humane program for becoming a happy person, and it remains valid to this day. Aristotle provides everything you need to avoid the realization of the dying protagonist of Tolstoy's *The Death of Ivan Ilyich* (1886), that he has wasted much of his life scaling the social ladder, and putting self-interest above compassion and community values, all the while married to a woman he dislikes. Facing his imminent death, he hates his closest family members, who won't even talk to him about it. Aristotelian ethics encompass everything modern thinkers associate with subjective happiness: self-realization, finding "a meaning," and the "flow" of creative involvement with life, or "positive emotion."[1]

This book presents Aristotle's time-honored ethics in contemporary language. It applies Aristotle's lessons to several practical real-life challenges: decision-making, writing a job application, communicating in an interview, using Aristotle's chart of Virtues and Vices to analyze your own character, resisting temptation, and choosing friends and partners.

Wherever you are in life, Aristotle's ideas can make you happier. Few philosophers, mystics, psychologists, or sociologists have ever done much more than restate his fundamental perceptions. But he stated them first, better, more clearly, and in a more holistic way than anyone subsequently. Each part of his prescription for being happy relates to a different phase of human life, but also intersects with all the others.

Becoming subjectively happy as an individual, Aristotle insisted, is your unique and momentous responsibility. It is also a great gift—it is within most people's power, regardless of their circumstances, to *decide* to become happier. But understanding happiness as an internal, personal state is still ambiguous. What is happiness, then? Modern philosophers come at subjective happiness from three different directions.

The first approach is connected with psychology and psychiatric medicine, and suggests that happiness is the opposite of depression, a private emotional state experienced as a continuous sequence of moods. It involves a positive, upbeat attitude. It could, theoretically, be enjoyed by someone without aspirations, who sat watching television all day every day, but felt permanently in good spirits. This might be a matter of temperament, perhaps inherited (a cheerful disposition does seem to run in families). According to some eastern philosophies, this emotional state can be cultivated by techniques like transcendental meditation. Western philosophers speculate it may even be related to naturally high levels of the chemical serotonin, the neurotransmitter many physicians and psychiatrists believe is crucial to the maintenance of mood balance and that is deficient in depressed people. A buoyant disposition is enviable, but many of us are not born with it. Modern antidepressants, which can benefit people either in temporary grief in reaction to life events, or suffering from "endogenous," persistent depression, mostly enhance the levels of serotonin. But is a cheerful outlook happiness? Can a life spent watching television qualify as happiness? Aristotle, for whom happiness required the fulfillment of human potentialities, would have said no. John F. Kennedy summed up Aristotelian happiness in a single sentence: "The full use of your powers along lines of excellence in a life affording scope."

The second contemporary philosophical approach to subjective happiness is "hedonism"—the idea that happiness is defined by the total proportion of our lives we spend enjoying ourselves, experiencing pleasure, or feeling delight and ecstasy. Hedonism (the word comes from *hedone*, the ancient Greek word for "pleasure") has ancient roots. The Indian school of philosophy known as Charvaka, founded in the sixth century BCE, espoused the view that "the enjoyment of heaven lies in eating delicious food, keeping company of young women, using fine clothes, perfumes, garlands, sandal paste. A fool wears himself out by penances and fasts."[2] A century later, one of Socrates' students, Aristippus from Cyrene in North Africa, developed a system of ethics called "hedonistic egoism." He wrote a book *On Ancient Luxury* about the exploits of pleasure-seeking philosophers. Aristippus averred that everyone should experience as much physical and sensory pleasure as soon as possible, without concern for the consequences.

Hedonism became fashionable again when the utilitarians, beginning with Jeremy Bentham (1748–1832), argued that the correct basis for moral decisions and action was whatever would achieve the greatest happiness for the greatest number. Bentham believed that this principle could help in the creation of laws. In his 1789 manifesto, *An Introduction to the Principles of Morals and Legislation*, he actually designed an algorithm for quantitative hedonism, to measure the total pleasure quotient produced by any given action. The algorithm is often called the "hedonic calculus." Bentham laid out the variables: how *intense* is the pleasure? How long will it last? Is it an inevitable or only possible result of the action I am considering? How soon will it happen? Will it be productive and give rise to further pleasure? Will it guarantee no painful consequences? How many people will experience it?

Bentham was interested in the total amount, rather than the type of pleasure. Quantity not quality. If film actor Errol Flynn was telling the truth about his mental experience in his dying words—"I've had a hell of a lot of fun and I've enjoyed every minute of it," reportedly—then according to the quantitative hedonist, he had been a very happy man indeed.

But what did Errol Flynn mean by "fun" and "enjoyment"? For Bentham's disciple, John Stuart Mill, "quantitative hedonism" did not distinguish human happiness from the happiness of pigs, which could be provided with incessant physical pleasures. So Mill introduced the idea that there were different levels and types of pleasure. Bodily pleasures that we share with animals, such as the pleasure we gain from eating or sex, are "lower" pleasures. Mental pleasures, such as those we derive from the arts, intellectual debate or good behavior, are "higher" and more valuable. This version of hedonist philosophical theory is usually called prudential hedonism or qualitative hedonism.

Few twenty-first-century philosophers advocate hedonistic approaches to achieving subjective happiness. The theory was dealt a severe blow in 1974 when Harvard professor Robert Nozick published *Anarchy, State, and Utopia*, in which he envisioned a machine capable of giving people continuous pleasurable experiences throughout their lives. These people would not be able to differentiate these simulated machine experiences from "real life." Would anyone choose to be hooked up to the machine? No. We want reality. Therefore, logically speaking, people do *not* regard favorable sensations as the exclusive determining factor in overall subjective happiness.

Nozick was writing just before the dawn of the age of mass ownership of computers and the idea of virtual reality. His thought experiment grabbed the public imagination, and was associated with the "Orgasmatron" machine in Woody Allen's movie *Sleeper* (1973). Maybe a day will come when most humans would opt for the certainty of perpetual simulated delight over the risky business of lived experience, but not yet. We want to be happy, and seem to believe that happiness consists of more than just favorable experiences. It requires doing something more sustained, meaningful, or constructive. This something is what, long ago in classical Greece, Aristotle was interested in. He thought happiness was a psychological state, a sense of fulfillment and satisfaction about your conduct, your interactions and the way your life is going. It implies some element of activity and goal-directedness. This, rather than the positive-mood or hedonist approach, is the third modern philosophical approach to subjective happiness. It is a philosophical approach based on analyzing and modifying your own ambitions, behavior and responses to the world. It comes directly from Aristotle.

Aristotle believed that if you train yourself to be good, by working on your virtues and controlling your vices, you will discover that a happy state of mind comes *from habitually doing the right thing.* If you begin deliberately to smile in a welcoming way every time your child approaches, you start doing it unconsciously. Some philosophers question whether a virtuous way of life is more desirable than its opposite. But "virtue ethics" have been rehabilitated in philosophical circles of late, and accepted as beneficial. Aristotle saw all virtues as part of an integrated bundle, but recent thinkers have tended to divide them into subcategories. James Wallace, in *Virtues and Vices* (1978), describes three different groups: self-discipline virtues, such as courage and patience; conscientiousness virtues, such as honesty and fairness; and virtues entailing benevolence toward others, such as kindness and compassion. The first two virtues can favorably influence the success of the individual's projects and of the whole community. Benevolence virtues are less clear-cut, but they can increase your liking for yourself and everyone else around you. So virtue has *extrinsic* benefits: you are more likely to be happy if those around you are happy, and thus it is in your enlightened self-interest to be virtuous. But Aristotle, along with Socrates, the Stoics and Victorian philosopher Thomas Hill Green, believed it also had direct *intrinsic* benefits. Virtues directed toward other people make a constitutive contribution to your own happiness.[3]

In *Nicomachean Ethics*, Aristotle discusses the cause of happiness. If it is not god-sent, he says (and Aristotle did not believe that gods involve themselves in human affairs), "then it comes as the result of a goodness, along with a learning process, and effort." The constituents of happiness can be described and analyzed, like the subject matter in any other branch of knowledge, such as astronomy or biology. But this process of studying happiness is different from those sciences because it has a precise goal: the achievement of happiness, which makes it more like medicine, or like political theory.

Moreover, says Aristotle, happiness could potentially be widespread, "since it can be attained through some process of study or effort by all persons whose capacity for virtue has not been damaged." Aristotle knows that the capacity for goodness can be damaged by certain circumstances and life events. But for the majority of people, happiness is indeed available if they decide to apply themselves to its creation.

Almost anyone can *decide* to think herself into happiness. This is not just something for a tiny minority of people with a degree in philosophy.

"Almost" is a key word here, of course. He is not offering a magic wand to erase all threats to happiness. There are indeed some qualifications to the universal capacity for pursuing happiness. Aristotle accepts that there are certain kinds of advantages that you either have or you don't. If you have the bad luck to have been born very low down the socio-economic ladder, or have no children or other family or loved one, or are extremely ugly, your circumstances, which you can't avoid, as he puts it, "taint" delight. It is harder to achieve happiness. But not impossible. You do not need material possessions or physical strength or beauty to start exercising your mind in company with Aristotle, since the way of life he advocates concerns a moral and psychological excellence rather than one that lies in material possessions or bodily splendor. There are also more difficult obstacles: having children or friends who are completely depraved is one such obstacle. Another— which Aristotle saves until last and elsewhere implies is the most difficult problem any human can ever face—is the loss of fine friends in whom you have invested effort, and especially of children, through death.

Yet, potentially, even people poorly endowed by nature or who have experienced terrible bereavements can live a good life, walking on the virtuous side. "This sort of philosophy, which everyone can do, is different from most other types of philosophy," Aristotle explains, since it has a hands-on aim in real, daily life: Ethics, he adds, "unlike the other branches of philosophy, has a practical aim. For we are not investigating the nature of being a good person for the sake of knowing what it is, but in order that we may become good, without which result our investigation would be of no use." In fact, the only way to be a good person is to do good things. You have to treat people with fairness repeatedly. You need to offer cheerfully to share fifty-fifty the weekend childcare with your co-parent and always pay your cleaning person in full if you cancel her session. Aristotle thinks many people imagine that talking about good behavior is enough: rather than "doing good acts, they instead just discuss what goodness is, and imagine that they are pursuing philosophy and that this will make them good people." He compares such people with "invalids who listen carefully to what the doctor says, but entirely neglect to carry out his prescriptions."

Thinking as Aristotelians means using our understanding of human nature in order to live in the best way possible. It means that nature, rather than a concept beyond nature—such as god or gods—is the fundamental basis of our analysis of our affairs and our decisions. This was the single most important difference between Aristotle and his teacher, Plato, who believed that humans needed to find answers to the problems of existence in an invisible world of intangible ideas or essential "Forms" beyond the material world they could see. Aristotle, however, focused on the thrilling phenomena in our perceptible here-and-now, as the poet and classicist Louis MacNeice wrote in *Autumn Journal*, canto 12:

Aristotle was better who watched the insect breed,
    The natural world develop,
Stressing the function, scrapping the Form in Itself,
    Taking the horse from the shelf and letting it gallop.

Aristotle put human experience at the center of all his thought. Thomas More, Francis Bacon, Charles Darwin, Karl Marx and James Joyce all deeply admired him for this. Modern philosophers, including some outstanding women born in the twentieth century—Hannah Arendt,

Philippa Foot, Martha Nussbaum, Sarah Broadie and Charlotte Witt—
have written important works deeply influenced by, or devoted to,
Aristotle.

Aristotle insists that creating happiness is not a matter of fanatically
applying big rules and principles, but of engaging with the texture of
life, in every situation, with every galloping horse, as we meet its
particularity. There are general guides; just as in medicine or navigation, the doctor or the captain will be equipped with knowledge of
certain principles, but every single patient and every single voyage will
present slightly different problems, which call for different solutions.

In your own life, as a moral agent you "have to consider what is
suited to the circumstances on each occasion." There will be weekends
when you need to do all the childcare, or none of it. It is not just a
matter of each occasion being different: every *individual* is different,
and being a good person through daily acts will vary from individual
to individual. Aristotle here uses the analogy of some athletes needing
bigger portions of food than others. He cites Milo of Croton, the most
famous wrestling champion Greece ever produced, as an example of a
big eater. Each of us needs to acquire self-knowledge and decide what
sort of ethical sustenance we need to provide for ourselves. Is it offering
help, relinquishing grudges, learning to apologize, or something else
entirely?

I don't think I'm exceptionally worthy or nice. I struggle with some
unpleasant character traits. After reading Aristotle on virtues and vices,
and talking honestly with people I trust, I believe my own worst faults
are: impatience, recklessness, excessive bluntness, emotional extremes
and vindictiveness. But Aristotle's idea of the ideal mean between
extremes, which we call "the golden mean," explains that all these are
fine *in moderation*—people who are never impatient don't get things
done; people who never take risks live limited lives; people who evade
the truth and do not express pain or joy at all are psychologically and

emotionally stunted or deprived; and people who have no desire what-soever to get even with those who have damaged them are either deluding themselves or have too low an estimate of their own worth.

Evil abounds in the world. We all know, or hear about, people and groups who do seem to be addicted, or at least habituated, to commit-ting bad acts and hurting others. But most of us remain passably convinced that a substantial proportion of human beings, if given sufficient basic resources not to be forced to be selfish in order to survive, enjoy being benevolent and socially interconnected. They feel good when they help other people. Living cooperatively in association with other people, in families and communities, seems to be the *natural* desire and state of the human being. The hallmarks of an Aristotelian thinker are living in these social groups, thinking rationally, making moral choices, using wholesome pleasure as a guide to what is good, and fostering happiness in self and others.

Other ancient philosophical systems have found advocates in modern times, especially the Stoicism of Marcus Aurelius, Seneca and Epictetus. But Stoicism does not encourage the same *joie de vivre* as Aristotle's ethics. It is a rather pessimistic and grim affair. It requires the suppres-sion of emotions and physical appetites. It recommends the resigned acceptance of misfortune, rather than active, practical engagement with the fascinating fine-grained business of everyday living and problem-solving. It doesn't leave enough room for hope, human agency or human intolerance of misery. It denounces pleasure for its own sake. It is tempting to agree with Cicero, who asked, "What? Could a Stoic arouse enthusiasm? He will rather immediately drown any enthusiasm even if he received someone full of zeal."

Aristotle wrote for people energetically involved in their communi-ties. The Epicureans encouraged people to renounce all ambition for power, fame and fortune and to live a life as free of disturbance as possible. The Skeptics, although sharing with Aristotelians the conviction that we must challenge all assumptions, were sure that true knowledge is impossible and claimed that setting out general principles for living a constructive life, lived together, was impossible. The Cynics agreed with Aristotle that humans were advanced animals, and that the goal of life was happiness, attainable through reason. But the route they recommended was more unconventional: happiness could be achieved through asceticism, by renouncing domesticity, material possessions and ambition for social rewards such as fame, power and wealth. The most famous Cynic, Diogenes (an older contemporary of Aristotle well known at Plato's Academy), lived semi-naked out of doors. He had neither wife nor household, and renounced any involvement in society. Many of us long for a simpler world, but few want to abolish the family and the state and become isolated vagrants.

Although Aristotle was not himself religious in any conventional way, he lived in a culture which practiced a religion to which nobody today adheres, and hundreds of years before Christianity and Islam were even invented. This means that his thought is not affiliated with any contemporary political or ideological camps. Over the centuries he has in fact inspired philosophers alike from Christian, Jewish and Muslim backgrounds, and more recently Hindus, Buddhists and Confucians. Aristotle is the exclusive property of no contemporary intellectual or cultural tradition. There is comfort in a dialog with a human mind from so long ago, because it makes you realize how little has changed about the human condition, despite all our supposed technological advances. It makes you feel part of a continuing human club and supported in a way that succeeds in transcending human mortality and time. Some philosophers since Hume and Kant have questioned the idea that human nature is useful in ethics, since human culture has varied so widely, and individuals even within communities are temperamentally different. But Aristotle describes an astonishingly constant set of human ethical problems. When he uses the pronoun "we," he often means the entire human race as a collective, past, present and future. In one of the most resonant passages in his *Metaphysics*, he criticizes the mythical, unscientific accounts of the origins of the universe given by the earlier Greek poets such as Hesiod. He says that Hesiod and the other cosmologists "gave no consideration to *us*. For they make the first principles gods or generated from gods, and say that whatever did not taste of the nectar and ambrosia became mortal." Instead of thinking about "us," the human race, the earlier cosmologists had thought about "them," the privileged deities, to whom "we" were merely an afterthought.

When you read Aristotle describing people who are mean with money, or quick to anger, you see all-too-recognizable human types who behave just the same today. He is also a fine role model for people at almost any time of life. Not only did he make a success of his own life, family and friendships, but he even managed to survive the most turbulent political events to achieve his personal ambition, after half a century of waiting and preparation, of founding an independent university and getting most of his ideas down on papyrus.

Aristotle was born into a medical family in Stageira, a small, independent Greek city-state, in 384 BCE. Stageira is perched on the twin peaks of a craggy peninsula jutting into the northern Aegean. His father Nicomachus was a doctor, and seems to have excelled at his profession; he was hired as personal physician by the then king of Macedon, Amyntas III. But Aristotle's childhood was disrupted. Both his father and mother died when he was about thirteen years old, against a backdrop of ever-increasing military strife in the Greek-speaking world. He succeeded in behaving ethically in a time and a place where standards of moral conduct were often shockingly low. He turned the problem into an opportunity, and spent much of his life refining his findings. A man named Proxenus, who was married to Aristotle's sister, took the boy into his own family and took charge of his education.

In his seventeenth year, Aristotle moved to Athens and enrolled in Plato's Academy. After two decades, when Plato died, he accepted the invitation of Hermias, ruler of a kingdom based at two cities in north-west Asia Minor, Atarneus and Assos. He later sealed the friendship by marrying Hermias' daughter Pythias. At around the age of forty, Aristotle sailed to the island of Lesbos, where he conducted the research into wildlife which enabled him to found the discipline of zoology. But everything changed in 343 BCE, when he was summoned by Philip II to Macedon to teach Philip's young son Alexander, later to become known as Alexander the Great. Philip had a school built for Aristotle at a sanctuary of the nymphs—which means somewhere with a fresh-water spring—in a spectacular, verdant valley at Mieza, thirty miles south of the Macedonian capital at Pella. The international political situation became explosive as Philip expanded the Macedonian Empire, and Aristotle may have spent 338–336 BCE, when Philip was assassi-nated and Alexander became king, keeping a low profile in Epirus and Illyria (the western Balkans).

At nearly fifty years old, Aristotle grasped his opportunity. He did not accompany Alexander on his campaign to the east, despite what is claimed to have happened in Robert Rossen's epic movie *Alexander the Great* (1956) starring Richard Burton. He was not a young man and he had been at the beck and call of others—whether Plato as the head of the Academy or his rich royal patrons Hermias and Philip—since he was a teenager. His time had come. He arrived in Athens and founded his Lyceum, the first research and teaching university in the world. Although he had been writing and thinking since his teens, most scholars think that it was only in the golden twelve years of his mature life as the head of the Lyceum that he wrote the treatises which survive, in addition to all the others—at least 130—which do not. One which has sadly been lost is the second book of his *Poetics*. (Just what a loss this has been to world culture was best illustrated by Umberto Eco's 1980 medieval detective story *The Name of the Rose*, made into a film starring Sean Connery in 1986. At the climax of both book and film, the last surviving manuscript copy of Aristotle's thoughts on comedy are destroyed in a blaze started by a monk who believed all laughter to be sinful. Eco's idea here may actually reflect the true reason why this precious work was not transmitted to the modern world; any writings on comic theater were far less likely to be copied out in medieval Christian monasteries than, for example, those on logic or moral philosophy.)

Although he is often characterized as an austere, uncompromising and arduous writer, there are dozens of moments in Aristotle's surviving works which come suddenly and compellingly to life. He is quietly humorous, and observes human foibles with a real twinkle in his eye. At a party drinking with philosophers, for example, he encountered a man who comically repeated the maxims of Empedocles—one of the more obscure Greek thinkers, who expressed his views in lengthy hexameter poems. Aristotle knew many poets personally, and found that they tended to be obsessed with their *own* literary creations, "adoring them as parents adore their children." He loved anecdotes illustrating harmless human eccentricity; for example, the story of a man in Byzantium who became an expert weather forecaster by observing the northerly or southerly walking directions of his pet hedgehogs, or the toper from Syracuse who kept the eggs his chickens laid warm until they hatched by sitting over them and partying with a continuous supply of wine.

Aristotle cared about his relationship to his body. He believed profoundly that sex, food and wine, enjoyed in constructive ways with people we love, offer crucial clues to human happiness. He was fascinated by the sensation of taste, by food and cooking; he knew what people grew to eat in domestic gardens. He enjoyed a rub-down and a warm bath in the gymnasium. The amount he knew about music and indeed about the practicalities of learning instruments suggests that this was an important aspect of his life. His usually measured tone evanesces entirely when he talks about the self-willed but irresponsible women of Sparta, suggesting he experienced a difficult relationship with one. He was a father and an uncle, and described the type of gift people make to children—a ball, or a personal oil-flask, for example.

Yet the treatises, based on his own research and the lecture notes he used in teaching his students, are often dense and strenuous, even in the most up-to-date and sympathetic translations. But he gave a great deal of thought to the difference between the way a philosopher or scientist needed to address the general public and a trained academic audience, and was convinced of the equal status of both styles of discourse. Far from looking down on "popularizing" works, Aristotle actually wrote many himself. We know that he wrote and delivered a different kind of lecture to public audiences, known in antiquity as his exoteric works ("exoteric" just means "outward-facing" or "designed for the public"). These works were almost certainly in the accessible, readable dialog form which Plato had popularized. Aristotle himself appears as a discussant in his dialogs, just as Socrates appears in the philosophical dialogs of Plato and Xenophon. Cicero, who knew all there was to know about literary style, said that Aristotle's public talks were written "in a popular way" (*populariter*), and was almost certainly thinking of them when he said that Aristotle's prose flowed "like a river of gold." The most famous of all his exoteric works was his *Protrepticus*, or *Encouragement to Philosophy*. This was a popular classic of philosophy for "everyman"; a philosopher named Crates came across it one day "as he sat in a shoemaker's workshop" and read it all in one go. The text expresses Aristotle's passion for philosophy, and describes what differentiates humans most from other animals: the sheer power of the human mind. It also brings them closest to what Aristotle simply called "god"—although the Greeks worshipped many gods, philosophers had a concept of a unitary higher divine power which ultimately motored the universe. And the few surviving fragments of the *Protrepticus* include phrases stressing how much fun it can be. "It is pleasant to sit down and get on with it."

But, in any attempt to revive Aristotelian philosophy, especially for a woman, there is the contentious issue of his prejudice, as a prosperous ancient patriarch and householder, toward women and slaves. In the first book of *Politics*, he notoriously defends slavery, at least in the case of Greeks enslaving non-Greeks, and states unequivocally that women are cerebrally inferior to men. I have not dwelled on the (actually extremely infrequent) passages where he reveals his error in thinking that women or non-Greek slaves were not born with the same intellectual potential as Greek men.[4] Instead, I stress Aristotle's consistency in arguing that *all* opinions must *always be open to revision.*

In the *Nicomachean Ethics*, for example, he writes that even though steadfastness is essentially a virtue, there are times when it can be damaging to adhere too rigidly to fixed opinions. If you receive incontrovertible evidence that your opinion is wrong, then changing your mind, which some people might condemn as inconstancy, is worthy of high praise. As often, he shows how deeply he thought about the ethical examples portrayed in tragedy. He cites the case of Neoptolemus in the *Philoctetes* of Sophocles. Neoptolemus had been persuaded by Odysseus to lie to the lame Philoctetes, but when he sees Philoctetes' suffering and learns more information about his plight, he changes his mind and refuses to participate in the deception. He revises his opinion. I like to think that if we could talk to Aristotle, we could persuade him to revise his opinion of the female brain.

Although he thinks traditional opinions (*endoxa*) need to be taken seriously, and if necessary refuted systematically, Aristotle has little time for the argument that something is good just because it is inherited from our ancestors. He believes that primitive humans were just like the less sophisticated people in his own day, "so that it is odd that we should abide by their notions." He thinks that written codes of law can also be revised to advantage, "because it is impossible that the structure of the state can have been framed correctly for all time in relation to all its details."

The traditional name for Aristotle's school of thought is Peripatetic philosophy. The word "Peripatetic" comes from the verb *peripateo*, which in Greek, both ancient and modern, means "I go for a walk." Like his teacher Plato, and Plato's teacher Socrates before him, Aristotle liked to walk as he reflected; so have many important philosophers since, including Nietzsche, who insisted that "only ideas gained through walking have any worth at all." But the ancient Greeks would have been puzzled by the romantic figure of the lone wandering sage first celebrated in Rousseau's *Reveries of the Solitary Walker* (1778). They preferred to perambulate in company, harnessing the forward drive their energetic strides generated to the cause of intellectual progress, synchronizing their dialog to the rhythm of their paces. To judge from the magnitude of his contribution to human thinking, and the number of seminal books he produced, Aristotle must have tramped thousands of miles with his students across craggy Greek landscapes during his sixty-two years on the planet.

There was an intimate connection in ancient Greek thought between intellectual inquiry and the idea of the journey. This association stretches far back in time beyond Aristotle to the opening of Homer's

Odyssey, where Odysseus' wanderings allow him to visit the lands of many different peoples "and learn about their minds." By the classical period, it was metaphorically possible to take a concept or idea "for a walk": in a comedy first produced in Athens about twenty years before Aristotle was born, the tragedian Euripides is advised against "walking" a tendentious claim he can never substantiate. And a medical text attributed to the physician Hippocrates equates the act of thinking with taking your mind out for a walk in order to exercise it: "for human beings, thought is a walk for the soul."

Aristotle used this metaphor when he began his own pioneering inquiry into the nature of human consciousness in *On the Soul.* He says there that we need to look at the opinions of earlier thinkers if we hope "to move forward as we try find the necessary direct pathways through impasses": the stem word here for a "pathway through" is a *poros,* which can mean a bridge, ford, route through ravines, or passageway through narrow straits, deserts and woods. He opens his inquiry into nature in his *Physics* with a similar invitation to us to take not just to the path but to the highway with him: the road (*hodos*) of investigation needs to set out from things which are familiar and progress toward things which are harder for us to understand.

The standard term for a philosophical problem was an *aporia,* "an impassable place." But the name "Peripatetic" stuck to Aristotle's philosophy for two reasons. First, his entire intellectual system is grounded in an enthusiasm for the granular, tactile detail of the physical world around us. Aristotle was an empirical natural scientist as well as a philosopher of mind, and his writing constantly celebrates the materiality of the universe we can perceive through our senses and know is real. His biological works suggest a picture of a man pausing every few minutes as he walked, to pick up a seashell, point out a plant, or call a pause in dialectic to listen to the nightingales. Second, Aristotle, far from despising the human body as Plato had done, regarded humans as wonderfully gifted animals, whose consciousness was inseparable from their organic being, whose hands were miracles of mechanical engineering, and for whom instinctual physical pleasure was a true guide to living a life of virtue and happiness. As we read Aristotle, we are aware that he is using his own adept hand to inscribe on papyrus the thoughts that have emerged from his active brain, part of his well-exercised, well-loved body.

But there is just one more association of the term "Peripatetic." The Greek text of the Gospel of Matthew tells us that when the Pharisees asked Jesus of Nazareth why his disciples didn't live according to the strict Jewish rules of ritual washing, the verb they used for "live" was *peripateo*. The Greek word for walking could actually mean, metaphorically, "conducting your life according to a particular set of ethical principles." Rather than taking a religious route, Aristotle's walking disciples chose to set out with him on the philosophical highway to happiness.

I have always loved walking, and now do much of my best thinking along the muddy bridleways of Cambridgeshire. At thirteen years old, and the daughter of an ordained Anglican priest, I lost my religion. The most difficult challenge to my fast-disappearing faith was the church's insistence that being a good Christian required belief in supernatural occurrences and worshipping entities invisible and inaudible to my senses. I just couldn't get in touch with the Invisible Friend I had previously called God any more. But coming to my secular senses left a big hole in my life. As a younger child, I was in no doubt that I would go to heaven if I was good. Now I felt like Antonius Block in Ingmar Bergman's classic movie *The Seventh Seal* (1957), a religious skeptic during the fourteenth-century plague, desperate to find some meaning to life: "Nobody can live with death before his eyes if he thinks oblivion lies at the end." It may be no coincidence that Bergman was also the child of a Protestant priest. I no longer believed there was anyone or anything "out there" in the cosmos who policed my life, or rewarded and punished me for virtuous and immoral acts respectively. I did not know what to put in His place. Yet I still longed to be a good person, live a constructive life, and ideally leave the planet a better place than I had arrived in it.

In my mid-teens I experimented briefly with astrology, Buddhism and transcendental meditation, and then, even more fleetingly, with more arcane phenomena including psychotropic drugs and spiritualism. I read Dale Carnegie's classic *How to Stop Worrying and Start Living* (1948) and other self-help manuals, but was left still searching for a workable, interesting and fundamentally optimistic moral system. When, as an undergraduate, I discovered Aristotle, he supplied the answer. He explains the material world through science, and the moral world by human standards rather than those imposed by an external deity.

Aristotle would have been the first to insist that no form of philosophical or scientific work can be purely theoretical. Our ideas, self-understanding and explanations of the world around us are integrally bound to our lived experience. He lived in eight diverse Greek places (see the map at the beginning of the book), and in April 2016 I visited them all to better understand his experiences. I followed in his life's footsteps and tried to get some sense of the real world lying behind the man, the paths he actually paced as he developed his philosophical ideas in response to the challenges and opportunities which life threw at him.[5]

One of the greatest ancient commentators on Aristotle, Themistius, said that he was "more *useful* to the mass of people" than other thinkers. It is still true. Philosopher Robert J. Anderson wrote in 1986, "There is no ancient thinker who can speak more directly to the concerns and anxieties of contemporary life than can Aristotle. Nor is it clear that any modern thinker offers as much for persons living in this time of uncertainty."[6] Aristotle's practical approach to philosophy can change your life for the better.

Chapter 1

———— ∞∞ ————

HAPPINESS

At the beginning of *Eudemian Ethics*, Aristotle quotes a line of wisdom literature inscribed on an ancient stone on the sacred island of Delos. It proclaimed that the three best things in life are "Justice, Health, and Achieving One's Desires." Aristotle trenchantly disagrees. According to him, the ultimate goal of human life is, simply, happiness, which means finding a purpose in order to realize your potential and working on your behavior to become the best version of yourself. You are your own moral agent, but act in an interconnected world where partnerships with other people are of great significance.

Aristotle's own teacher was Plato, himself the disciple of Socrates who famously said "the unexamined life is not worth living." Aristotle regarded this is as somewhat harsh. He knew that many people—perhaps the majority—live intuitively and often unreflectively, but they enjoy great happiness, on "autopilot" as it were. He would have shifted the emphasis to practical activity and to the future, and his alternative motto might have been: "the un*planned* life is unlikely to be fully happy."

Aristotelian ethics put the individual in charge. As Abraham Lincoln saw, "Most folks are about as happy as they make up their minds to be." Rather than working on autopilot, Aristotelian ethics put you as sole pilot at the full control panel. Other ethical systems place far less emphasis either on your individual moral agency or on your responsibilities toward others. Aristotelian ethics share the starting point of the moral agent with ethical egoism, associated with the early modern philosopher Bernard Mandeville (1670–1733), but nothing else. This system recommends that every individual consciously act so as to maximize their own self-interest. Imagine you are hosting a tea party for ten of your neighbors. You know that two are vegans. But vegan sandwiches are three times as expensive as ham sandwiches. If you buy two servings of vegan sandwiches, there will be less food all round for everybody. The egoist would ignore everyone else's needs and choose whether to cater for the vegans depending on her own personal eating habits. If she were not a vegan, then she would certainly not want her helping of ham sandwiches diminished by having to cater for anyone else's different preference. If she *were* a vegan, then she would ignore the deprivation suffered by all eight carnivores receiving smaller helpings and simply ensure that there was plenty of vegan food available for herself, and order a private extra serving.

Utilitarians, on the other hand, seek to maximize the happiness of the greatest number, thus focusing on *consequences* of actions: for utilitarians, a result involving eight happy carnivores completely trumps the accompanying problem of two miserable vegans. Utilitarianism gets difficult when the minorities are very large: a tea party with, say, four miserable vegans and only six happy carnivores would begin to feel decidedly unfestive. Followers of Immanuel Kant emphasize duties and obligations, asking whether there should be a universal and fixed law about the proportion of different kinds of sandwiches available at tea parties. Cultural relativists, on the other hand, have insisted that there is no such thing as a universal moral law. Everyone, they say, belongs to a group or groups which do have their own *internal* laws and customs. Across the planet, there are many cultures and communities which eat no pig products at all; there are others which cannot comprehend vegetarianism or even tea parties.

Aristotle would instead realize that the decision about the sandwiches could not be made abstractly in a vacuum. He would set aside time to think about the problem and make plans. He would look behind catering plans to make his *intention* conscious—if it is to make all ten neighbors feel welcomed and well fed, because that would make the whole community nicer for everyone to live in, conducing to individual and collective happiness, then his decision would need to maximize the possibility of that intention being fulfilled. There would be little point in offending even a minority of the guests. He would then consult interested persons, including the invitees and the caterers, to test the water on possible reactions. He would think about previous parties he had held or experienced, review precedents and very likely discover a way round the whole problem from looking at the history of tea parties—serving non-dairy cakes which everyone liked, for example, rather than the divisive sandwiches. He would also make sure that he personally enjoyed the types of cake he then chose, because unnecessary self-denial has no place in his philosophy of respect toward self and others.

Aristotle's ethical system is versatile, flexible and practical to implement in daily life. Most of the real-world psychological steps toward increasing contentment outlined by psychologist Sonja Lyubomirsky in *The How of Happiness: A Practical Guide to Getting the Life You Want* (2007) bear a startling resemblance to Aristotle's philosophical recommendations, and she indeed cites him with approval. His leitmotifs are working with the situation you find at hand, forethought, an unrelenting focus on *intentions*, flexibility, practical common sense, individual autonomy and the importance of consultation with others. The basic premise of Aristotle's notion of happiness is wonderfully simple and democratic: everyone can *decide* to be happy. After a certain amount of time, acting rightly becomes ingrained as a habit, so you feel good about yourself, and the resulting state of mind is one of *eudaimonia*, Aristotle's word for happiness.

This Aristotelian pursuit of *eudaimonia* is often attractive to agnostics and atheists, but is in fact compatible with any religion which emphasizes the individual's moral responsibility for their own actions and does not assume that frequent guidance, reward or punishment come from any external divine being. But since Aristotle himself did not believe that god interfered in the world or was interested in it in any way, his program for achieving happiness was a system in itself. The Aristotelian will not expect to find rules about tea parties in any sacred text. But she will not expect to be hit by god-sent retribution if her tea party goes badly wrong, either. Living in a competent and planned manner is something you elect to do to control your life and destiny. Since this control is traditionally assigned to a god or the gods, there is a sense in which it can make *you* "godlike."

Eudaimonia, however, is not so simple to explain. The *eu-* prefix (pronounced like "you") means "well" or "good"; the *daimonia* element comes from a word with a whole range of meanings—divine being, divine power, guardian spirit, fortune or lot in life. So *eudaimonia* came to mean well-being or prosperity, which certainly includes contentment. But it is far more active than "contentment." You "do" *eudaimonia*; it requires positive input. In fact, for Aristotle, happiness is activity (*praxis*). He points out that if it were an emotional disposition which some people are either born with or not, then it could be possessed by a man who spent his life asleep, "living the life of a vegetable."

Aristotle's definition of happiness is not constituted by material prosperity of any kind either. A century earlier, another northern Greek thinker, Democritus, whom Aristotle admired, had talked about "happiness of the soul," and had insisted that it definitely did not derive from the possession of livestock or gold. When Aristotle uses the word *eudaimonia*, he likewise means "happiness of the soul," as experienced in the consciousness of the sentient human. According to him, life itself consists of having an *active mind*. Aristotle was convinced that most people get most of their pleasure from learning things and wondering about and at the world. Indeed, he regarded the attainment of an understanding of the world—not just academic knowledge, but understanding of any aspect of experience—as the actual goal of life itself.

If you believe that the goal of human life is to maximize happiness, then you are a budding Aristotelian. If the goal of human life is happiness, the way to achieve it is by thinking hard about how to Live Well, or being alive in the best way possible. This requires *self-conscious habit*, which Aristotle does not think other animals are capable of. The deceptively simple adverb "well" can mean "competently" in a practical sense, "morally" in terms of being kind, and "fortunately" or "with felicity" in terms of enjoying happiness and pleasant circumstances.

On 4 July 1776, the brand new United States Congress ratified the text of the Declaration of Independence drawn up by Thomas Jefferson. Its epoch-making first sentence reads: "We hold these truths to be self-evident, that all men are created equal, that they are endowed by their Creator with certain unalienable Rights, that among these are Life, Liberty and the pursuit of Happiness." It is well known that the ancient Roman Republic was a model for the Founding Fathers of America, but that telling phrase "the pursuit of Happiness" shows that Jefferson was immersed in the philosophy of Aristotle as well. Four years later the constitution of Massachusetts (1780) followed suit: government is instituted for the common good, "for the protection, safety, prosperity, and happiness of the people."

Aristotle believed that the way we educate future citizens is crucial to whether they can fulfill their potential both as individuals and in communities. The 1787 Northwest Ordinance could not have sounded more Aristotelian when it stated that schools were necessary to "good government and the happiness of mankind." Everyone in the world who lives in broad agreement with the principles that were espoused in the bright new dawn of American independence is, whether they know it or not, an Aristotelian committed to the project of human happiness.

The most famous statement by Aristotle—so famous that it was (inaccurately) quoted in an exchange between Pope Francis and Donald Trump in February 2016—is that man is a "political animal" (*zoon politikon*). Aristotle meant that man is distinguished from other animals by naturally tending toward gathering together to live in a large settled community, a *polis*, or city-state. Aristotle always arrives at definitions by making a series of distinctions, and in his *Nicomachean Ethics* he asks crucially: what are the distinctive features of the human being? Humans, like animals and plants, partake in the basic activity of living, obtaining nutrients and growing. If other animals and plants live, get nourishment and grow, then this is not distinctive to humanity. Animals, like humans, also have senses with which they discern the world around them and other creatures. So sentient life can't be the distinctive and definitive feature of being human, either. But no other living being shares "the active life of the being that has reason." Humans do things, and are able to think before, during and after these activities. That is the human *raison d'être*. If you, as a human being, don't fulfill your ability to act while exercising your rational faculties, then you are not fulfilling your potential.

Exercising your reason to Live Well means cultivating virtues and avoiding vices. Being a good person *will* make you happier. There is a reason why Frank Capra's feel-good fantasy *It's a Wonderful Life* (1946) is the most popular Christmas movie of all time: its message resonates so deeply with the generous and cooperative values most humans share. George Bailey, played by James Stewart, is a troubled philanthropic businessman, persecuted by a rapacious capitalist. He is planning suicide on Christmas Eve. A guardian angel, Clarence, arrives from heaven, and through flashbacks shows George episodes from his past life where he has unselfishly helped others; he has been a devoted family member and offered loans allowing the poor to buy their own houses. Clarence persuades George out of suicide by showing him an alternative version of history in which he had never existed, his family had been deprived of him and the poor had to live in slums. George sees that his "wonderful life" had connected him to other people by his efforts to support them. The movie is also Aristotelian in that it presents life as a project, a continuous arc, which is as wonderful as we choose to make it. However cheesy the film may now seem, it strikes an authentic emotional chord.

La Promesse (1996), by Belgian filmmakers Jean-Pierre and Luc Dardenne, eschews all sentimentality, showing how a young person on the brink of adulthood, and full moral agency, learns the gratification of goodness. At the beginning of the film Igor is only fifteen years old, a trainee mechanic, but he faces an extreme ethical challenge and succeeds in establishing moral independence from his unscrupulous father. The plot involves the accidental death of an illegal immigrant and Igor's father's insistence that Igor help to conceal it. Igor comes to moral maturity and a degree of serenity by assisting the bereaved family in the face of an unfeeling father, feelings of guilt, social vulnerability and fear of the law.

The emphasis on the connection between happiness and virtuous action is one of the fundamental differences between Aristotle's recipe for happiness and that of the other philosophies such as egoism, utilitarianism and Kantianism. In his *Politics*, to illustrate the difficulty of achieving happiness *without* trying to be a good person, Aristotle offers an extreme caricature of the vice-ridden and consequently miserable person:

> Nobody would call a man ideally happy that has not got a
> particle of courage nor of self-control nor of decency nor sense,
> but is afraid of the flies that flutter by him, cannot refrain

from any of the most outrageous actions in order to gratify
a desire to eat or to drink, ruins his dearest friends for the
sake of a penny, and also in matters of the intellect, similarly,
is as senseless and mistaken as any infant or lunatic.

George Washington put the same virtue/happiness correlation differently in his 1789 inaugural speech, when he told his New York City
audience that there is "an indissoluble union between virtue and
happiness."

Deciding to pursue happiness by Living Well means practicing
"virtue ethics" or more simply "Doing the Right Thing." Aristotle's
virtues, likewise, are translated into portentous nouns like "justice,"
which really just means treating other people fairly and decently. Virtue
ethics have always attracted humanists, agnostics, atheists and skeptics
precisely because they offer, to people who want to live contented,
decent and constructive lives, a considered way in which to do so.
Virtue ethics will help you approach decisions, morality, and the "big
questions" about life and death, trusting in your own judgment and
ability to look after yourself, your friends and your dependants. But
the lack of idiomatic translations of the Greek has been one reason
why Aristotle's sensible and effective program of pursuing happiness
through deciding to Do the Right Thing has not become more widely
understood among the general public. If people understood that personal
happiness was down to their own conduct, then happiness, he wrote,
would become "more common because it would be possible for more
people to share it." Aristotle goes so far as to say that, ideally, "all
humankind would be seen to be in agreement with the views that will
be stated," but, failing that, they should sign up to at least part of the
program entailed by virtue ethics, "for *everyone* has something to
contribute."

Aristotle wrote the first books ever devoted to the question "how should I act?" Nobody, even Plato, had thought about this separately from other issues such as religion or politics before. Aristotle wrote two big books on ethics, the *Nicomachean Ethics* which seem to have been addressed to his son Nicomachus, and the *Eudemian Ethics* named after his friend Eudemus, who may have edited the manuscript. He does not seem to know or use these titles themselves, although in his *Politics* he does mention previous writings about "character," *Ethika* (the ancient Greek for a character is *ethos*). The *Eudemian Ethics* was probably written earlier than the *Nicomachean*, and later partially revised in light of it. These two great works follow similar basic lines. They both tackle the fundamental project of *eudaimonia* near the beginning, and then move through the nature of virtue in general (*arete*) and the discrete virtues (*aretai*) which need to be cultivated in human animals if they are to Live Well, flourish and be happy. Friendship and pleasure are also covered, and (briefly) humans in relation to the divine. There is also a smaller book, which contains an explanation of Aristotle's ideas but which may be by one of his followers, confusingly called the *Magna Moralia* ("Big Ethics").

There are few hard-and-fast rules or general instructions supplied by Aristotle's works on ethics. There is no strict formula or "moral code." The intention is always to improve our lives and direct them toward well-being, but the ethical dimension of each decision will be different and require different analysis and responsive action. Two of your employees may take money from the till, but one may feed her children, repaying at the end of every month, while the other may have a drug habit. Aristotle thought that general principles are important, but without taking into account the specific circumstances, general principles can often be misleading. This is why some Aristotelians call themselves "moral particularists." Each situation and dilemma requires detailed engagement with its nitty-gritty particulars. When it comes to ethics, the devil really can be in the detail.

Aristotle knows that there are people who aren't able or ready to live in this flexible but principled way. Such people may simply be immature—and he carefully points out that maturity is not a matter of biological age, since there are young people who are extremely emotionally mature, and older ones who never grow up psychologically or morally. But Aristotle also thinks that people who repress their emotions too much are not able to live life in a way which effectively pursues a good goal: in this he sounds very modern and Freudian. Individuals who do not take any account of their emotional responses and natural inclinations are no more able to achieve good goals than individuals who do not exercise their moral reasoning powers. In the *Nicomachean Ethics*, he suggests that the relationship between reason and emotion is not one of polarity but "like the convex and concave sides of a curve."

He also points out that many people mistake certain kinds of good things—pleasure or wealth or fame—for the type of constructive good thing he is really talking about. The problem with such goals as these is that they can be radically affected by chance, whereas misfortune doesn't damage more socially constructive goals. If wealth is your goal, and you remain poor or suddenly lose your money because of bad luck, then you will never achieve the happiness that *eudaimonia* means.

Yet living a self-consciously ethical life is not for everybody. Aristotle divides humans aiming at goals into three groups. The first group are only interested in the kind of "good" which comes from physical pleasure: he compares such people with cattle, and says that unfortunately there are plenty of prominent people whose sole goal is bodily pleasure. He cites the mythical king of Assyria, Sardanapalus, as an example: his motto was "Eat, drink, play, since nothing else is worth the snap of the finger." Aristotle did think that physical pleasure was important, and a guide to what was good for *all* animals. But for the human animal, it is a good thing because it is instrumental in guiding people to happiness, rather than constituting happiness itself. The second group consists of people of action who spend their lives in the public or political sphere. Their goal is fame or honor—recognition. The problem, however, is that they are keener *on being recognized,* than *on actually being good people.* What matters is the accolades and not the reason for them. But the third group consists of people whose goal is to learn about the world and satisfy their minds. It is much more difficult for this goal to be sabotaged by factors beyond your control, such as luck; it does not require other people to recognize or compliment you. It is something you can do yourself and which is inherently connected with self-sufficiency.

Self-sufficiency or self-reliance (*autarkeia*) is a key element in Aristotle's concept of living a good and therefore happy life. It is a term often found in an economic context; the autarkic or self-sufficient person can be one who is financially independent and does not need economic support from anyone else. This in turn makes him independent in a moral sense—he does not have to pander to anyone else's whims or take orders. This is the more important sense for Aristotle. To Live Well requires being able to act as an independent moral agent and not have your deliberated choices of action limited by obligations to others. Adequate income can be an important factor in freedom to be a good person and pursue happiness. But this also puts a responsibility on the person who wants to Live Well and be happy to find in themselves the necessary character resources. Toward the end of the *Nicomachean Ethics* Aristotle suggests the most self-sufficient life is the life of pure philosophical contemplation, because it requires no other person. But even here Aristotle says that the full-time philosopher, although he can philosophize alone, "might do better if he has colleagues sharing in the contemplation." If you are intending to become happy through practicing fairness in your dealings, you need someone to be fair toward.

This concession distinguishes Aristotelian thought sharply from that of the ancient philosophical schools which advocated living in isolation, like a religious hermit, in retreat from relationships and the affairs of the world. For Aristotle, even the self-sufficient person's life is enhanced by having friends. He opposes outright those philosophers who argue that the person Living Well has no need of friends. As inherently good things to have in your "outer" life, why on earth would the happy man not want to have them? He might be able to manage without them if circumstances so conspired, but why would this ever be his preference?

So you can keep your friends on the road to happiness. There is more good news. You don't even need to be "naturally talented" at Living Well and Practicing Virtue in order to become the Best Possible You. Aristotle takes care in book 3 of the *Nicomachean Ethics* to argue *against* those who say that people are born either bad or good. You can take responsibility for your own happiness and decide to Live Well at any point in your moral career. What's more, in *Nicomachean Ethics* book 9, he insists that people who want to Live Well and treat others fairly need at all costs to love *themselves*. People brought up in strict religious households, being told that they are sinners who have committed trespasses, and need to beg God for forgiveness, often find this refreshing.

Long before Freudian psychoanalysis encouraged people to understand their primal urges as natural rather than morally contemptible, and before Ohioan psychiatrist Dr. W. Hugh Missildine asked us all to embrace our inner child in *Your Inner Child of the Past* (1963), Aristotle argued that happiness is not compatible with self-loathing. People who cannot respect themselves and believe in their own fundamental decency cannot even like *themselves*, let alone other people. Completely depraved and criminal individuals hate themselves as well as others. His analysis of self-hatred deepens. Unlike most religions and other ethical systems, Aristotelian ethics are surprisingly non-judgmental about immoral people, for he sees that they are fundamentally miserable. Immoral people are always *conflicted*. They do what gives them pleasure, but at some level know that the pursuit of pleasure for its own sake is not conducive to happiness. Equally conflicted are people who know what the right thing to do is, but are prevented from going through with it "out of cowardice or laziness."

Aristotle, who lived in his forties at close quarters with the tyrannical Macedonian royal family, the ruthless Philip II and his scheming wives, concubines and lieutenants, all jockeying for position at court, seems to have meticulously observed the misery of immoral people. He knew serial criminals who simply committed suicide. He watched bad men "who constantly seek the society of others and shun their own company, because when they are by themselves they recall much that was unpleasant in the past and anticipate the same in the future, whereas with other people they can forget." These miserable reprobates, who can't stand to be alone with themselves, can't even fully experience "their own joys and sorrows, as there is civil war in their souls." They feel as if they are physically being torn asunder. They enjoy indulging their cravings for a few minutes, but "they regret it a little later, and wish they had never developed the tastes they have, since the bad people are always changing their minds." Leo Tolstoy, who was well read in ancient Greek literature and philosophy, sounds as though he had been reading Aristotle when he opened *Anna Karenina* (1877) with the observation, "All happy families are alike; every unhappy family is unhappy in its own way." For Aristotle had asserted that "the good is simple, whereas the bad is multiform; and also the good man is always alike and does not change in character, whereas the wicked and the foolish are quite different in the evening from what they were in the morning."

No better dissection has ever been performed of the multiform psychological miseries which the immoral inflict upon themselves by their
own inconsistent behavior.

Aristotle was born in Stageira, into a prosperous and apparently
loving family in a free, self-governing city-state in a beautiful location
washed by the sea and with a backdrop of woods and mountains. I
think his idea of happiness as consistent virtuous activity within a
flourishing community was fundamentally informed by his childhood
memories. In later life he remained loyal to his childhood home town.
Philip of Macedon conquered it and destroyed some of its buildings in
348 BCE. He enslaved all the surviving inhabitants. But he relented
when Aristotle begged him to rebuild it and restore the citizens'
freedom. In the town center are the remains of a marble colonnade,
with an inbuilt bench, where the free, self-governing Stageirites,
including Aristotle's father, gathered for debate.

I agree with Aristotle, who may have had these happy childhood
memories, that children can't be happy in the full sense, because they
have so little of their lives under their belts and are so swayed by the
desire for instant gratification that thinking long-term is quite impossible. This makes me very sympathetic to young adults as well; not
only are they often financially and emotionally insecure, but they have
far more opportunity remaining to them for serious random misfortune
than the middle-aged or elderly. The only advice is that they should
be true to themselves. Their state of mind will not be constantly liable
to complete change or annihilation, like "a chameleon, or a house built
on the sand" as Aristotle puts it.

The most serious threat to securing happiness is sheer bad luck. In
the *Eudemian Ethics* Aristotle devotes many pages to the relationship
between your internal self as a moral agent—your ability to determine
your own behavior and control your destiny—and the random bad luck
you may encounter which is utterly beyond your control. Aristotle's

favorite example of unlucky suffering on an epic scale is Priam. The king of the prosperous and happy Trojan realm, with fifty children, lost both his kingdom and all his sons to the invading Greeks before dying an ignominious death on his own city's altar. And he had done *nothing to deserve any of this.* My own example is Sonali Deraniyagala, an economics lecturer at London University, who lost both her children, both her parents and her husband in the 2004 Sri Lankan tsunami. She has been through indescribable pain since. She has no religious faith, and says that it was only through the disciplined use of deliberate recollection (an intensely Aristotelian technique) that she has managed to stay alive and, with extraordinary psychological efforts, recover parts of her old "self" at last. She recorded the whole experience in her beautifully written memoir *Wave* (2013). It is humbling. Small changes, caused by luck, as Aristotle says, "clearly do not change the whole course of life"; on the other hand, "great and frequent reverses can crush and mar our bliss both by the pain they cause and by the hindrance they offer to many activities."

Yet Sonali Deraniyagala is still alive, sees friends, works again and occasionally laughs. Aristotle would have commented that it *is* possible to undergo even apparently unendurable disasters and still try to Live Well: "even in adversity goodness shines through, when someone endures repeated and severe misfortune with patience; this is not owing to insensibility but from generosity and greatness of soul." In this sense, the Aristotelian imperative to pursue happiness at all costs is a profoundly optimistic moral system.

A primordial Greek proverb maintained that nobody could ever be called happy until they were dead. It was a favorite saying of Solon, an Athenian leader and one of the "Seven Wise Men" of the Greeks. He once visited the fabulously wealthy king of Lydia, Croesus. Croesus wanted Solon to agree that he, Croesus, was the happiest man in the world. He was annoyed when Solon chose an ordinary Athenian named

Tellus, who lived a long life, lived to see all his grandchildren, all of whom survived him, and died fighting for the country he loved. Solon's point was that misfortune could strike at any time, and so a person's total happiness cannot be assessed until after they have died. This turned out to be eerily prophetic: Croesus' son was soon afterward killed in an accident, his wife committed suicide and he lost his kingdom to the Persians. Aristotle cites Solon's precept, and approves of it insofar as it requires thinking about your future and how you are going to face the challenges it brings.

Solon's advice "look to the end" is timeless. It doesn't matter whether you are a teenager beginning to plan your life, a burned-out midlife professional, or a pensioner wanting to make the most of the remaining years of your life. None of us wants to be haunted on our deathbed either by guilt or the knowledge that there was something we didn't achieve simply because we were too scared to try. In 2012 Bronnie Ware, a palliative nurse who has attended to many people during their last few weeks, published a moving account of the most common regrets they have expressed to her.[7] These chime almost miraculously with the pitfalls Aristotle advises us to avoid as we create happiness over our lifetimes. People say "I wish that I had let myself be happier," thus acknowledging that they had somehow let the opportunity to be self-sufficient and *choose* to make their own happiness pass them by. They wish they had made more effort with friendships (one of Aristotle's most important principles). But the most frequently expressed regret is this: "I wish I'd had the courage to live a life true to myself, not the life others expected of me."

Chapter 2

—∞∞∞—

POTENTIAL

What does being "true to yourself" really mean? To Aristotle, it means realizing your potential, and so it is never too late to start to become "true to yourself." The English word "realize" has two meanings—becoming conscious of, and turning into reality—and Aristotle's idea involves both.

Problems and frustrations faced Aristotle at various times in his adult life, and he was unable to devote himself full-time to writing and teaching philosophy—fulfilling his own unique potential—until he was nearly fifty. But he must have been conscious that he had been exposed to consistent intellectual stimulation all the way from birth until his mid-thirties. As a physician, Aristotle's father Nicomachus was able to introduce the boy to the most advanced scientific ideas and methods known to the Greeks. In the ancient world, medicine was a hereditary profession, and Aristotle could have followed in his father's footsteps; he remained convinced throughout his life that medicine and philosophy were affiliated. The concept of human potentiality could well have been a topic Nicomachus discussed with his little son as they walked, gathering medicinal plants, in the wooded hills which stretch inland into Chalkidiki from Stageira. Perhaps the topic arose when Nicomachus asked, as parents do, "What do you want to be when you grow up?"

Aristotle's ancestry also gave him a family reputation to maintain. Nicomachus was one of a long line of doctors, who claimed they were descended from Machaon, one of the Greeks' legendary healers at Troy. Machaon was the son of Asclepius, the god of medicine, no less; Asclepius had been given special medicinal herbs from Cheiron, the original Centaur-doctor himself. Aristotle's father also wrote six books about medicine and one on natural philosophy, setting an example to his clever son.

Aristotle's enormous natural gifts, apparently identified by caring adults when he was still small, could develop and flourish. His potential to become the most eminent philosopher and scientist of his generation, and some say in world history, could be realized in these circumstances. Too often then, as now, the potential of many people was wasted. Creating happiness means, above all, spending our lives enabled to do what we are best at and enjoy.

Of all Aristotle's key concepts, most of which he uses in both his philosophical and his scientific works, the most inspirational is *potentiality*. Every object in the universe, according to Aristotle, has a purpose for which it exists. Even an inanimate object like a table has a purpose: somewhere for people to sit at and put things on. But *living* things have a different kind of potential, a *dynamis*, which is to develop into the mature version of whatever they are: a seed or acorn has the potential to develop into a plant or a tree; a chicken egg, if fertilized, has the *dynamis* to develop into a cockerel or hen. In the case of animals (including the human animal), Aristotle's idea of *dynamis* eerily anticipates our modern concepts of genetic encoding and DNA, and has been recognized as such by modern biologists and geneticists: the horns on an animal are produced from the interaction of form and matter which always had an inherent *potential* programmed within them to produce horns. These have a specific purpose, end or *telos*: the self-defense of the animal.

The idea of potentiality, for Aristotle, is linked with one of his most famous doctrines: that everything has *four fundamental causes*. A statue, for example, has (1) a material cause (the stone it is made out of), (2) an efficient cause (the sculptor who chisels it), (3) a formal cause (the precise design and shape of the statue which the sculptor implements), and (4) a final cause, which is the reason and purpose of its existence (to stand in a sanctuary and receive the offerings due to it). Potentiality, in a human, is closely allied to the final cause, which explains the reason and purpose of your existence. A human being's material cause (1) is the organic matter—blood, flesh, bone—out which you are made. Your efficient cause (2) is the parents who made you. Your formal cause (3) is the DNA which determined your genetic makeup, appearance, and constitution. The only cause in your own control is your *final* cause (4), the reason and purpose of your existence. A universal commitment to the full realization of human potential in the Aristotelian sense just might solve the problems today facing the human race.

The word Aristotle uses for potential and potentiality is *dynamis*, from which we derive *dynamic*. Alfred Nobel originally called his revolutionary new explosive "Nobel's Blasting Powder," but he was thinking of the ancient Greek noun when he changed it to dynamite. This is why, unfortunately, the word is associated with sudden destruction rather than long-term and constructive self-development. Since early Greek poetry, the word *dynamis* meant the power or capacity to do something. Doctors and scientists had already used the term to explain motion and change. But it wasn't until Aristotle that a systematic discussion of *dynamis* in terms of human beings and their life experience took place.

Aristotle explains what he means by *dynamis* in the ninth book of his treatise called *Metaphysics*. One can have the potential to breathe, or grow, or walk. Plants, animals, and humans can fulfill this kind of potential unconsciously. But there is a type of *dynamis* which is special, and superior. He calls this a "rational potentiality." Only humans have this kind of potentiality. It cannot be realized without conscious thought.

A person who is a good doctor was born with the intellectual potential to learn medical lore. Once trained, a doctor has the potential to heal a patient. But she can decide not to treat the patient, or to treat the patient in a way which will be damaging rather than beneficial. It is only rational activity—thought—intentionally applied to the goal of healing the patient which will actualize the doctor's potential to heal. The doctor needs to *decide* to help the patient back to health, and also needs to deliberate about which treatments are most likely to achieve that goal. Being a good doctor requires all four of these things: potentiality, training, intention and reasoning. So does being a good and happy person.

Even an inanimate object often requires a combination of elements to achieve its end, and different activities contribute. Aristotle offers the example of building a temple. For a temple to reach its appropriate *telos* as a complete and fully ornamented edifice, foundations need to be laid, stone blocks need to be prepared and fitted together, columns need to be fluted and ornamental friezes carved. But none of these processes will alone result in a completed temple. The actual assembly of the whole structure, on the foundations, out of the blocks, fluted columns and decorative parts, is far more important. The full realization of the temple can only come when each of these discrete processes has taken place.

Similarly, a human needs to be conceived, born, nourished, protected, housed, cuddled, stimulated and educated. If she or he is to achieve their full potential, they need to have their talents and what makes them happy (which Aristotle regards as the same thing) identified and brought to fruition with specialist training. Helen Keller, who fulfilled her remarkable potential as a campaigner for the disabled, felt she had discovered the source of true happiness: "It is not attained through self-gratification, but through fidelity to a worthy purpose." But if her parents, doctors and especially her instructor, Anne Sullivan, had not worked so hard to help her, Keller's combined deafness and blindness would have made it impossible for her intellect, passion and energy to have been recognized and supported. On the other hand, in the absence of potentiality, no amount of training, intention or reasoning can result in success. There is therefore nothing more important than finding out what each individual is *potentially* good at. It is sadly all too possible for a potential that needs rational realization never to be realized.

In *Generation of Animals*, Aristotle attempts to explain how the raw matter out of which a new animal is created acquires its form. He incorrectly thinks that matter is the female menstrual blood inside the mother's body, and that the potential form is given to it by male semen. He is not clear about the quantitatively equal role played by male and female genetic inheritance. But that is not the important point. Aristotle realized that all living things *are in a process of continuous change and development.* He saw that some changes take many months or years, even though they are inevitable once conception has originally taken place. He recognized the *delayed impact* of the form or "code" which he felt was imparted to the newly conceived animal at conception. In the human animal, the time lapse between conception and the fully phys-ically mature male, Aristotle believed, was at least thirty years; intel-lectually, he thought that a man did not realize his full potential until he had gained plenty of experience and learned many kinds of lessons, at the age (and Aristotle is curiously precise) of forty-nine.

Aristotle used the twin ideas of potentiality (*dynamis*) and actual-ization or realization of that potential in practice (for which his term is *energeia*) in works ranging from ethics, physics and metaphysics to psychology and cognition. *Dynamis*, in your own case, means the bundle of natural qualities, talents and aptitudes nature gave you. If you are a mature adult, only you can assess what these really are, based on your own desires and experiences, perhaps in discussion with honest friends or counselors. Daring to name and face even wild dreams or ambitions others call crazy is crucial: few people on their deathbed regret *trying* to achieve their dream, but many certainly regret not even making the attempt.

We all have a duty to help the young identify their potentialities and actualize them; parents and those of us in teaching or caring professions may do this full-time. Some potentialities are inevitably actualized and nothing will stop them; others need the right conditions. A human being needs to be in the "circumstances appropriate" to its potentialities. This means it needs to be in a condition which allows it to be supported and acted upon by external circumstances and agents. If the young human is not fed, cuddled, and exposed to the alphabet, they will be malnourished, psychologically damaged and illiterate. We now know that the "rational" part of the human brain, the frontal cortex, does not even get fully "wired up" until the mid-twenties, which means that we need to continue supporting the young long after they are legally adult, and often for years after their formal education ceases. Put another way, humans can be brought up and looked after in ways which allow them to fulfill everything of which they are potentially capable, but they can also have their potential stunted or left unfulfilled.

If we embrace Aristotle's *dynamis* in one of the contexts he found it most fascinating—*intellectual* potentiality—we remember that it may or may not be actualized depending on whether circumstances are right. Moreover, it is not going to be identical in type or quantity in every human. Humans as a species share certain kinds of potential, but Aristotle saw different categories of human as possessing different kinds and levels. Thus, for example, children are not yet capable of rational deliberation, but are fully endowed with the potential for it. We can be sure that Aristotle maintained that *individual* humans also have different potentials—indeed, in *Generation of Animals* we can see him trying to work out how much is given to each embryo by an individual father which makes the potential human individuated from other humans. What makes Aristotle more like his father Nicomachus than like other fathers in his northern Greek home town of Stageira? And how much of his potential was simply determined by the "species" code which will allow the embryo to grow into a human, a *Homo sapiens*, like any other?

■

Have *you* identified and actualized *your* unique potential? Did you long to do something with your life and were never supported in developing a talent or natural proclivity? Did you want to be a painter, politician or master chef? Aristotle didn't really get going until his fifties, so you almost certainly still have time! But, at any age, long-term thinking is essential. Happiness, in the Aristotelian sense, means deciding what you want to do, and why, and then implementing a plan to achieve it.

He opens his most important work on morals, the *Nicomachean Ethics*, by emphasizing that everything we do has a positive goal, which he calls "a good." In medicine the good thing is health; in shipbuilding, it is a ship; for household budgeting, it is financial prosperity. Every individual can decide for themselves what good things they want to achieve, and then apply themselves to acquiring the skills, situations and partners which will make it possible to achieve the goal. The most succinct statement of the need for finding yourself a purpose in life comes in the *Eudemian Ethics*:

> Everybody who is able to live according to their own purposive choice should set before themselves some goal [*skopos*] to aim at through living in a good way—the goal could be achieving recognition, or distinction, or wealth, or culture—on which they will keep their eyes fixed in everything they do. It is clearly a sign of foolishness not to create order in your life in terms of having an end [*telos*].

An un*planned* life is indeed less worth living.

In the *Nicomachean Ethics* Aristotle makes a striking comparison. Discussing what makes good things good, Aristotle makes, as often, an analogy from the visual arts. He suggests that the discussion can begin by describing the "outlines" of what is good, "by making a rough sketch, and [filling] it in afterward. If a work has been well laid down in outline, to carry it on and complete it in detail may be supposed to be within the capacity of anybody." Some details can only be worked out over the course of time. We can transfer this image to the process of thinking about life goals. The really important things we want to do need only to be in our heads in rough outline: the details can be filled in, like a painting, as we proceed.

In my own case, I wanted a partner who loved me and to raise children with him. But I also wanted, while avoiding boredom (I was always aware that I needed a good deal of brain stimulation), to leave the world a better place than I entered it. The first part of the outline (spouse and children) did not start to be achieved successfully until I was in my mid-thirties, mainly because I did not know how to recognize a partner with similar objectives in life and kept going out with handsome lizards and moral invertebrates. It also took me a long time to work out how even to attempt to fill in the second part of the sketched outline (doing something interesting and constructive). But then I was helped in my late twenties by a wise mentor, a lecturer in English literature called Margot Heinemann, who in a very formal conversation did me the biggest favor of my life. She assessed my potential. She pointed out that my only assets were a clean driving license, an analytical brain, communication skills, and academic qualifications in classics. I had to figure out how to contribute to the human project by harnessing those assets. So at thirty-one—quite late in comparison with most academics—I finally got a doctorate, my first university post, and a reasonably coherent set of unfulfilled dreams. I decided to use the

Greeks and Romans, as far I was able, to further the "goods" of collective enlightenment, entertainment and social progress.

The greatest gift is to help someone identify their potential and provide the right circumstances for its development. There are vast numbers of children in the world who will never fulfill their potential because they are poor, uneducated or forced to work at a young age. But there are also vast numbers of children even in wealthy countries, with compulsory schooling, who will never fulfill their potential either. This is either because they are hot-housed and pressurized too early (remember that frontal cortex which remains underdeveloped until the age of twenty-five?) or because nobody tries to help them. Every child is good at something, and usually they enjoy what they are good at. The pleasure means that the talent, once identified, could be a useful guide to what kind of employment or career to choose. Exposing your child to many different stimuli and activities, while watching out for signs of an enthusiastic response, is not so very difficult. But it is amazing how few parents help their progeny identify their natural talent.

Among my own circles of often hyper-educated friends and colleagues in the chattering classes there are far too many parents who impose their own vision of the ideal career or lifestyle on their children. One imagined, on zero evidence, that his three-year-old son was destined to become a world-class solo pianist (ten years later the son refused ever to practice the instrument again). What the boy actually liked doing, it seemed to me, was cooking, camping and orienteering. Another acquaintance ignored her daughter's passion for engineering and forced her to take literary subjects at school and university; she has ended up bitter and frustrated, but at least gets to fix things now that she's become a plumber.

When deciding a plan the most important principle is pleasure. Aristotle regards pleasure as a wonderful tool for scientific, social and psychological analysis of any kind. This is because he believes nature uses pleasure to help all sentient animals find and do what they need to flourish. Different animals are endowed with slightly different ways of feeling pleasure: asses like eating chaff, but dogs like hunting game birds and small mammals. Humans are remarkable because they evince such a *diversity* of pleasures, distributed across the population. "One man's meat is another man's poison." You may like eating fish; your spouse pork sausage. But this wide diversity applies to far more than our taste in food.

Aristotle argues that occupations which afford pleasure are the ones which we should all be aiming at:

> Life is a form of activity, and each person exercises his activity upon those objects and with those faculties which he likes the most: for example, the musician exercises his sense of hearing upon musical tunes, the student his intellect upon problems of philosophy, and so on. And the pleasure of these activities perfects the activities, and therefore perfects life, which all men seek. Men have good reason therefore to pursue pleasure, since it perfects for each his life, which is a desirable thing.

Aristotle noticed that people who get pleasure from their work are almost always best at it. He says that only people who delight in geometry become proficient at it, and the same goes for architecture and all the other arts.

Some inborn talents require more training than others. Nobody is born with full knowledge of geometry or music or architecture. In *Rhetoric*, for example, Aristotle says that stage acting is largely a natural talent and is not so greatly affected by training as some other professions. But when it comes to the ability to be good at enlivening your speech or writing by quoting previous authors, sayings and proverbs, success may come either from natural talent, or from hard work studying literature (or both). This last example is probably most representative of most jobs people do today. You may be naturally good at communication and analyzing facts, but only a rigorous training will make you a great barrister. You surely need both a natural gift and application to learning if you are ever to become a nonpareil—Aristotle calls it "a wise man," (*sophos*)—in your particular field, however humble. He gives the example of a harp player, and keep in mind that in the fourth century BCE, expert musical instrumentalists were by no means afforded the respect and high social status they enjoy today. But he is nevertheless emphatic that a harpist can consciously decide for or against practicing to be good at harp-playing.

The trick is to find out what you like doing and have an aptitude for, and then *stick at it*. This may seem more easily said than done. But at least, as a human, rather than an elm tree or a gazelle, you can make a rational choice. Aristotle also names the sculptors Polycleitus and Pheidias, who made the famous statue of Athena for the Parthenon on the Athenian Acropolis. They had become pre-eminent in a single field by natural gift plus sustained application. But he acknowledges that some people are deeply versatile and their innate gifts can allow them to turn their hands to many different activities. (There are also, sadly, just a few who unfortunately are either almost completely untalented, or fail to find their true métier. He quotes a comic epic poem, the *Margites*, to illustrate his point. Of some poor person the poet had said, "Neither a labourer nor a ploughman him / The gods had made, nor wise in anything else besides." It is unlikely that anyone who has chosen to read this book is quite as unwise as that.)

Some occupations are challenging or competitive, and there may well be times when you need to earn a living at something you do not enjoy because you have dependants to support. But the general principle that you choose the type of work you do, and therefore the training it requires, according to the activity which makes you feel happiest, is of unchallengeable validity. If you are stuck in a demanding job you hate, even if you have a young family to support, you would do well to review all possible alternatives immediately. Most children would rather have a parent who worked in a local shop and was around for them often at home than a middle-class income any day. I have a friend, a brilliant physicist, who turned his back on an academic career because it would have meant moving a continent away from his child. He took a job stacking supermarket shelves, which allows him to think while he is doing it, instead. The family is happy and he publishes research as an independent scholar anyway. Aristotle himself gives you permission if your work actually makes you suffer: "If a person finds writing or doing sums unpleasant and irksome; for he stops writing or doing sums, because the activity is painful."

There is a utopian tendency to Aristotle's thought. This was one reason why Thomas More once wrote that Aristotle was the philosopher "whom I love above many," and in his own *Utopia* (1516) says that his radical traveler Raphael Hythlodaeus took several of Aristotle's books with him on his voyage of discovery. Aristotle has more recently been reclassified as belonging to the category of utopian thinker because his works on ethics and politics assume that creating circumstances in which humans can flourish, achieve their full potential and be happy, was the goal of human life. He also envisaged a world where machines could take over most manual labor, thus freeing humans to devote themselves more fully to the contemplative life. The human race, today, despite all our computers, nuclear and steam power, internal combustion engines, machines and robots, is still not remotely exploiting its own intellectual potential. Many billions are not put in a situation where their mental *dynamis* is actualized by education. The ecological and political challenges facing the human race have never been more acute, and yet we are by no means nurturing all the aggregate brainpower with which we are endowed.

Unlike his more elitist tutor Plato, who was skeptical about the intelligence of the poor and working classes, Aristotle frequently stresses that the greatest experts on any given topic are likely to be those people with common sense who have accumulated experience of it, however low their social status. In the *Nicomachean Ethics* he admits that people who have considerable hands-on experience of an activity may be much *more* useful than those who have studied its underlying theoretical principles. He suggests that there were dietary advisers in ancient Greece who never went to the market or did any cooking. "If a man knows that light meat is easily digested and therefore wholesome, but does not know what kinds of meat are light, he will not be so likely to restore you to health." It will be the cook, not the student of dietetics, who is more likely to know the difference between pork belly and chicken. In his *History of Animals* he describes "experienced fishermen" who have seen and even fished up strange creatures—stick-shaped black ones and red ones resembling shields—that he would like, as a zoologist, to be able to classify. He is unfortunately unable to do so because the sightings have been so rare.

The trust Aristotle felt in the general good sense of humanity even enabled him to find language in which to express his prototype of the modern idea of the "smart mob"—that is a group which, rather than behaving in the loutish manner often associated with crowds, draws on universally distributed intelligence to behave with maximum efficiency. The idea, introduced by Howard Rheingold in *Smart Mobs: The Next Social Revolution* (2003), emerged from observations of modern groups, which can transmit and access information in an actualization of the potential for collective intelligence. Aristotle certainly formulated an ancestor of the idea of collective intelligence in his *Politics* book 3:

For it is possible that the many, though not individually good men, yet when they come together may be better, not individually but collectively, than those who are so, just as public dinners to which many contribute are better than those supplied at one man's cost; for where there are many, each individual, it may be argued, has some portion of virtue and wisdom, and when they have come together, just as the multitude becomes a single man with many feet and many hands and many senses, so also it becomes one personality as regards the moral and intellectual faculties. This is why the general public is a better judge of the works of music and those of the poets, because different men can judge a different part of the performance, and all of them all of it.

Our collective intelligence, quite simply, is much greater than the sum of its parts.

Some of Aristotle's most inspiring sentences on human potential occur in his *Metaphysics*, which begins with the famous statement, "All human beings by nature yearn for knowledge." He then defines philosophy—wondering at and asking "why?" about the universe—as something distinctively human and tremendously exciting. Part of the excitement is that it is not a directly productive activity—it does not lead to material enrichment of any kind. He describes how he came to this view "from a consideration of the first philosophers. It is through *wonder* that men now begin and originally began to philosophise; wondering in the first place at obviously perplexing things, and then by gradual progression raising questions about the greater matters too, for example about the changes of the moon and of the sun, about the stars and about the origin of the universe." Aristotle says that earlier humans used myth to explain these things (he is thinking of Hesiod's creation myth in his *Theogony*), and as such were, in a sense, philosophers. They wondered at the mysteries of the universe, felt that they were ignorant, and tried to come up with answers.

Aristotle knows that philosophy and science began about 200 years before he was born, and that at first the exercise of "wonder" at puzzling things was a pastime. It could only really begin in a place and at a time when people had enough to eat and time for recreational thinking. The practical necessities of life were already supplied. Asking "why?" is a natural tendency for humans, he argues, but one which requires time *over and above* fulfilling the physical needs created by the pressures of mere survival.

The word Aristotle uses for wondering at the world is *theoria*—our word "theory." If one phrase from Aristotle's own *oeuvre* were inscribed on his tomb, it should be this: "We have the *dynamis theoretike* (the potential to theorise about the world)." Yet Aristotle's idea of human intellectual potentiality is now hardly ever discussed. This huge waste of human talent and potential is rarely noticed, let alone regretted. Instead, Aristotle's revolutionary concept of potentiality has long been monopolized by Catholic moral philosophers in a single, narrow sphere: the debate on the legitimacy of abortion.

Such Catholic thinkers argue that embryos should never be aborted because they possess in potential form the attributes that they will later possess in developed form. Potentiality became locked forever into the vocabulary of the abortion wars in 1973, when the U.S. Supreme Court made some abortions legal in its landmark decision of the *Roe* v. *Wade* case of 1973. But it also stressed that the state has an "important and legitimate interest in protecting the potentiality of human life from the 24th week of pregnancy." The Supreme Court ruling meant that Aristotle's idea of potentiality has subsequently been discussed, in relation to the moral status of the unborn child, by bioethicists, philosophers and theologians. It is most usually referenced by those who oppose abortion, but is also part of the argumentative toolkit of their opponents, many of whom are openly feminist, when they argue for women's right to choose whether to bear a child. Here the controversy over potentiality becomes the competing rights of a potential human and an actual, pregnant one.

Potentiality, surely, is relevant to more than embryology. Potentiality is actually a political issue because it can help us think about the future, both of individuals and of societies. Potentiality can help us to imagine futures, to try to bring imagined futures into reality (Aristotle would have called this to *actualize* them), or indeed to resist undesirable futures—environmental pollution, global warming, or extinction of rare species of animal. Humans who have achieved adulthood also have potentiality, and they have traveled much further along the road to its development than first-trimester embryos.

Aristotle himself received continuing support to make real his potential both in infancy and as he grew to adulthood. He had constant contact with the Macedonian court, to which the wealthy kings invited the most innovative inventors, scientists, shipwrights and artists in the known world. He studied with the best philosopher of his day at the Academy in Athens. In his thirties, he lived on the island of Lesbos for two years, studied the marine biology of a great lagoon there, and conversed with his friend Theophrastus, another natural scientist, who had local expertise as a native of that island. Later, Aristotle remained in contact with Alexander the Great's armies as they went ever eastward, probably receiving regular reports of natural and social phenomena from his great-nephew Callisthenes, who crossed the Hellespont with the king. Aristotle could also compare political systems from direct experience: he had lived under both democracy and monarchy, as well as tyranny with Hermias, and oligarchy in Lesbos. After Alexander's conquests, he saw what was then the largest ever system in the hands of just one man.

The eighth book of his *Politics* opens with this famous dictum: "None will doubt that the legislator should direct his attention above all to the education of youth; for the neglect of education does harm to the constitution." He means that education at all levels, from small children through to young adults, is of such fundamental importance to the flourishing of the community under *any* form of constitution that it must be *publicly* determined and can't *possibly* be left to be decided ad hoc by each parent. Since the goal of any city-state is to ensure that its citizens live the good life, "it is manifest that education should be one and the same for all, and that it should be public, and not private." He does not believe that leaving every parent to make private arrangements for education serves the community well. It would be much better if all citizens received the same education about all matters which he describes as those "of common interest."

It is not that Aristotle asserts a "one size fits all" curriculum for everyone. He has watched sports trainers who adapt their training techniques to the particular athletes involved. He uses the analogy of medicine to point out that although rest and fasting are often good for a fever, "they may not be best for a particular case." Careful empirical study of a particular patient may even mean that someone who is not a doctor—a close relative, perhaps—may know best what treatment will work; we all know some self-medicators, muses Aristotle, who "appear to be their own best doctors, though they could not do any good to someone else." Some students need carefully tailored special treatment even under a universal system of education. "Presumably," concludes Aristotle, "a Professor of Boxing does not impose the same style of fighting on all his pupils." But it remains his conviction that there should be a proper system of public governance of education. Parents today who reluctantly resort to private schools because they are not happy with what is offered by the state can take comfort from his concession that "when the matter is neglected by the community, however, it would seem to be the duty of the individual to assist his own children and friends to live good lives, or even if not able to do so successfully, at all events to make this the aim."

But what is this ideal education system, which would be organized by the state to train all citizens "in things which are of common interest"? The only state in which the curriculum is actually laid down by law, warlike Sparta, Aristotle does not admire: there the young free children, rich and poor, are all given an identical training. (In his *Politics* he says that this is one of the paradoxically *democratic* features of the otherwise extreme Spartan oligarchy.) There would be little room for the sort of individual adjustment Aristotle recommended.

On the other extreme he offers the example of the mythical giants, the Cyclopes, one of whom, Polyphemus, is the "star" of *Odyssey* book 9. Polyphemus is the archetypal primitive, who lives alone and has not even formed the most basic of partnerships with a wife. Sociologically minded Aristotle has noticed, however, that there are other Cyclopes living on the same island. The other Cyclopes *do* have wives and children, but still have formed no kind of partnerships between their households that would constitute a community and facilitate state involvement in education. The Cyclopes have no parliament or shared legislation. Each male is the king of his own cave in the mountains, and makes the laws for his own children and wives, and does not care about the others.

In our own society, what would be the "matters of common interest" all young people should understand? Urgent sociopolitical and environmental problems, certainly. Aristotle would insist that this education should be the same for all, so that everyone in the community can understand the issues and can engage in fruitful dialog with their fellow citizens. Universal education would thus mean *maximizing* the possibility of individuals with the relevant *dynamis* coming up with solutions to the problems facing everyone. Really able humans can appear in any community, at any time. Intelligence really is randomly distributed. By failing to identify and actualize human intellectual potential we are placing shackles on our ankles at the starting line of our race against time. How much wasted mental potential is out there was painfully brought home to me in 2015. A report compiled for the government uncovered the appalling statistic that 37% of working British adults believe that their job is pointless and not making a meaningful contribution to the world.

Surely responsible citizens of the global village need to take the initiative and argue for an education which covers the "things which are of common interest" for their fellow citizens. Aristotle would have agreed with Dr. Martin Luther King Jr., who on 7 January 1968, a few weeks before he was murdered, delivered a sermon at Ebenezer Baptist Church, Atlanta. It was entitled "What Are Your New Year's Resolutions?" One of the things he said was this:

> I said to my children, "I'm going to work and do everything that I can do to see that you get a good education. I don't ever want you to forget that there are millions of God's children who will not and cannot get a good education, and I don't want you feeling that you are better than they are. For you will never be what you ought to be until they are what they ought to be."[8]

We cannot as twenty-first-century citizens fully achieve the actualization of our own Aristotelian *dynamis* until we make part of our work ensuring that everyone else on the planet is given the education and support that allows them to fulfill *their* potential as well. For we will never be fully what *we* ought to be until the human race can do so in entirety.

Chapter 3

───── ∞∞∞ ─────

DECISIONS

Much of the recent research, mostly by psychologists and neuroscientists, into decision-making emphasizes the sheer number of daily choices we make—some estimates running into many thousands—rather than their relative magnitude. In affluent societies, we are indeed bombarded incessantly with hundreds of choices about what to eat, wear, buy and watch on television. These require little thought because the consequences are ephemeral. But there are decisions that have such significance for our lives, and sometimes the lives of others, that they deserve a serious investment of time and active reflection.

When to settle down with a particular man or woman, whether to get married, whether and when to have children, where to live, whether to have an affair or get divorced, or whom to leave money to in a will. Our decisions may relate to people for whom we are responsible. We need to decide what to name our children, what behavioral boundaries to set, what childcare arrangements we need to put in place, and what school they should attend.

Some occupations have repeated decision-making locked into their inherent structure: doctors, judges, politicians and even stockbrokers must daily make choices with enormously significant consequences, and they are equipped to do so by being trained in the decision-making procedures specific to their sphere of competence. But most people have no training in basic decision-making techniques at all.

The popular craving for help in decision-making was revealed by the global success of the bestseller *Thinking, Fast and Slow* (2011) by psychologist and Nobel laureate Daniel Kahneman. He emphasizes the differences between swift, intuitive decisions we take all the time (his System 1) and the slower process of logical deliberation (System 2), while emphasizing that the two often operate in close conjunction with each other. More than twenty-three centuries ago, Aristotle offered almost identical advice, although he was far more interested in luck's capacity to torpedo the best-laid plans (having lost both his parents by his early teens, he was speaking from experience). He also provided one further indispensable guideline neglected even by Kahneman: the importance of examining *precedents*.

One of the most important decisions of Aristotle's life was taken when he was a teenager. After his parents' death he was adopted by his brother-in-law, Proxenus, and between them it was decided that the ideal place for this exceptionally intelligent youth was the best university in the world—Plato's Athenian Academy. The most brilliant student Plato had ever taught, Aristotle was thus enabled to throw himself into every branch of study available, as well as several in which Plato himself had little interest—the natural sciences. Aristotle developed into the first philosopher to describe in practical terms the best way to make a decision, written in a lively, matter-of-fact manner without complicated jargon. The method entails deliberating competently about all alternative courses of action which may or may not conduce to achieving your goals, attempting to anticipate the consequences of each course of action, and then choosing and sticking to one.

The Greek word for the whole process of competent deliberation and decision-making is *euboulia*: the verb "to deliberate," *bouleuesthai*, is related to Latin words such as "volition" and the English verb "to will." *Euboulia* designates the ability both to deliberate for one's self and to be able to recognize good deliberation and rational decisions in others. It therefore includes soliciting advice from well-chosen advisers. The Greek grasp of deliberation was intimately tied up with a sophisticated understanding of government: if even the most ordinary people are to exercise executive power well, they need to be "competent deliberators." The Greek term *deliberate* is therefore from exactly the same root as the word for the Athenians' democratic Council, where 500 citizens of all classes would take advice on and mull over policy and legislative measures before votes were cast upon them in the Assembly. George Washington was thinking of the Athenians' deliberative council when he concluded his inaugural address of 30 April 1789 by neatly summarizing the Aristotelian purposes of government. God had blessed the American people with "opportunities for deliberating in perfect tranquility"; they could work together for "the advancement of their happiness" through "the temperate consultations, and the wise measures on which the success of this Government must depend."

Aristotle believed the decision-making process mattered equally for both large decisions, like how much the government should spend on defense, and small decisions at home, like how to handle a rebellious teenager.

From all Aristotle's works, but especially the *Nicomachean Ethics* and *Eudemian Ethics*, we can extract a kind of "formula" for the best kind of deliberation, a set of instructions or "rules" to follow whenever we have to make a decision of any size. I have talked about the "rules" of Aristotelian deliberation to teenagers at many secondary schools, and have always found them intensely responsive to this kind of moral philosophy. Deliberative skills need time to improve; they begin as self-consciously applied common sense but blossom into what Aristotle calls "practical wisdom" (*phronesis*) if applied daily to real situations. It is significant that the historical individual whose *phronesis* Aristotle singles out for praise is Pericles, the near-legendary Athenian statesman who had led Athens for several decades in the mid-fifth century BCE and was voted into office time and time again. Pericles sustained good decision-making with extraordinary consistency, and the Athenians prospered, allowing them to create great artworks including the buildings of the Acropolis and the tragedies of Sophocles and Euripides. Pericles' evolution as statesman showed no signs of slowing down as he advanced in practical wisdom: his career was curtailed only by his death from the plague, a classic example of the kind of random bad luck against which Aristotle, like British philosopher Bernard Williams in his superb book *Moral Luck* (1981), well knew that deliberation can prove no defense at all.

Aristotle dwelled on bad luck more than most modern experts. The trouble with bad luck is its very randomness. This means that life is unfair and fate is not providential. Bad people and incompetent deliberators often succeed while good people who take decisions with infinite care often suffer. The rhetorician Isocrates, a prominent intellectual figure in Athens when Aristotle first arrived there, expressed the standard Greek understanding of the competing influences of chance and deliberation, insisting that true courage is tested during deliberations in the Assembly rather than in the face of the dangers of war, since "what takes place on the field of battle is due to fortune, but what is decided here is an indication of our intellectual power." Aristotle would have agreed with the distinction (although, with his more sophisticated models of analysis, he would have insisted that skill as well as luck was involved in success on the battlefield). But he would have been most in sympathy with Herodotus' philosophical Persian Artabanus, who insists that it is *always* worth deliberating properly. Even if a competently deliberated plan fails, it is important, in hindsight, when analyzing the reasons for the outcome, to recognize that it was because of chance and not lack of effort.

In the eighth book of his *Eudemian Ethics*, Aristotle observes that some people are lucky. There are spheres of activity in which luck is paramount to success (playing dice would be an example), and in which even really foolish people can triumph. There are other matters in which, although skill is necessary, success nevertheless depends to a large extent on luck (here Aristotle cites military strategy and navigation).

How should we explain the phenomenon of luck? Aristotle, the first philosopher in world history to subject it to intensive analysis, says most people think that luck is inborn, like having blue eyes or brown eyes. Others say that it is not an inherent quality, but that the lucky man, however deficient morally and intellectually, is nevertheless loved by God. He is like "a badly built ship" which "often gets through a voyage better, though not owing to itself, but because it has a good man [i.e., God] at the helm. But on this showing the fortunate man has the deity as steersman."

Aristotle is not satisfied by these popular explanations, pondering the possibility that some people *use* arbitrary good luck better than others, thus harnessing whatever natural capacities they do possess to the cause of turning random happenstance—serendipity—into life success and happiness. When people win vast fortunes on a national lottery, some of them squander it all, lose their friends by getting "above themselves" socially, and see their marriages and families fall apart before they descend into worse poverty than before their windfall. Phenomenal good luck turns out to be misfortunate. Others invest such winnings in their children's education, reward loyal friends and family by buying them appropriate houses, and even set up charitable foundations. By deliberation and reason, they succeed in turning random good fortune into circumstances which are really conducive to non-random but planned and well-executed *eudaimonia*.

Perhaps, as Aristotle suggests, in many cases good luck is not so unaccountable at all. He offers us an extraordinarily sophisticated picture of the individual who does by nature have certain qualities—strong desire for getting good things in life or for self-improvement, and (even if "on autopilot" rather than reflectively) the energy and commitment to pursue these goals. Today we might call such persons self-starters, optimists and aspirational. These qualities are natural to them and impel them, without them giving it any thought, onto courses in life where they are, as it were, *more likely to be lucky*. They do not necessarily need developed intellectual skills like deliberation. The parallel Aristotle offers here is of "musical people who have not learned to sing and yet have a natural aptitude for it." There are people completely untrained to achieve happiness or success, and who could therefore not teach ethics. But they intuitively act like a self-conscious virtue ethicist. Think of the good singer who has never been trained, but nevertheless pleases everyone when he performs. Looked at this way, virtue ethics and deliberation as learned skills can help people *make up for the unfairness* which has made some people born with a greater natural proclivity to doing what will produce happiness.

Practical wisdom, however, is cumulative: perfecting the art of deliberation takes practical experience. You need to do it repeatedly, and assess the results, before you become a competent, let alone expert, deliberator. It is not, Aristotle says, just like learning mathematics, which can be absorbed from first principles without application in practice. The sooner young humans start trying to deliberate rationally, the better. Education in moral decision-making procedures makes the world a better place for everyone.

The young urgently need education because, as Aristotle warns, deliberation can be fiendishly difficult. There are easy circumstances to know right from wrong; the basically decent person will know intuitively a fair way to apportion money or food or opportunity across groups of people. But, Aristotle says, the exact way to perform that right action is "a harder task than to know what medical treatment will produce health." Ethics are far more fluid and complicated even than human physiology. Ever the doctor's son, Aristotle adds that even in medicine, actually *effecting a cure* is far trickier than simply knowing information about "honey, wine and hellebore, cautery and surgery."

First, however, we have to define deliberation. For Aristotle, deliberation has a very specific sense. It is not about our final ends—a doctor does not deliberate about her intention, which is obviously to produce health in her patient. It is about choosing the best *means* to achieve our ends. The doctor deliberates about what course of action and treatment will restore the patient's health. Analogously, we know happiness is our goal, but deliberate about the means of achieving it—the courses of action which are most likely to secure happiness for ourselves, our loved ones, and our fellow citizens.

Deliberation is, for Aristotle, a distinctive activity; there are many things we do not deliberate about, such as the laws of nature or proven facts, for example whether a particular object is a loaf of bread. It is only *uncertainties* about which we deliberate, and this does not even include uncertain phenomena over which we have no control, such as the weather, or the serendipitous discovery of treasure: we only deliberate "about things that are in our power and can be realised by action." We deliberate *in order to act*, and this is why deliberation is prominent in the spheres of ethics and politics, which are concerned with *doing* things.

Deliberation is also about what we are going to do in the future, not what happened yesterday, or even what we did yesterday. We may *regret* a decision we made yesterday, as a doctor may regret having decided to give a particular treatment if it has had an adverse effect. Aristotle's example is as big an event as he can imagine: "no one *chooses* to have sacked Troy" and thus kill thousands of people, wiping out an entire civilization. No human, not even a god, can un-besiege Troy or un-spill milk; "what has happened cannot be made not to have happened." Aristotle quotes with approval a poet named Agathon, who wrote, "The only thing denied even to God is the power to undo what has been done."

This is all about taking responsibility for your own life and not expecting happiness to land in your lap (as women have been trained since time immemorial to expect in the form of a "handsome prince" who will miraculously appear, without any effort on their part, to provide them with a purpose). To show this, Aristotle gives the example of men who "wish for some things that they know to be impossible, for instance to be king of all mankind and to be immortal." Deliberation is what Aristotle calls a "purposive choice," something "which necessarily rests with yourself." This does not include becoming king of the world or mutating into a deity. Perhaps thinking about the advance of Alexander the Great's army ever eastward across Afghanistan, Aristotle tells his audience in Greece that there is no point in deliberating about "affairs in India," for "they do not rest with us" any more than it is within our remit "to turn a circle into a square."

Aristotle acknowledges that some people are too weak to be able to take full responsibility for the things which necessarily rest with themselves. They are unlikely to be able to learn to deliberate well or to implement deliberated policies. But the bottom line is this: if you want to achieve happiness, you *must* take responsibility for your own actions and indeed failures to act. "Of things which it depends on a person to do or not to do, he is himself the cause, and what he is the cause of depends on himself," Aristotle writes, asserting that we all have the free will to act as good or bad people. The same person "clearly commits voluntarily all the acts that he commits purposely. It is clear, then, that both goodness and badness are voluntary."

This is fundamental to our morality: Aristotle goes so far as to say that "it is by a man's purposive choice that we judge his character—that is, not by *what* he does but what he does it *for*." Aristotle has been struck by an example in a tragedy where Pelias was killed by his daughters. This mythical Greek king was old and infirm. The sorceress Medea persuaded the sisters that the liquid in her cauldron had the power to rejuvenate him. She even proved it empirically by an experiment with a ram. The Peliades deliberated, and decided for the best of filial reasons, backed up by apparent scientific evidence, to cut Pelias into joints and put them in the cauldron. He did not survive. But with deliberation, the daughters of Pelias would have considered what private agenda might be driving Medea (she wanted Pelias' throne for her husband) and would certainly never have taken advice from her.

Aristotle recommends founding your goals, which should be tough but achievable and commensurate with your own abilities and resources, on good intentions. Deliberate systematically about the precise course of action which will achieve them. Compare different courses of action and then choose one (Aristotle's term for this type of choice, *prohairesis*, means something more like "preference"). Then single-mindedly put those actions into effect. That way lies Aristotle's idea of true, deep, satisfying and lasting happiness. Because it is self-made it can't be taken away from you except by random bad luck, such as catching the Athenian plague. Even then your achievements prior to catching the plague are likely to be recognized and also mean that you die a happier person than if you had lived an aimless and undeliberated life.

Aristotle sees an intense connection between deliberation and causes and effects: we aim for achieving an end *all the more purposively* when we have deliberated about how to achieve it. Those people least given to deliberation, as Aristotle has noticed, are excitable, impulsive, and without much sense of purpose in life. There is also a large category of individuals who deliberate competently enough, but lack the discipline to follow through and implement the policies which their deliberations have led them, temporarily, to adopt.

We have all of course been in this position: how many of us deliberate every January about cutting back on food and wine and joining a gym, in order to become healthier, but abandon the policy before February is through? This turns each one of us, sometimes, into Aristotle's "unrestrained person who does not keep to the resolve he has formed after deliberation." It means that, at least in regard to food consumption, many of us resemble "a state which passes all the proper enactments, and has good laws, but which never *keeps* its laws."

There is a preparatory step before you even start to deliberate. You need to decide whether you actually do have a choice at all. As the educationalist John Dewey (who was much influenced by Aristotle) put it, "A problem well-defined is a problem half solved." Sometimes you have no room for maneuver, for example, if you are held captive. There are also circumstances when you *seem* to have a choice but actually, if your priorities are right, you don't. Here Aristotle cites an example which makes one wonder what he saw happen in the Macedonian court, run by autocratic kings: if a tyrant arrests your parents and your children, and tells you he will kill them if you don't do something reprehensible for him, you may not have a choice about what to do. So Aristotle believes that relationships with loved ones outweigh moral scruples. I find this very refreshing—I once queue-jumped in a hospital in a way I would normally regard as utterly out of order. But one of my children, then aged eighteen months, was extremely ill. I was not going to put my normal moral fairness—respecting people ahead of me in the queue—above her well-being. I feel ashamed of the queue-jumping, but Aristotle explicitly exempts wrong actions done for the sake of your children's lives from "normal" moral assessment. Loss of a child is one of what he describes as the "penalties that impose too great a strain on human nature, and that no one could endure."

When it comes to putting lives above property, sometimes right-thinking people choose abnormally. For example, if you are on a voyage and a storm threatens the life of yourself and your shipmates, would you throw all your possessions overboard to save yourselves? "Any sane person would do so," insists Aristotle in *Nicomachean Ethics* book 3. He would not have been impressed on 8 September 2015, when a British Airways plane caught fire on a Las Vegas runway. Asked to evacuate the plane and leave all their bags behind for safety's sake, many passengers wasted time by looking for their hand baggage and taking it out of the overhead lockers.

When Aristotle and his students discussed deliberation, they were building on a long and rich tradition of Greek wisdom literature. It developed out of the conviction that since there are arbitrary factors at play which you can't control—that is, luck—you can never guarantee that you will take the correct decision. But you *can* guarantee that you prepare for the decision-taking in the manner which maximizes your chances of success and happiness. A treatise actually called *On Deliberation* was circulated by Simon the Cobbler, the "workbench philosopher" and friend of Socrates and Pericles (his actual shoe shop, complete with hobnails and part of a pot inscribed "Simon's," has been discovered in the Athenian marketplace). Aristotle himself wrote a book called *Peri Symboulias* ("On Deliberation or Giving and Taking Advice"), which presumably fleshed out what he says about taking decisions in his surviving works. Deliberation in western literature is inaugurated in the *Iliad*, where Achilles speaks about the choice between two alternative destinies—a brief but glorious life, or a long one ending peacefully at home in old age (9.410–29).

So what are Aristotle's "rules" for deliberation—both those he explicitly discusses and those which he takes for granted as part of accrued Greek wisdom? Imagine that you are trying to decide whether to leave your significant other. Perhaps you have heard a rumor that they are having an affair. The first rule followed by the competent deliberator according to the ancient Greeks is "don't deliberate in haste." Impulsiveness has no place in deliberation. You may want to leave your partner after a row, but things often look different next week. There was in fact an ancient Greek proverb, "deliberate at night" (we would say "sleep on it"). In the days before e-mail, we would write real letters when angry, and put them by the front door, ready to post in the morning. They often got torn up when we awoke and realized in the clear light of day that we did not actually want to get divorced, resign or emigrate with immediate effect. The Internet has made hasty correspondence a much greater hazard; e-mail and social media are best avoided in the heat of passion altogether. Aristotle actually says that the speed at which serious deliberation takes place is not itself significant—he recognizes that some people can do it swiftly and others, although needing much more time, are nevertheless outstanding decision-makers.

The second rule is to verify all information. A correct decision can never result from incorrect knowledge. Othello needed to ask a few more questions about the provenance of that handkerchief before he decided to kill Desdemona. Aristotle had studied at the Academy, where a central, recurring topic was the difference between true knowledge and opinion or rumor. And a rumor that your partner is having an affair is not a fact. This can be difficult: a friend of mine, also an academic, had a husband who was so convinced she was having an affair that he hired a private detective to get a photo or video recording which would prove it. All that he found was that she was inseparable from the primitive Atari computer on which she was word-processing lecture handouts. Hiring a detective is extreme, but there are other ways to verify, including directly asking your partner how they respond to the nefarious rumor in circulation and watching whether their breathing changes.

On the level of global politics, failing to verify information can have truly catastrophic consequences. On 6 July 2016 Sir John Chilcot's report on the UK's policy on Iraq 2001–9 was published, which concluded that "judgments about the severity of the threat posed by Iraq's weapons of mass destruction" had been presented by Tony Blair's government "with a severity that was not justified." Worse, Chilcot stated that it was clear "that policy on Iraq was made on the basis of flawed intelligence and assessments. They were not challenged, and they should have been." The innumerable British and Iraqi deaths which resulted were based on exaggerated and flawed information. Aristotle would not have been surprised.

Verifying information is closely related to the third rule, to consult *and listen to* an expert adviser. The Athenians went to great lengths to get advice about the navy from expert mariners, and designs for their splendid temples from only the best architects. These specialists did not have to be Athenian: expertise was expertise. The Athenians would have applauded President Obama when, in his speech at Rutgers in May 2016, he pointed out that one would never want to board an airliner piloted by someone untrained in aviation. Aristotle says if you are not an expert on a particular matter, then consult one: he quotes the archaic wisdom poet Hesiod in confirmation:

> The best man is the one who can give himself good advice, after considering everything, and the future, and his aim. The man who follows good advice is also good. But the one who neither thinks for himself nor keeps in mind the advice of another, is a man who brings no benefits at all.

The adviser needs to be *disinterested* (not *un*interested), and not standing to gain or lose from your decision. Othello should never have believed that Iago could have offered him disinterested advice. Your employee is by definition never disinterested. Your best friend—the person most of us instinctively turn to in times of emotional distress or quandary—is even worse. She or he has their own agenda precisely because you mean so much to them. Instead of acting on your friend's gossip, seek advice from a relationships guidance counselor.

The fourth imperative is to consult or at least look at the situation from the perspective of all parties who will be affected. It is not just you and your partner who will be affected if you split. So will your families, friends, colleagues, neighbors, and especially your children if you have them. You are simultaneously engaged in many different types of partnerships, and the domino effect of altering one relationship can hold nasty surprises.

Rule number five is to examine all known precedents, both those in your personal life and history. When the decisions are trivial this part of deliberation can be highly amusing. If you are trying to decide what to give someone for their birthday, there is a good deal of sense in remembering what you gave them last year. When you are making a seating plan for a dinner party, you do not put two people who you know loathe each other side by side. But on more serious questions there is far more to be learned from the past. What happens to humans when relationships break up? What happens to you personally when you are emotionally traumatized? How does your partner behave under stress?

Rule number six: calibrate the *likelihood* of different outcomes and prepare for every single one you think is possible. Here the Chilcot Inquiry chillingly revealed how the Blair government ignored this rule in going to war in Iraq: "Despite explicit warnings, the consequences of the invasion were underestimated. The planning and preparations for Iraq after Saddam Hussein were wholly inadequate." Your own decisions may never have this scale of consequences, but they do need equal calibration of likely outcomes. Are you 99% sure that your partner will behave like a decent human if you leave him or her, and not hit you, rip you off, or abduct your children? If you are less than 99 percent certain, then you need to think pre-emptively, visit a lawyer and take the necessary precautions. You need *to plan* to deal with any of the probable or possible consequences. Under stress, having a preprepared strategy to meet unfolding events can prove invaluable.

Besides likely and predictable outcomes, the seventh rule requires that you also think about that inconsiderate factor of *luck*. Factor in all the *random* possibilities you can possibly envisage. What unanticipated events might drastically affect how things proceed? What if you suddenly became too ill to look after dependants? Bad luck can never be fully pre-empted, but awareness of its sinister possibility is part of the deliberative process.

On a lighter note, most ancient Greek discourse on deliberation includes the injunction "don't drink and deliberate." Aristotle would certainly concur with this, since the intemperate man inflamed by drink often features in his works as an example of the type of person who is incapable of virtue ethics at all. This is not to say that Aristotle disapproved of wine-drinking; on the contrary, he thought such pleasures were to be recommended, in moderation. He certainly read Herodotus, and I sometimes wonder what he made of that historian's account of the method by which the Persians took collective decisions about matters of national consequence. They voted when they were drunk together, but then, crucially, reviewed the verdict when they were sober. Action was only taken when both verdicts were the same: heart and head in perfect harmony, or the archetype of Daniel Kahneman's fast and slow thinking combined. I admit that I have betrayed my Aristotelian commitment to moderation by occasionally imitating the Persians, along with my husband, when making important family decisions. In my experience the method works. But we have always ensured that we have assiduously followed Aristotle's rules for deliberation before *either* vote is taken.

So there it is. I have omitted as anachronistic rule number nine, which says that slaves can't deliberate, and number ten, which is "women and deliberation don't mix." Aristotle, sadly, believes that the deliberative part of women's minds is "inoperative," or needs "steering" by a man, depending on how you translate the adjective in question (*akuron*). Yet he might have been persuaded that he was wrong, even in his own day. Some ancient Greeks always recognized that some individual women could deliberate with unquestionable competence. In a tragedy by Euripides called *Suppliant Women* the profound advice of Aethra, the mother of King Theseus of Athens, leads Theseus to make the only morally decent decision in the circumstances; in Aeschylus' *Agamemnon*, the exceptionally articulate and cerebral Queen Clytemnestra of Argos is said to have "a mind that deliberates like a man's."

Aristotle's work on deliberation had a long future. Erasmus chose deliberation as a topic in his Renaissance best-selling *Adagia* (1500), and a few decades later, the English queen's own adviser Francis Bacon published his treatise *Of Counsel* (1597). Aristotle's thoughts on decision-making are coming back into fashion in modern philosophical circles. Political theorists apply it to the deficiencies and merits of group decision-making in democracies, and (in ways that overlap with cognitive psychology) the workings of the individual moral agent's subjectivity. A fascinating cluster of contemporary philosophical studies attempt to define the ideal deliberator, but all of them lead back, like Kahneman the psychologist, to Aristotle, and focus on a quality or procedure which Aristotle had already considered in some detail. Good deliberation has recently been defined, for example, as evaluation of ends on the basis of full and correct information (which may well require seeking expert advice from a disinterested party). Sometimes this means using precedent and experience to calibrate the likelihood of outcomes. Another model focuses on the stability of the deliberator's intuitions and judgments.

Finally, although thinking about and practicing the rules of deliberation can be time-consuming, you will enjoy life more by not *worrying* so much. The imperative to deliberate competently simply does not apply when you can't change anything. If the patient has an incurable condition, there is no point in a doctor deliberating about how to cure it—only how to make it more tolerable. This apparently simple truth is quite difficult to absorb, but it provides extraordinary relief to individuals with overdeveloped senses of responsibility. Time spent worrying about things which you cannot change is wasted.

I have myself worried far too much, at the last minute, about the imminent performance of my students in their exams when I have in fact done everything I could weeks, months and years ahead to ensure that they are well informed, motivated and prepared. I would have much better spent that time around their exams thinking about how my experience teaching them could help me improve the way I teach the next generation. I have also wasted months of my life anguishing about what to do about the alcoholism of someone of whom I am very fond. It took me a long time to understand that there was nothing whatsoever in my power: it was up to them.

There is no point in trying to change anything beyond your control. It may well rain on the day you have arranged to hold a wedding, for example. But there *are* ways that you can use moral reasoning to decide what you would do if it *did* rain. Aristotle would simply supply an alternative indoor venue for photographs, a stand full of wedding-themed umbrellas, and extra hairspray for the bride.

Chapter 4

───── ∞ ─────

COMMUNICATION

Aristotle broke ground by insisting that rhetoric, like logic, is a *neutral* skill, which can be used for good and evil. Rhetoric, in fact, is essential for any individual pursuing happiness: "It is absurd to hold that a man should be ashamed of an inability to defend himself with his limbs, but not ashamed of an inability to defend himself with speech and reason; for the use of rational speech is more distinctive of a human being than the use of his limbs." He compared the individual trained in rhetoric with his favorite figure of the medical practitioner. The consummate medic uses his complete repertoire of techniques for healing, even though he cannot cure every single patient. The rhetorician, similarly, needs to have a total understanding of the techniques available, and how to implement them—even if he may not always succeed in persuading everyone.

Aristotle knew this from painful experience. Toward the end of his life, he was denounced for impiety before the court of the Areopagus by an Athenian priest named Eurymedon. The main charge was that he held beliefs which were in conflict with the Athenians' religion. He seems to have appeared in court, for some ancient sources speak of the defense speech he wrote and delivered for himself, exercising the skills in rhetoric about which he had written so eloquently. But the prejudices of his opponents meant that this speech, however brilliant, did not result in his acquittal.

The study of verbal persuasion was nevertheless revolutionized by Aristotle's *Rhetoric*, because its emphasis was on what made speech *work*, the nuts and bolts of argumentative technique, instead of how to get power in the city-state by being a clever speaker. The treatise opens with a statement that must have seemed quite threatening to many educated men of his day: rhetoric is a skill which can be taught and absolutely everyone can learn it. All people "attempt to criticise or uphold arguments, to defend themselves or accuse others." Most people do this all the time, at home or work, without thinking about the process consciously, having become familiar with argumentative techniques from habit and from hearing others use them. But since it is clearly a learned process, it is also "clear that matters can be reduced to a system."

Aristotle thinks that rhetoric should not be studied as a skill under the rubric of preparing for a political career, but simply as a capacity for argument in any social sphere, political or otherwise. His students learned rhetoric so they could better express themselves in any intellectual discipline whatsoever. It is revealing that he asks why nobody takes any notice of pleasing the audience when they are teaching geometry. Why not? Teachers of any subject, even if its content is wholly objective and factual, will be more effective if they study rhetoric. So will any human being, for that matter.

If you apply Aristotle's basic rules from *Rhetoric* to any situation, whether a job or in negotiating housework, they will help you to succeed. The very way we all argue with each other has been fundamentally informed, over the centuries, by Aristotle's *Rhetoric*. It is not just that his book has been studied intently, but that all the other ancient rhetoricians, such as Cicero and Quintilian, whose work has also influenced speechwriters and educators, absorbed Aristotle's precepts.

Another reason is that Aristotle's theory of persuasion was developed integrally with the rest of his works. Emotions and thought underlie

Aristotle's virtue ethics, but are also integral to his advice on persuasion. Some of his most interesting empirical observations on cognition through speech—how people take in information delivered in words—also occur in the *Rhetoric*. His entire theory is built on the relationship between the communicator and the audience, and how emotions and language create that relationship.

The Greeks had been studying speeches for centuries by the time Aristotle wrote his *Rhetoric*, and had written manuals on the tricks of the trade. But rhetoric had acquired a bad reputation. It was seen as a suspect knack by which unscrupulous politicians could make bad arguments look good, and persuade citizens into amoral or self-destructive collective decisions on the basis of no evidence. In the dialogs of Plato, there is a major structural distinction between philosophers, who look for the truth, and sophistic rhetoricians, who are only concerned with influencing opinion.

Aristotle is not taken in by rhetorical tricks. He offers examples of how speakers put a positive or negative "spin": one man's terrorist is another man's freedom fighter. Aristotle's example is that you can call Orestes, who killed his mother, Clytemnestra, in revenge for her killing of his father, either a "father-avenger" or a "mother-murderer" depending on whether you want your audience to sympathize with him or loathe him. Aristotle also remarks that in his day, "robbers" had begun to "talk themselves up" by describing themselves as "purveyors." And he points to the example of the poet Simonides, who was asked to write an ode celebrating a competitor's victory at one of the athletics contests in the race for mules. Simonides declined, thinking that it was impossible to write an ode—an inherently elevated verse genre—on such an undignified animal. But when the commissioning customer offered him enough money, he decided to "talk up" the mules, and wrote "Hail, daughters of storm-footed steeds!" Simonides would have made a good spin doctor.

Persuasion can be used for laudable ends. In his late thirties, Aristotle went to live in the towering clifftop kingdom of Assos and Atarneus in Asia Minor and teach its ruler Hermias philosophy. He seems to have been appointed as some kind of official state aide, and to have convinced Hermias that he needed to run a more democratic regime. But by then Aristotle was also well aware, having lived for twenty years in democratic Athens, that the speeches and oratorical style of lawyers and politicians often appeal to volatile, prejudiced or ill-informed crowds.

He criticizes previous manuals of rhetoric (none of which has survived) because they were more interested in dimensions of speech-making that were extraneous to the actual topic: they gave advice on distracting the audience from important evidence, defamation and disparagement of opponents and rivals, and how to inflame emotions such as pity by wiles including the display of your small children weeping in courts of law. Rhetoric of this kind is successful not because the speaker makes a better case but because they pander to the audience's taste for the sensational or histrionic.

Aristotle sees that abandoning the study of rhetoric is to throw the eloquent baby out with the demagogic bathwater. Aristotle sees rhetoric as simply a toolkit which enables you to argue the facts *relevant* to the case in the most convincing manner, allowing the audience to form rational judgments. The most convincing argument is *always* one which is centered on proof, which Aristotle labeled an *enthymeme*.

Most successful enthymemes start out from beliefs already held by the audience. In a job interview, these would be that the interviewers want to choose the most qualified candidate, and that both parties agree on those qualifications. In the case of an interview for the job of a taxi driver, the enthymeme would assume the possession of a clean driving license, no criminal record, and verification of several years of problem-free work for another taxi company. *Everything* comes down to proof judged according to generally assumed beliefs (*endoxa*). Documentable proof is considered to be by far the most cogent element in the process of persuasion.

Aristotle's *Rhetoric* is usually discussed alongside his *Poetics,* but in fact it is more intimately connected with his six works on logic, which later ancient philosophers put together and named his *Organon* ("Instrument"). The *Organon* has been seminal in the historical evolution of philosophy, science and mathematics. Aristotle was not content with *using* arguments: he thought that the reasons we use for supporting or refuting theories are complicated and require analysis in their own right. He saw that a discipline was needed which studied not a "content"—plants in botany, or human behavior in ethics—but the form taken by the arguments we use when we apply reason. In this he was a pioneer, as he well knew: "In the case of rhetoric there were many old writings on which to draw, but in the case of logic we had absolutely nothing at all to say until we had spent much time in laborious research."

The simplest but most important forms of argument are simply statements or "premises." From putting two statements together we can deduce or infer a third statement which constitutes a conclusion or a truth. This is similar to the rhetorical enthymeme but called a *syllogism* (which in Greek just means "a process of putting arguments together"). Here is a successful syllogism:

Premise 1:   All philosophers are human.
Premise 2:   Aristotle is a philosopher.
Conclusion: Therefore Aristotle is a human.

Aristotle was the first thinker to see that this could be written out in a universal form: all philosophers (x) are human (y). Aristotle (z) is a philosopher (x). Therefore Aristotle (z) is a human (y).

Once he had defined the idea of the syllogism, Aristotle saw that most syllogisms fell into certain categories, depending on the form taken by the premise and the modifying adjectives—"all philosophers" or "some philosophers," for example. A modifier could even be negative—"no philosophers"—for Aristotle realized that slightly more complicated syllogisms involve negative statements:

Premise 1:   Aristotle and Theophrastus *are not both* at the Lyceum today.

Premise 2:   Theophrastus is at the Lyceum today.

Conclusion: Therefore Aristotle is not at the Lyceum today.

If both premises are true, the conclusion is certain to be true. *If* the premises are correct, a valid and useful conclusion can be drawn.

The devil with formal logic, however, is in the detail. By the age of seven most children can spot a faulty, illogical conclusion, as in this:

Premise 1:   All Britons are human.

Premise 2:   Some humans like bananas.

Conclusion: Therefore all Britons like bananas.

If only *some* humans like bananas, then we cannot assume that *all* Britons do. The conclusion does not follow: it is a non sequitur. We would need more information in order to derive that conclusion. Yet it will take most children much longer to learn to question a *premise* that is presented to them:

Premise 1:   Aristotle is a philosopher.

Premise 2:   All philosophers are pedants.

Conclusion: Therefore Aristotle is a pedant.

The first premise here is indisputable. Even the conclusion derives logically from the premises *if you accept them.* The problem lies in the second premise. Experienced philosophers, politicians and lawyers know well that the clever place to hide a logical problem or tendentious viewpoint is in the second premise. The vulnerable point is *always* the middle of the syllogism, because if the listener has accepted your first premise, they are put in the frame of mind which regards you as plausible and makes them more willing to accept your second. Most arguments relying on racial or other discriminatory prejudice house an incorrect statement—often a generalization—in their second premise: all Irish people are lazy, all redheads have a temper, no woman can park a car.

A colleague of mine, Susan, who is an archaeologist, was quarreling all the time with her husband, a philosopher. Like Spock in *Star Trek*, he could always pick holes in her conclusions, and say she was illogical. Her deductions, he claimed, were all non sequiturs. But she didn't at the time realize that the place he was hiding his own logical problems—incorrect generalizations—was in the second premise:

His premise 1:   Susan is in psychotherapy.

His premise 2:   People go to psychotherapy because they are psychologically inadequate.

His conclusion: Therefore Susan is psychologically inadequate.

Once Sue had read, marked and inwardly digested all of Aristotle's works on logic via a competent précis of them in a philosophical encyclopedia, her husband could no longer get away with that surreptitiously inserted false second premise. She had previously spent all her time trying to prove that she was an *exception* to his second premise, instead of refuting it altogether. But she was able, via learning the rules of the logical premise, to restate his syllogism like this:

Premise 1:   Susan is in psychotherapy.

Premise 2:   By signing up for psychotherapy, people prove their psychological intelligence and adequacy.

Conclusion: Therefore Susan is psychologically intelligent and adequate.

The couple are still together and somewhat happier! Training our young in elementary logic, and especially in questioning premises rather than just focusing on drawing logical conclusions, would give them a peerless weapon. They could use it to defend themselves not only in significant relationships, but against unscrupulous people, especially bigoted politicians who want to exploit their naivety.

One example of a false premise was used by President George W. Bush when arguing for the introduction of educational reforms which dramatically increased the role of testing in grades 3 to 8 under the No Child Left Behind Act 2001. He stated:

Premise 1:   Children are failing too often in basic literacy and numeracy in schools.

Premise 2:   Everybody opposed to dramatically increased testing has no interest in holding schools accountable for their failures in teaching literacy and numeracy.

Conclusion: Only dramatically increased testing will improve literacy and numeracy in schools.

The first premise expressed a truth and one which was widely accepted. But the second premise was not true. Bush's opponents were indeed extremely interested in making schools more accountable for their performances, and had developed several different proposals for reforms, but they did not include increased testing. This meant that the conclusion Bush had drawn was false. He had not for one minute proved that the *only* way to improve literacy and numeracy was by increased testing. Bush frequently used such misrepresentation of the opposition's views in his second premise in putting the case for his proposals to the public.

Or take the false syllogism on which support for the 2003 invasion of Iraq was raised by both President Bush and Tony Blair:

Premise 1:   Intelligence reports tell us that Iraq holds weapons of mass destruction.

Premise 2:   We would not lie to you, distort or exaggerate evidence.

Conclusion: Therefore we must invade Iraq and disarm Saddam Hussein.

Emotive language was used to draw attention away from the fuzzy glossing over of the details of the "evidence" in Premise 1, and the appeal to their own moral integrity in Premise 2. Blair insisted that Iraq's weapons of mass destruction program was "active, detailed and growing," while Bush said that the invasion was necessary before Saddam "threatens civilisation." Many other tragic historical events have been caused by failure of voters to see the invalidity of such a logical syllogism.

But what are you trying to achieve by rhetoric? There are three constituents in the process: you the communicator; your audience; and your "script," the words which you deliver to them in a letter, an e-mail, a speech or a lecture. Aristotle divides "scripts" into three fundamental categories. First, there are speeches, for example speeches in law courts, which describe things that have happened already, and are therefore in a kind of "past tense": Socrates had introduced new gods, said his opponents in their prosecution speech. Second, there are speeches in a present tense which discuss or celebrate people or institutions in the present—a good example here would be a speech at a wedding praising the newly married couple: Aristotle and his wife, Pythias, both *love* zoology and so are perfectly suited. But, third, there are speeches about future action in which people are trying to decide *what should be done*. These speeches, designed to persuade interlocutors to choose certain types of conduct, are in a future tense and a conditional or subjunctive mood: "Philip, Your Majesty, *if* you rebuild my beloved home town of Stageira, I *shall* be friends with you again." This rhetoric is related to Aristotle's notion of deliberation. Aristotle is far more interested in this "deliberative" rhetoric because it has the potential to alter the course of history, even on a minor scale. It can powerfully affect what happens in relationships, careers and politics. Skill in "deliberative," persuasive rhetoric empowers its possessor. And the beauty is it can be learned.

Aristotle's *Rhetoric* is three books long and enthralling. I have here tried to condense his most important "rules" for effective communication into a few pages. In my own experience, as an academic, the situation where effective communication has had the greatest consequences for people's lives has been the job application. There are regularly 200 applicants even for poorly paid temporary teaching posts in today's universities. It can be almost impossible to get onto a shortlist, and even more difficult to persuade a committee in twenty-five minutes flat that you are a better bet than the other five people they are interviewing. An academic job application is no different from any other except in details of content, so the following would be as relevant to any employment application. Say that we are asking Aristotle what to write in our covering letter, and how to prepare for the interview: the

"ABC" of effective communication, according to Aristotle, is audience, brevity and clarity.

Before you start writing, find out as much as possible about your audience—the members of the appointment committee and anyone else (e.g. the head of personnel/human resources) who is likely to be reading your application. It is not usually difficult to discover who will be involved in the appointment; many public employers are obliged to publish the names, and, in most professions, word gets out. It is essential to make your audience, the people drawing up the shortlist, feel that you have researched and thought seriously about who they are, that you respect and admire them, and have some understanding of what working with them would be like. For Aristotle, rhetoric is above all an *emotional* transaction: you want to make the recipients *feel* good about themselves and *desire* to meet you or see you again. The trick is to do this without demeaning yourself by resorting to unctuous flattery. Avoiding any negative tone is obviously sensible: when applicants report in their letter that they hate their current job and have fallen out with their boss, the letter goes straight in the waste-paper bin. The statements may be true, and even justifiable, but marketing yourself as a conflict-prone melancholic is absurd.

So "audience research" is crucial, both in your application and once you have secured an interview. I have a friend who was offered a competitive job he had applied for in business because he was the only interviewee who had discovered the political biases of the most powerful individuals on the committee and that one of them was obsessed with Wagner. In academia, it is important to check out the publications of every single interviewer. This enables you to steer the dialog in directions which you know will interest them. It also allows you to know the areas of the syllabus where the faculty has fewest available teachers, making you able to paint a word-picture of the lectures you could deliver addressing the gaps, thus promising to lighten their own workload. But even in the application letter there needs to be a sentence or two showing you have thought about what the appointee could do to complement the skills of the staff.

Thinking about the audience, and adapting your letter of application to create the right emotional response, takes effort and time. So does pitching the tone perfectly in tune with your audience. I have read application letters that are laughably portentous and affected, beginning "Esteemed sirs," but I have also read ones where the author comes over as almost insultingly nonchalant ("Hi, Profs!"). There is an unaffected but dignified Aristotelian mean between these extremes ("Dear members of the appointment committee") but each letter must be tailored to suit the individual recipients. It is of course much easier and quicker to print off and send the identical letter to every employer to whom you are applying. But it will not get you onto many shortlists.

The second of Aristotle's cardinal rules of rhetoric is brevity. When it comes to persuading other people, less is *always* more. The only speeches where length has value for its own sake are *not* concerned with future actions. They are created for other purposes. A speech where extension is in itself a desideratum would be one intended to entertain (if you are hired to give a half-hour's after-dinner speech and only go on for ten minutes, your customers would be entitled to complain). Another would be the obituary speech at a funeral. This describes things that have already happened—events in the life of the deceased. If it is too short it can justifiably be seen as disrespectful. But if you are trying to persuade someone to *do something in the future*, however immediate—for example offer you a job—succinctness is essential. With the details laid out in a CV, I would go so far as to say that if your covering letter goes on for more than one or at the most two pages of A4 in twelve-point type, you need to rethink your arguments.

There are only two components to effective persuasion about future action, according to Aristotle. *Anything* else is superfluous and will detract from or obscure your case. The first component is the statement of what you want to happen (e.g. that you are offered the job in question). The second is the evidence which proves that you are the most desirable candidate. In longer speeches of persuasion than a job application, such as a speech in Parliament proposing to bring in a new law, it can become necessary to sum up, in a conclusion, what has already been said. Aristotle had discovered that there are fairly universal limits to the amount of information which any human can absorb and retain if the whole rhetorical performance—whether it is heard or read—lasts for more than about five minutes. But where it takes less than five minutes to hear or read, even the summation is dispensable. In a one-page letter of application, it is redundant.

In this kind of letter, the statement of what you want to happen, and why, requires exactly two sentences. "I would like to apply for the lectureship in spectromorphology (Job ref. F3400) in the music department at St. Wenceslas College, advertised in the *Daily Educator* for 16 April 2016. I am currently in a fixed-term post at Postlethwaite University, where I have been happy, but am now looking to secure a permanent position in a larger and more internationally prominent department." The remainder of the letter *briefly* specifies the supporting evidence that you are the ideal candidate. This evidence can only fall under a limited number of headings, some relating to the past and present you, and some relating to the future you. You already possess the suitable qualifications, past achievements, experience and attitude. You believe that you and the employer would make a particularly good fit in the future. Name the most important piece of evidence in each of these categories, and you will already have written a letter which is superior to that submitted by at least 75% of the rival candidates.

The third crucial quality of the piece of rhetoric is clarity. If people do not understand your case, you *will* fail to persuade them. It is astonishing how many aspiring lecturers' dossiers don't state when, where and exactly with what result they took their final examinations or PhD in the past, nor what precisely they are doing right now, let alone what contribution they would offer the department in the future. If you are reading through 200 applications, having to hunt even for a minute for this kind of information is sufficient reason to discard one immediately.

People are not stupid and your appointment committee will spot either ambiguity or vagueness. Both make the speaker/writer look evasive and makes the hearer/reader irritated or nervous. So Aristotle's advice is to be specific: in your letter of application, do not say "I will apply for research grants for my project on the Greek gods after a number of months," but "I will apply for research grants for my project on cult centres of Apollo in the Cyclades islands at the end of my first year in post." Or "I will use the projected profits from the Portsmouth outlets to establish new branches of Peter's Plimsoll Retailers in the eastern suburbs of Greater Manchester in September next year." Then be prepared to explain in the interview *exactly* what this project will involve and the ways in which you will finance it.

Aristotle is also instructive on the alienating effect on your audience of opaque and mystifying forms of expression. His particular example is Heraclitus, perhaps the most impenetrable of all the ancient Greek philosophers. He quotes a sentence by Heraclitus where the word order makes it quite impossible to be sure what is meant: "Although this reason exists forever men are in a state of doubt." It is not clear whether it is the *reason* which exists forever, or whether it is *men* who are forever in doubt. The sentence badly needs either punctuation, or a change of word order which would elucidate which part of the sentence the adverb "forever" qualifies.

So let us suppose that this flawless letter, combined with the well-organized CV, gets you an interview. At this point your bodily self-presentation comes into the limelight, and for Aristotle, an important component of this is the "D" in the alphabet of successful rhetoric—delivery.

Aristotle's close friend Theophrastus wrote a whole treatise on delivery, the surviving scraps of which suggest that they shared a lively interest in the topic and would discuss the delivery styles of public speakers in Athens. The ancient Greek word for this is actually *hypokrisis*, the word used for what stage actors do when they perform; in English, the same term has become distorted into the word for *faked* moral sensibility, hypocrisy. But the idea of acting a role is not unhelpful when preparing for a rhetorical performance. A glamorous friend was once in court, charged justifiably with using a monochrome television set without a license. She dressed up in a frumpy frock with flat shoes and her hair in a scruffy bun. She mumbled to the judge that she was a botanist and a teacher and did not understand the law relating to the licensing of televisual appliances. She apologized earnestly. She got off with the lowest fine available.

What sort of character do you want to come over as possessing in a job interview? You may well be a work-shy, irresponsible freeloader who, if appointed, will exploit your colleagues. But you do not want to give this impression to your prospective employers. The opening chapter of the second book of Aristotle's *Rhetoric* contains this trenchant statement: to produce conviction in hearers, the speaker must "(1) make his own character look right and (2) put his hearers, who are to decide, into the right frame of mind. As to his own character, he should make his audience feel that he possesses good sense, moral virtue and goodwill." If you are a practicing Aristotelian, of course, you will have been working on acquiring these qualities as ingrained habits, and should by now have few problems in conveying that to your interviewers.

But Aristotle develops further the picture of the sort of individual who is generally well liked. These are people who do not live off others but earn their living by hard work. Even if your past success is a result of amoral means, such as flirting with your superiors or cheating in your exams, pointing to some sheer hard graft in your past *always* pleases potential colleagues who are probably creaking under the weight of their own workloads.

Aristotle expands his definition of universally likable people. "Those who are agreeable to live or spend the time with; for example, those who are good-tempered and not given to carping at our mistakes, and are neither quarrelsome nor contentious." Good cheer, buoyancy and affability are invaluable. Getting humor right is also essential: you *must* be able to take humor directed *at* you as well as dish it out, and you need to dish it out *tastefully*: "We like people who are adroit at making or taking a joke." Having said that, even if an interviewer *does* do something as unprofessional as cracking a joke at your expense, the interview is not the moment to return it, even in the best possible taste. One piece of helpful Aristotelian advice is to respond to aggressive comic attacks with gravity and earnestness. Sarcasm and irony wither in the face of authentic statements of feeling and opinion. Aristotle knows that irony can often mask contempt and that you can turn ironic attacks on you to your own advantage.

It is *not* true that all interviewers make up their mind about you within the first two minutes of the interview. Experienced interviewers know that at around the seventeenth minute some candidates forget the "role" they are playing, especially overconfident ones who have started to feel comfortable and allow themselves a little too much of a self-aggrandizing tone. But more superficial factors can affect interviewers' responses to you. First impressions matter, as Aristotle knows well. In his works on ethics, he discusses clothes and personal grooming. The great-souled man needs to achieve the mean between off-putting sartorial extravagance on the one hand and looking as if he doesn't care about his appearance at all on the other. Aristotle shrewdly comments that excessive shabbiness is a form of ostentation in itself. In my profession, many colleagues used to affect a complete disregard for their appearance, in order to imply that their minds were somehow on higher things. This extended not only to their clothes but a failure to use deodorant and shoe polish, let alone the services of dentists, hairdressers or dry-cleaners. Thankfully, things have improved among the younger generation. The best advice here is always the same, to both women and men: nobody ever failed to get a job because they were wearing a *plain* but well-cut dark suit with a crisp white shirt, or a businesslike dress, and well-maintained but plain dark shoes. It *is* worth putting money into good tailoring. This can be hired if you can't afford to buy it.

The first impression consists of more than your physical appearance. It *is* helpful to make eye contact, consecutively, with everyone in the room, and sustain that ocular relationship with them all, especially when it is their turn to put a question. In his *On Delivery*, Aristotle's colleague Theophrastus said that a speaker who fails to meet his audience's gaze makes as poor an impression as an actor with his back turned. And your initial responses carry great weight: the opening of any rhetorical performance, whether it is designed to be read or heard, offers an unparalleled opportunity, as Aristotle underlines, to grab or repel the attention and interest of your hearers. Aristotle tells us that the most famous tragic actor of his day, Theodorus, insisted on having all the classic plays rewritten to make sure that the character he was playing had the opening speech, simply because that is the best moment in a play to establish a bond with the audience.

Among Aristotle's advice on persuasive speech there are several other helpful observations. First, the opening of your interview or speech is the moment when you are most likely to have everyone's attention, but their minds can start wandering soon afterward. Keep up your personal concentration as a performer, but more important retain the attention of your listeners, as "attention slackens everywhere else rather than at the beginning." He has been proved correct in numerous experiments conducted by cognitive scientists in pedagogical contexts. Repeated studies of the human ability to focus in lectures have shown that almost everyone stops concentrating between five and twenty-five minutes in. A golden rule, therefore, is to change tack or introduce a completely different type of information at about the seventeenth minute, and, in a fifty-minute lecture, again at about the thirty-fifth. And point out the gear change firmly. Aristotle cites the philosopher Prodicus, who, whenever his audience "began to nod," would say, "I am going to tell you something more strange and wonderful than you have ever heard!" He would then treat his audience to a special free excerpt from his most famous display speech, the fee for which, on other occasions when he performed the whole thing, was the considerable sum of fifty drachmas.

Finally, Aristotle thinks that analogies are invaluable in persuading your listener. A well-chosen analogy is of far more use in producing conviction than any other rhetorical ornament, such as the insertion of unusual words: "The greatest thing by far is to be a master of metaphor. It is the one thing that cannot be learnt from others; and it is also a sign of natural talent, since a good metaphor implies an intuitive perception of what is similar in dissimilar things." Here he is talking specifically about metaphor, but I use the word "analogy" because Aristotle does not believe there is any *functional* difference between a simile ("the sun's rays at dawn were like rosy fingers") and a metaphor ("the rosy-fingered sun dawned"): it makes the listener imagine the appearance of the early-morning sun and its rays as a hand with pink fingers. Aristotle was primarily interested in the *cognitive* role of such comparisons. He correctly believed that they accelerated learning. Because the listeners need to consider in what respect the two things being compared are similar (why are the rays of the sun like fingers?), they actively participate in a process of learning something about the appearance of both suns and hands.

The ability to draw original and instructive parallels, rather than recycle tired old analogies, is one of the very few things which Aristotle thinks is a natural gift and cannot be learned. There are certainly some individuals who have earned reputations for their outstanding use of comparisons. Winston Churchill was one of them, and used images to heighten his listeners' detestation of their enemy: "This whipped jackal Mussolini, who to save his own skin has made all Italy a vassal of Hitler's empire, comes frisking up at the side of the German tiger with yelpings not only of appetite—that can be understood—but even of triumph." Author Dorothy Parker was renowned for her acerbic and amusing comparisons: "A little bad taste is like a nice dash of paprika." "His voice was as intimate as the rustle of sheets." The images used by the man to whom she bequeathed her estate, Dr. Martin Luther King Jr., helped to do what the best rhetoric can, which is change history for the better. His epoch-making speech "I have a dream" was rich in visual imagery through metaphor and simile, much of it evoking the grandeur of the American landscape: "With this faith, we will be able to hew out of the mountain of despair a stone of hope." But some of the images are delivered through quotation: "We cannot be satisfied so long as the Negro in Mississippi cannot vote and the Negro in New York believes he has nothing for which to vote. No, no, we are not satisfied and will not be satisfied until justice rolls down like water and righteousness like a mighty stream." As many of his Bible-trained followers well knew, King was here alluding to the Old Testament prophet whose vision of the future had historically provided so much comfort to African Americans, Amos 5:24: "But let justice roll down like waters, and righteousness like an ever-flowing stream." It was shrewd of Barack Obama to quote King, quoting Amos, in 2007, when he announced his candidacy for the U.S. presidency: "We welcomed immigrants to our shores. We opened railroads to the west. We landed a man on the moon. And we heard a King's call to let 'justice roll down like waters,' and righteousness like a mighty stream. We've done this before." He thus made the image of the elemental, ineluctable momentum of racial justice do double work. It made abstracts like "justice" feel visceral and material, but also invited his audience to resurrect King in their minds, speaking before the Lincoln Memorial, and compare the changes which Obama now proposed to oversee as president with those brought about by the 1960s civil rights movement.

Aristotle seems to have prided himself on his own dazzling analogies. He knew he was naturally endowed with the ability to do what we call "horizontal thinking" or "thinking outside the box." Time and again he succeeds in clarifying a tricky concept by drawing an analogy with another dimension of experience altogether. In his public *Encouragement to Philosophy*, he compared contemplation of the nature of the universe to what spectators do at the theater or athletics competitions. In order to explain the educative potential of tragedy, he says that learning from watching an enactment of suffering was like learning from looking at a diagram of an ugly, primitive life form. He compares equity in questions of justice with the flexible measuring ruler of the builders he had seen at work on Lesbos. A good teacher who adapts the curriculum to each pupil is like the "Professor of Boxing" who trains all his students in the same sport, but adapts the exercise program to suit their individual gifts. A man who rejects his fellow citizens and opts for the loner's life is like "an isolated piece at draughts."

Some of Aristotle's most helpful comparisons in his ethical works are with famous mythical episodes in the Homeric poems. When arguing that the state needs to be involved in determining the curriculum studied by its children, he reminds us that it is the mark of a brutish race like the Cyclopes for each male cave-boss to determine unilaterally what education his own young receive. And when considering the importance of long-term thinking, such as threatening the stability of your household by committing adultery, he recommends imagining you are the Trojans looking at Helen of Troy. Her presence may be something you desperately desire, but it will destroy your city if you don't say no.

Finally, the observation of Aristotle's that has most potential to transform your own persuasiveness is that there is far less difference than usually assumed between effective speech and effective writing. "Generally speaking, whatever you write should be easy to read or easy to utter, which is the same thing." It is true that in Aristotle's day silent reading was the exception rather than the rule. Most people used their voices in reading, as children do today. But that does not lessen the importance of his advice. If a sentence does not roll off the tongue, it will not roll into the cognitive part of your reader's brain either. Sentence *length* is crucial here. As Aristotle says, if it is too short, it jars on the reader. A two-word sentence can occasionally be effective, but only once or twice in any particular text or presentation. Sentences that are too long are even worse, because, as Aristotle says, the reader or listener can't keep track of the meaning. You might as well not speak at all. So when you are writing a letter of application for a job, read it out loud before you send it off. One member of the appointing committee may well end up reading out loud or quoting part of your letter to the others, or (which is worse), back to you in the course of the interview.

Chapter 5

---※---

SELF-KNOWLEDGE

Even for those of us satisfied in both our working and personal lives, there usually comes a point where we feel we could do better. A difficult experience, such as a divorce or a feud, may have left us feeling vaguely guilty and wondering how much personal responsibility we need to take for other people's misery. The arrival of a first baby may have made us step up morally because selfishness and parenthood do not mix. Or we have met someone whose conduct and contribution to human happiness we want to emulate and so work toward self-improvement. Aristotle's categories of virtues and vices offer self-knowledge, allowing us to discover our own best and worst characteristics. Self-appraisal followed by *action*, expanding your virtues and minimizing your vices, will not only make other people around you happier, but also increase your own happiness.

Aristotle's most extended pieces of advice concern the good qualities which the happy person cultivates—virtues—and their correlative shortcomings. The relationship between happiness and these good qualities is pivotal to his whole ethical outlook. As we have noted before, he regards it as self-evident that individuals deficient in the basic virtues can never attain happiness: "For nobody would call a man ideally happy that has not got a particle of courage nor of self-control nor of decency nor sense, but is afraid of the flies that flutter by him, cannot refrain from any of the most outrageous actions in order to gratify a desire to eat or to drink, and ruins his dearest friends for the sake of a penny."

Aristotle believed that human well-being required justice, courage and self-control—the type of "virtues" which have given rise to philosophers labeling his overall moral system "virtue ethics." The nouns he used for the "good qualities" (*aretai*) and "bad qualities" (*kakiai*) are basic and everyday words in ancient Greek, without specifically moral associations. Their traditional translations as "virtues" and "vices" have rather off-putting connotations. "Virtue" has a suggestion of priggishness, and "vice," associated with viciousness, drugs cartels and prostitution, is a far more loaded term in English than the Greek *kakia*.

"Virtue ethics" itself may sound affected and grandiose. But instead of deciding to practice "justice," say to yourself that you have decided to be fair to everyone and fulfill your responsibilities, while helping people, including yourself, fulfill their human potential. Instead of "practicing courage," think in terms of facing things you are frightened about and training yourself to be less fearful. Instead of taking a vow of "self-control," figure out what is the "golden mean" or appropriate level of response to strong emotions, personal interactions and desires (which is what Aristotle's "self-control" entails).

Aristotle's writing on virtues and their associated vices in the *Eudemian Ethics* and *Nicomachean Ethics* constitutes a practical instruction manual in morality. The "virtues," or "routes to happiness," are not so much qualities of character as habits that can be learned through practice. After repeated performance, they become so ingrained, like our unconscious reflexes when we drive a car, that they may indeed seem (to other people, at least) to be a permanent quality (*hexis*) of your character. The process takes a lifetime, but many people get better at it in middle age when some of their fiercest desires become more easy to control. Almost all of us can improve morally if we want to. As

Aristotle says, we are not like stones, which cannot be "trained" to move upward through the air on their own accord—if you release them, they will *always* drop downward. He sees a virtue like any other skill, such as playing the harp or building, which can be "learned." If you play the harp cacophonously or build walls that collapse, and make no effort to improve, you will obviously deserve a reputation for being bad at harp-playing or construction work. "The same then is true of the virtues," says Aristotle. "It is by taking part in transactions with our fellow men that some of us become fair-minded and others iniquitous; by acting in dangerous situations and forming a habit of fear or of confidence we become courageous or cowardly. And the same holds good of our dispositions with regard to our bodily appetites, and anger; some men become self-controlled and gentle, others profligate and irascible."

It is perhaps easiest to see this in the case of courage. Many of us have phobias or terrors which we overcome through repeated exposure to the feared object or experience. I was attacked by a dog as an infant, and for many years would go to enormous lengths to avoid dogs of any kind. Aristotle would have told me not to be too hard on myself. Like a man he mentions who was pathologically frightened of weasels, I had become afraid through trauma. But the trauma was equivalent to a disease and therefore treatable. It was only when my husband persuaded me to take on a puppy, and I (at first reluctantly) engaged with Finlay on a daily basis, that after a couple of years I became (almost) entirely confident with almost all dogs (although I remain strict about keeping them away from small children). In a more compli-cated example, a friend of mine sabotaged all his early relationships with women by being incapable of expressing anger or discontent for months, until he would suddenly explode and walk out altogether (or they would sense his emotional inauthenticity and leave first). It was only in his early thirties, by committing himself to being clear about how he felt with the mother of his children, that he was able to negotiate problems as they arose rather than months too late.

Humans are not born with the skills entailed by Aristotle's virtues, which involve a combination of reason, emotion and social interaction, but instead with the potential to develop them. Aristotle's "virtue ethics" can be read as a record of discussions he had when walking in company with all his students, whether as Alexander's tutor in Macedon or later at his own Lyceum in Athens, about the way to be a decent and moral person. Although his moral philosophy is applicable to any one of us, when he does seem to have a particular type of student in mind, they are (perhaps inevitably) male, rich, and destined for public prominence. Occasionally this becomes suddenly and comically apparent, for example when Aristotle is discussing the benefactions required of rich men in certain city-states: most of us will never be invited to choose between financing a theatrical chorus at the national theater, a warship, or a public banquet. But the point is that such privileged youths have no excuse *not* to aim to perfect *all* the virtues. If they succeed in this, they will deserve Aristotle's ultimate accolade—to be thought to have developed a great soul (to be *megalopsychos*, from the Greek for "big" plus the Greek for "soul" or "psyche"). The nearest English word comes via the Latin, and is "magnanimity." I can hear Aristotle describing the deportment appropriate to the great-souled man to a tutor group of rowdy Macedonian teenagers: "a slow gait, a deep voice, and a deliberate utterance; to speak in shrill tones and walk fast denotes an excitable and nervous temperament."

The path to happiness comes through taking on a life's project of becoming a great-souled man or woman—of being magnanimous. You may not have the money to fit out a warship, and nor do you need to walk slowly or talk in a low-pitched voice. This kind of magnanimity, the state of mind of the truly happy individual, is the mark of the type of person almost all of us fundamentally aspire to be: he does not court danger for its own sake, but is prepared even to sacrifice his life for an important cause. He prefers helping other people to asking for assistance himself. He is never obsequious to the rich and powerful, and he is always courteous even to humble folk. He is "open both in love and in hate," because only a person who is afraid of what other people think of him needs to conceal his true feelings. But he avoids gossip because it is usually negative. He rarely criticizes other people, even his enemies, unless in an appropriate context (a lawsuit, for example), but equally he avoids excessively lavish praise. In short, being magnanimous means being quietly courageous, self-sufficient, non-sycophantic, polite, discreet and candid: this is a role model everyone can adopt with enthusiasm and sincerity. Just because it was written down more than twenty-three centuries ago does not make it any less inspiring.

The next step is to review all of Aristotle's characteristics and virtues from a self-analytical standpoint. Aristotle's list offers self-reflection for everybody capable of honesty with themselves. As one of the inscriptions on the Temple of Apollo had it, "know yourself" (*gnothi seauton*): Socrates, Plato's teacher, had also been fond of quoting this maxim. But if you do not "know yourself" or are not prepared to admit you are, for example, stingy, or fond of malicious gossip, then you might as well stop reading here. Aristotelian ethics require telling yourself home truths because they are not judgmental and are meant to be *feasible.* The imperative is *not* to judge yourself harshly and descend into self-castigation or self-dislike.

For Aristotle, character traits and emotions are almost all acceptable—indeed necessary to a healthy psyche—provided that they are present in the right amounts. He calls the right amount the "middle" or "mean" amount, the *meson.* Aristotle actually never used the term "golden mean"; it arose in English when his philosophical principle of the healthy "middle" in psychological traits and appetites was associated with a passage in the Latin poet Horace's *Odes* (2.10). Horace says that people who value the "golden mean," in Latin the *aurea mediocritas*, need not fear having to live in either a sumptuous palace or a squalid hovel. But whether we call this "mean between extremes" golden or not does not really matter.

A sexual appetite, since humans are animals, is a good thing in proportion. On the other hand, too much or too little sexual appetite are both conducive to unhappiness. Anger is essential to a healthy personality, and someone who never feels anger is not always going to do the right thing and will therefore not achieve happiness. Yet too much anger is also a shortcoming or defect—a vice. It is always a question of the right amount at the right time. Aristotle, of course, did not invent the other ancient Greek proverb inscribed on the Delphic Temple, "nothing in excess," but he was the first thinker to work out a detailed moral system to live in accordance with the principle.

One of the trickiest areas in ethics is the nexus of issues around envy, anger and desire for revenge. All three are central to the plot of the *Iliad*, Alexander's favorite book. He took it with him everywhere on campaign and will have discussed it at length with his tutor Aristotle. In this epic, the most important Greek king in terms of status, Agamemnon, envies Achilles, because Achilles is the greatest Greek warrior. Agamemnon humiliates Achilles publicly and also appropriates his beloved concubine Briseis. Achilles is furious. His wrath is increased when the Trojan Hector kills Patroclus, Achilles' best friend, in battle. Achilles gets his revenge on Agamemnon by receiving compensation and the restitution of Briseis. He slakes his thirst for revenge on Hector by killing him in single combat, mutilating his corpse, and also executing twelve entirely innocent Trojan youths by sacrificing them on Patroclus' pyre. This is excessive.

Aristotle writes with great acuteness about these three dark impulses: envy, anger and revenge. Aristotle was the target of envy both during and after his life. Despite being by far the best philosopher of his generation, when Plato died in 348 BCE, he was passed over for the leadership of the Academy where he had studied for two decades. The other Academicians found Aristotle's effortless brilliance hard to stomach and chose a dull philosopher called Speusippus instead. Later, they envied the admiration and support which Aristotle received, apparently without having to abase himself, from the kings of both Assos in Asia Minor, where he taught for two years, and of Macedon. As an Aristotelian who wrote a history of philosophy later put it, the great man incited so much envy simply "because of his friendships with kings and the sheer superiority of his writings." The Greeks were good at being honest about emotions that are often criticized today. Not everyone finds in Christian morality much help in dealing with any of the Aristotelian vices. Envy, for example, is a deadly sin, and the good Christian is supposed to "turn the other cheek" rather than retaliate if unjustly assaulted. But even if envy is not a major part of our characters, it is inescapable.

There is nobody who has not envied people with more money or better looks or better luck in love. If there is something we would like very much but that no amount of effort can guarantee—better health, a new baby, professional recognition or fame—then it can be almost unbearable to see others acquire them. The psychoanalyst Melanie Klein regarded envy as one of the primary driving forces of all our lives, especially in sibling relationships and other social peer relationships—that is, with our surrogate siblings. We cannot help envying those who seem to have received more blessings than we have. There is a sense in which this can be a healthy response, motivating us to remedy unfairness of any kind. It can be expressed at work by campaigning for legislation guaranteeing equal pay regardless of gender. It can be expressed politically in disapproval of a social system which allows a huge gap between rich and poor.

But envy of purely natural endowment, such as Aristotle's intellectual gifts, is a happiness-wrecker. It can warp the envious person's very personality and lead to obsession. It can lead to wholly undeserved attacks on the target of the envy; in the modern world these often take the form of vicious trolling or cyber attacks. In extreme cases, envy can result in the whole of society being deprived of works of genius if a gifted person's career is "successfully" stalled.

The toxic effect of this envy is beautifully dramatized in Peter Shaffer's 1979 play *Amadeus*, which he adapted to become the screenplay of Miloš Forman's multiple-Oscar-winning movie in 1984. The mediocre composer Salieri becomes obsessively envious at the ease with which his younger rival Mozart produces sublime masterpieces. He frustrates Mozart's career in every way he can, bad-mouthing him to the emperor. He plots to pass off Mozart's incomparable *Requiem* as his own. On his deathbed Salieri confesses that he had actually poisoned him. This means that not only did Mozart never complete the *Requiem*, but also, since he died in his mid-thirties, that the world may have been deprived of the dozens of wonderful works he might have produced if had lived for longer.

Although Salieri's murderous plot is fictional (indeed, he seems in reality to have been good friends with Mozart and he looked after Mozart's son when he was orphaned), the worldwide success of the film shows how much the portrayal of envy as an obsessive force resonated across cultures. Shaffer's own source for the story was an 1832 tragedy by Russian author Alexander Pushkin. In Pushkin's script, Salieri's dissection of his own predatory envy is expressed with brutal clarity: "I'll say it. / I am an envier. I envy; sorely, / Profoundly I now envy." He simply can't accept the *natural* unfairness of human society, in which some people are born more able or endowed than others:

Where, where is rightness? when the sacred gift,
Immortal genius, comes not in reward
For fervent love, for total self-rejection,
For work and for exertion and for prayers,
But casts its light upon a madman's head,
An idle loafer's brow . . . O Mozart, Mozart!

Aristotle recommends asking whether you are envying someone because they have acquired an unfair share of society's rewards or because they were born more naturally blessed than you. In the former case, your envy can energize you to seek justice and equality, but in the latter case, reflect on how that person's inborn gifts actually *enhance* your own life. If Aristotle's fellow Academicians had elected him their principal, he would have brought great prestige to their institution, rather than leaving and in due course founding his own rival university at Athens, the Lyceum. Their own reputations, which today are mediocre, would have been enhanced by being allowed to practice philosophy in his "slipstream," as it were. As philosophers themselves, they might even have learned to enjoy being in his company rather than resenting him.

Anger also fascinates Aristotle. The "mean" here is gentleness, or calmness, or kindness. He comments that there is actually no word in Greek which precisely means excessive gentleness. He suggests "lack of spirit"; we might call it apathy or indifference. This is a fault, says Aristotle, and "those who do not get angry at things at which it is right to be angry are considered foolish, and so are those who do not get angry in the right manner, at the right time, for the right length of time, and with the right people." If you don't feel or resent an injury, and are never angry, either on your own behalf or that of your friends when they are the victims, then this is a sign of a dysfunctional morality. People will think you have no self-respect and are incapable of sticking up for anything. Anger, says Aristotle, is sometimes virtuous and legitimate.

There are many causes of anger and of course ancient Greek literature affords hundreds of examples, from Medea's fury at her adulterous husband to the mighty warrior Ajax's wrath when he is not awarded the prestigious arms of Achilles when Achilles has been killed. But if you suffer from extremes of anger all the time, you may fairly be called culpably irascible. The irascible person may get angry with the wrong people (like the parent who takes work stresses out on their children rather than having it out with their boss). He may get angry for the wrong reasons (I have a neighbor whose husband did not speak to her for two weeks when she had merely locked the car keys in the hire car by accident on a family holiday). He may get angry more violently than is appropriate, fly off the handle far too quickly, or stay angry for too long even after an apology and compensation have been offered. Aristotle thinks that the last category is the most problematic. The best form of anger is that of the "quick-tempered, who display it openly by retaliating, and then have done with it." But people who are bitter, brooding and sullen by nature are seriously problematic: "they remain angry a long time, because they keep their wrath in." If you do not show your anger when you feel it, you "labour under a sense of resentment." Since your anger is concealed, nobody tries to placate you, "and it takes a long time to digest one's wrath within one. Bitterness is the most troublesome form of bad temper both to a man himself and to his nearest friends." So make sure you admit your anger to yourself and the actual perpetrator, explain the reasons clearly, and move on after the air is cleared. Many of us find this a challenge, and only begin to get better at this kind of emotional honesty in middle age. But Aristotle knows how difficult anger is to cope with when attempting to Live Well: "it is not easy to define in what manner and with whom and on what grounds and how long one ought to be angry, and up to what point one does right in so doing and where error begins."

In my own self-appraisal I discovered that while neither anger nor envy troubles me, I am by nature vengeful. I have over the last few years come to deal with this up to a point by learning from Aristotle, who was quoted by Dorothy Parker on the subject: "Living Well is the best revenge." Rise above the cesspool of envy and malicious backbiting and Be Happy! Ignore your detractors; if you are doing your best, criticism of you will *not* be well-intentioned. The truly great-souled man will get to the point of serenity where he "does not bear grudges, for it is not a mark of greatness of soul to recall things against people, especially the wrongs they have done you, but rather to overlook them." On the other hand, Aristotle does think that there is a time and a place not only for vengeful *feelings* such as anger, but for vengeful *action*. As might be expected from someone who spent so much time in the political atmosphere of Philip's Macedon, Aristotle's insights into vengeance are candid, profound and useful. In the fourth book of the *Nicomachean Ethics* he even argues that revengeful feelings can be virtuous and rational.

Aristotle does not dismiss altogether the pleasure of revenge. He also realizes that revenge is often about restoring our honor or status if we have been slighted. I have a close friend who made a point of being seen at a workplace party in a new dress with a handsome man, and thus making an ex-husband who had treated her badly both respect her and feel pain at losing her. She says that it was one of the best moments of her life and that it has made it much easier for her to move on and pursue happiness in a new relationship. But Aristotle's view is that desiring revenge is likely to be virtuous and thus conducive to your happiness *only* if a wrong has been committed which can be *righted* by revenge. Righting the wrong should help protect in the future from a similar wrong, at the hands of the same perpetrator.

When we are talking about righting wrongs, the issue of course becomes entangled with the law. In cases of serious crimes, such as slander, theft, assault, rape or murder, both victims and their loved ones may be entitled to having vengeful feelings satisfied by seeing the perpetrator legally punished. This is the thinking which underlies the campaigns for victims' rights and, in the USA, the right of relatives of murder victims to push for the death penalty. But what interests Aristotle are everyday slights which, although not reportable crimes, constitute a definite wrong.

In his *Rhetoric* book 2, Aristotle very specifically defines the anger of legitimate and virtuous vengefulness as "a desire accompanied by pain, for a patent revenge for a patent slight at the hands of people with no justification for slighting either oneself or one's friends." People who slight you or your friends without any justification are usually motivated by envy (so are Internet trolls who attack rich, beautiful or successful celebrities). If they slight you and hurt you publicly, it is fine to want public redress.

What does Aristotle mean by a "slight"? He says a slight can take three forms: contempt, spite and insolence. He gives two examples of what he calls contempt, or disrespect. The first will resonate with every person who has ever dealt with someone who uses "humor" to evade facing the seriousness of what you are saying. He calls them "those who reply with humorous levity when we are speaking seriously." The movie that makes this Aristotelian point to perfection is Patrice Leconte's *Ridicule* (1996), in which French aristocrats respond with arch jokes to the deadly serious pleas of local peasants to drain the marshland, which is causing their children acute disease. A woman professor I know complained to her personnel department because a colleague consistently delivered sexist wisecracks about women's inability to open doors for themselves. His response when called to account was to say that she couldn't "take a joke." The second example of contempt Aristotle describes as "those who treat us less well than they treat everybody else; it is another mark of contempt that they should think we do not deserve what everyone else deserves." Bullying, persecution or discrimination fall into this category. Any parent whose child has been bullied will agree that anger is perfectly legitimate, indeed virtuous, in such circumstances, as is a desire to see the wrong righted.

After contempt, the second category of slight for Aristotle is spite. The example he gives is "preventing another person from fulfilling their wishes," when your motive is *not* to get what you want for yourself. Your *only* motive is to hinder your victim. I can think of numerous examples of this kind of behavior in my professional life. Some individuals will go to extraordinary lengths to impede the career of someone they dislike but who is not even in competition with them. In academia, "blind peer review" is when scholars write anonymous reports on the articles other scholars have written. This can legitimize spiteful attacks. A bad review may negatively affect someone's career, especially if the article is rejected as a consequence. All too often, unfairly negative reviews are written with no justification at all. The system also protects spiteful reviewers from having to justify their stated opinion. In my personal life, this type of spiteful act is committed by women a bit like Dolly Parton's "Jolene." The "I" voice in that song is a less beautiful woman in love with a man. She begs Jolene, "Please don't take him just because you can." A friend once shared a house with a gorgeous woman who routinely seduced other women's husbands not because she wanted them, or had any intention of staying with them, but because she had a bad relationship with her mother and spitefully enjoyed stopping any married woman from being happy.

Aristotle's third and last category of slighting is insolence. He defines this as "doing things or acting in ways and saying things that bring shame on the victim when it can neither benefit you directly nor make up for anything that has happened to you, but purely for the pleasure entailed." The pleasure here is caused, says Aristotle, by the feelings of superiority over others which the insolent person gets by deriding or mistreating them. Simply demeaning someone else, bitching about them either to their face or behind their back, makes the insolent person feel, temporarily, better about themselves. Aristotle shows remarkable psychological acuity in seeing that people who need to criticize others constantly have a problem with respecting *themselves.*

Any type of slighting which uses laughter to denigrate a serious point someone makes calls into question how far humor is compatible with trying to be the Best Possible You at all. Now most of us like a laugh, and enjoy making others laugh. Humor is an extraordinarily helpful tool in all kinds of social situations, making difficult times much easier to bear, deflating pomposity and creating human bonds across political differences. But isn't laughter such a good thing that there are no limits on its role in the life of the person trying to practice virtue? It all comes down to our *intention.* People who are intent on turning *everything* into a joke care more about raising a laugh than about either "the boundaries of what is appropriate" on the one hand or the avoidance of "inflicting pain on the object of jesting" on the other. At the other extreme are joyless individuals, constitutionally incapable of being funny themselves: "it is right that they are considered churlish, boorish and morose." The golden mean is frequent humor that is neither indecent nor hurtful. This sort of joyous humor does not seem artificial, says Aristotle, but as if it springs authentically from a good-humored character.

There is one universal rule: only crack the kind of jokes you would be prepared to have cracked against you or in front of you. Imagine a young woman from a strict Christian background whose feminism is open to any kind of mockery from members of her intimate family, whereas her father's religious beliefs are sacrosanct. He may not be teased about them without reprisals. When it comes to laughter, it is crucial to be able to take just the same as you dish out. Or "do as you would be done by," as the nicer of the two aquatic spinsters in Charles Kingsley's *The Water Babies* (1863) maintained.

In the second book of his *Eudemian Ethics*, Aristotle provides a helpful table showing various qualities of character. He indicates in each case the "virtue" which is constituted by having this particular quality in the appropriate amount, along with its two correlative vices on either extreme, if it is present in excess or is deficient. Perhaps he sat the young Alexander and his peers down together in Mieza, the college Philip built for Aristotle in a lovely valley in Macedonia, to do it as a personality quiz—an exercise in self-assessment. You can use it as a checklist by yourself or with a trusted friend whom you can rely on to be honest with you, not try to score points, and not be judgmental:

Excessive	Appropriate	Deficient
insolence	respectfulness	shyness
self-indulgence	self-control	being insensitive to pleasure
envy	righteous indignation	a deficiency with no Greek label
avarice	financial integrity	financial gullibility
financial wastefulness	generosity	meanness
boastfulness	truthfulness about yourself	false modesty
fawning behaviour	friendliness	antagonism

obsequiousness	self-respect	arrogance
delicacy	endurance	invulnerability
self-importance	magnanimity	pettiness
extravagance	dignity	frugality
deviousness	prudence	gullibility

The virtue on which Aristotle expends most emotional intensity and colorful language is generosity. The related vices are prodigality—wastefulness with money—on the one hand, and meanness or parsimony on the other. It is obvious to me and my family which direction I personally err in here. I have often been described as "over-generous" or "generous to a fault," which Aristotle would call being "prodigal" with money—giving it away irresponsibly and in disproportion to your means. This threatens your ability not only to be self-sufficient economically, and look after yourself, but to look after other people dependent upon you. St. Francis of Assisi may have done a noble thing in giving a vagrant beggar his only cloak, but in doing so he fell sick himself and thus risked being no further use to anyone at all.

The most famous example of being "generous to a fault" in our culture is the central character in Shakespeare's late play *Timon of Athens*, based on an ancient Greek story with which Aristotle would have been familiar. Timon is a wealthy nobleman who is excessively generous: he pays off his friends' debts for which they have been imprisoned, helps a poor man wed the richer woman he loves, and throws lavish dinner parties entirely at his own expense. This excessive generosity inevitably leads to bankruptcy. Timon is miserably disappointed by the failure of his supposed "friends" to help him now he has fallen on hard times, and retires to a cave to live the life of an embittered, misanthropic hermit. The play makes it very clear that the problem is not generosity in itself, which is a noble and altruistic impulse, but that it is easily exploited by false friends who will not reciprocate when you are the one in need.

Aristotle writes with an intensity about financial meanness that convinces me he had someone particular in mind. Had his father Nicomachus, a middle-class doctor in the northeastern Greek city of Stageira, limited Aristotle's pocket money to a quarter of what his school friends received? Was Philip II, for all his commissioning of splendid statues, and his legendary drinking parties, tight-fisted when it came to his employees? Aristotle relishes some idiomatic and insulting words for the ancient Greek equivalent of Charles Dickens' Scrooge: *pheidolos* (miserly), *glischros* (sticky—i.e. money can't be removed from this person), and *kimbix* (a penny-pincher). Best of all is the *kuminopristes*, which means, literally, "one who saws even a cumin seed in half"; this reminds me of the proverbial miser who dries out and reuses his teabag. We shall probably never know the identity of Aristotle's personal cumin-seed-splitter, but his different rhetorical perspectives on the virtue of generosity still apply.

One angle, to do with very wealthy people, is decidedly political. Aristotle does not regard wealth as special. It is something which we can use, like other things we happen to have, if we do possess it; and things can be used well or used badly. Aristotle is unequivocal that to use wealth well involves generosity. The super-rich who never give to the less fortunate could never be happy, because they are living according to the vice of meanness rather than the virtue of generosity. The generous man is also concerned "with giving to the right recipients" at the right time, and spends more time considering this question than worrying about wealth acquisition. Aristotle accepts that the virtuous man must be sure that his money comes from honest sources. But since the generous man does not have much esteem for wealth *in itself,* he is unlikely to consider trying to obtain it from immoral sources.

Generous people don't usually ask for favors from others: the person "who confers benefits does not readily accept them."

Generosity, says Aristotle, is relative to an individual's resources. We do not assess the generosity of a gift according to its amount, but according to the intentions and character of the giver. A generous person thinks hard about how much they have and what proportion of it they can afford to give away without detriment to their own well-being or that of their dependents. In his own philosophical equivalent of the biblical story of the widow's mite, told by Jesus in the Gospels of both Mark and Luke, he tells us that "it is therefore possible that the giver of a smaller amount may be the more generous person," if she or he is giving "from smaller means."

The principle that pleasure can be virtuous takes an interesting form in the case of generosity. The generous person acting generously, to the right people at the right time, gives "with pleasure, or at all events without pain." If people give for some other motive (scenarios of emotional coercion or acquisition of power over another individual come to mind), they are obviously not generous at all. Nor is the person who feels pain when she gives money away. This person would not give it away if she thought her stinginess would go unnoticed. Yet Aristotle stresses that the truly generous person is always liable to the "vice" of giving away their money irresponsibly, to the extent that she actually leaves herself with less money than those receiving benefits from her, "for it is a mark of a generous nature to have little regard for oneself."

He has thought hard about financial meanness and its causes. "Men who have inherited a fortune are reputed to be more generous than those who have made one, since they have never known what it is to want." I am not sure that I agree with Aristotle here. I have known self-made businessmen who give nearly every penny away to good causes, and I have certainly known more than one pathologically stingy individual who was born into a sizable personal trust fund. But his reasoning is interesting. He assumes that having experienced poverty makes a person more tight-fisted (unlike some other ancient philosophers, who thought physical deprivation could enhance one's spiritual life, Aristotle has nothing positive to say about poverty). He is probably thinking about the views of some such ascetic sect when he comments that it is hard for a generous man to stay rich, because he is not good either at making money or keeping it, "while he is profuse in spending it and values wealth not for its own sake but as a means of giving. Hence people blame fortune because the most deserving men are the least wealthy. But this is really perfectly natural: you cannot have money, any more than anything else, without taking pains to have it." He also thinks self-made men are inclined to meanness because "everybody is especially fond of a thing that is their own creation: parents and poets show this."

Aristotle thinks that it is better to err on the side of excessive generosity, because this fault "is easily cured by age or by poverty." Since the person who spends too much on others is generous, he can be reformed into giving his money only when appropriate. The overly generous person "is foolish rather than evil or ignoble." The mean man, however, benefits absolutely nobody, not even himself, because he is incapable of being reformed and practicing the virtue of generosity. He will never Live Well and achieve true happiness. Aristotle regrets that more humans are by nature avaricious than generous, and that avarice seems to take a variety of forms.

Some people are mean with money because they are old or suffer from some serious debility of another kind, which is forgivable. Another group will sacrifice every moral scruple in order to "take from every source and all they can; such are those who follow degrading trades, brothel-keepers and all people of that sort, and petty usurers who lend money in small sums at a high rate of interest." Aristotle would have been the first to rebuke loan sharks and credit-card companies who encourage people to spend more than their income and amass debt, which they are then required to pay back at crucifying rates of interest.

A third group accumulates wealth on an enormous scale—Aristotle cites "princes who sack cities and rob temples." Philip II, of course, had done his fair share of city-sacking and primitive accumulation of capital by the time Aristotle went to Macedonia to teach Alexander, but the Macedonian king was usually careful to appear, at least, to conform with basic standards of piety and avoid sacrilege. Even so, it would be revealing to have been on the stroll round the royal college at Mieza when Aristotle told Alexander that such princes were guilty of far more than meanness—they were downright wicked. He puts them almost in a different category altogether from the petty criminal, "the dicer and the robber and the bandit," all of whom are certainly mean. They show "sordid greed," and in order to make a profit become immune to censure. Aristotle finds the dicer even more reprehensible than the bandit, who at least takes from people with whom he has no relationship, while the dicer "makes gain out of his friends, to whom one ought to give." Friends are not there to be financially exploited. If you take money from them, even in a game, they may not be your friends much longer.

Aristotle regards ambition as the hardest quality of character for anyone to get right. In fact, whatever you do in terms of ambition, you will be criticized: ambition seems to be a uniquely ambiguous element of character. People are praised both for having it and lacking it: at times "we praise the ambitious man as manly and a lover of honourable things, or praise the unambitious man as modest and temperate." But at other times people are criticized for being both too ambitious or not ambitious enough: "We blame a man for being ambitious if he seeks recognition more than is right, or from wrong sources; we blame him as unambitious if he does not care less about being recognised even on honourable grounds." By "ambition" Aristotle means a desire for public recognition and honor, not the more broadly defined and commendable desire to fulfill your potential *for its own sake*. Wanting to fulfill your potential, to develop your inborn talent to the maximum to be the best possible violinist, or footballer, or parent, or gardener, or scientist, is to be warmly encouraged and applauded in everyone. It takes a critic warped by irrational envy to object to anyone else being very good at what they do.

The tricky bit is monitoring one's desires for recognition and rewards. As a society, we do collectively enjoy bestowing fame, prizes and marks of distinction on successful people. There are literary prizes, Oscars, sports competitions, Nobel Prizes, knighthoods and the cover of *Time* magazine. There is nothing inherently wrong in enjoying the experience if one receives such an accolade. The problem comes when the thirst for fame takes over from the desire to be good at what you do for its own sake. This can happen easily. Fame can be disorientating, and addictive, especially in the political arena where it is allied with actual power. The ancient Greeks knew this well: Aristotle's favorite play, Sophocles'. *Oedipus Tyrannus*, portrays a leader who once worked for the good of the people but who has let the desire to be considered the world's most intelligent and capable leader, along with the enjoyment of power, go to his head. One of the best examples in modern culture is Willie Stark, the anti-hero of Robert Penn Warren's Pulitzer Prize-winning novel *All the King's Men* (1946), made into two fine movies in 1949 and 2006.

Stark develops into a narcissistic and corrupt governor of a southern state in the USA, who revels in the glory he receives as perceived champion of the "little man" and the applause he receives for his fire-brand speech-making. But Warren's novel stresses that Willie began as a restrained and honest lawyer in an agricultural area. It was only when he was catapulted into the limelight that all his humility was vanquished by his ambition to dominate the headlines. His negative ambition—a desire for glory—had supplanted his positive ambition, which was to lead and fairly represent his fellow citizens. Desire for what we now call "celebrity" is today even more of a live issue than it was in classical Greece. There are indeed many people devoid of all talent who crave and—at least briefly—achieve fame through "reality" TV shows, social media and gossip magazines. Aristotle would probably regard such fame junkies as seeking "recognition more than is right, or from wrong sources."

It is important to remember that "modesty" can be used as a stick to beat people with, especially women, who have historically been subjected to far harsher criticism for ambition than men, as was the case for Hillary Clinton in the 2016 U.S. presidential election. The question is always whether the ambitious person has lost sight of their original goals and replaced them with desire for maximum self-publicity.

Aristotle's standards are certainly exacting, but he is sympathetic to the struggle of identifying and sticking to the "mean." He interweaves into his discussion of the virtues and their related vices several encouraging observations about particularly tricky situations. He is, for example, strikingly clear that abusive experiences in childhood can make it difficult to do the right thing. He cites a man who is on trial for beating up his father. In his defense speech, the accused said, "Well, my father used to beat his father, and he used to beat his, and (pointing to his little boy) so will my son here beat me when he grows up; it runs in our family." A child brought up in a family culture of violence (even if we are surprised that Aristotle's example entails adult sons beating their fathers, rather than fathers beating their little boys) may find it impossible to control themselves when the same situation repeats generationally. Psychiatrists are well aware that suicide runs in families partly because precedent makes the choice seem a relatively "normal" response even to temporary unhappiness.

It is never too late to change your mind, according to Aristotle. If you discover new information, or have an emotional response which suggests you have assessed a situation incorrectly, then change your attitude or actions, however late in the day. Everyone has been in situations when new information or an emotional response has changed your mind. A friend of mine who works in business once had a protégée of whom he was very fond. He was told repeatedly that the protégée was bullying an assistant. Because my friend had never seen this side of the younger man's personality, and because he had invested time and effort in the relationship, he refused for several months to take the allegations seriously. It was only when the relevant e-mails were forwarded to him that the scales fell from his eyes. In due course the former protégée lost his job.

Aristotle knows how hard it can be to maintain the path of virtue in the face of strong affection or desire. He is an emotional realist. He is scathing about the Socratic idea that people never go off the rails or do wrong if they have all the available information. There are several reasons, Aristotle insists, why even individuals most committed to virtue ethics may slip up, so we should be more sympathetic to everyone. Passion, desire, madness and other threats to perfect self-restraint can afflict anybody and undermine their intellectual grasp on a situation. Ever the doctor's son, Aristotle says that "anger, sexual desire, and certain other passions, actually alter the state of the body, and in some cases even cause madness. It is clear therefore that we must pronounce people who are out of control to 'have knowledge' only in the same way as men who are asleep or mad or drunk." There is a gap between what they say, think and do, "just as if they are actors speaking their part."

The occasional and temporary loss of control, for Aristotle, is excused by extreme psychological pressure caused by pain or ecstasy or the humor of a situation. In a play about Philoctetes by Theodectes,

Philoctetes received the snake bite which disabled him, and apparently screamed in agony: to scream in such a situation is of course understandable, says Aristotle. If you discover that your father has had sex with your daughter (i.e. with his own granddaughter) and had a baby by her, as King Cercyon did, it would be astonishing if you *didn't* experience an emotional outburst. In his final example of acceptable loss of all self-control, he says that if we try to restrain a powerful impulse to laugh, eventually our "laughter explodes in one great guffaw, as happened to Xenophantus." Sadly, we do not know the reason for Xenophantus' hilarity, but we have *all* been in the situation where laughter has got the better of us on the most unsuitable occasions. At the funeral of one of my husband's relatives, the banality and pomposity of the rent-a-vicar's address at the crematorium made it altogether impossible for me to keep a straight face.

Even the best of us slip up and make mistakes. Regret or self-recrimination is not helpful. The important thing is to continue trying. It is interesting which example Aristotle uses here, given his absolute condemnation of adultery elsewhere; it even makes me wonder whether he ever desired another man's wife. Extreme desire, he says, may make a man commit adultery, but a one-off impulsive mistake which has not been deliberated does *not* turn an otherwise completely faithful man into someone we can fairly define as an adulterer. I have evolved a personal rule of usually allowing everyone a second chance in such cases out-of-control mistakes, but not a third one. Relationships can be developed with people who make one mistake, but *listen* to the pain it causes and resolve never to do it again: people who hurt you in the same way twice, however, are leopards who cannot change their spots.

Virtue ethics are so rich and sophisticated that they can indeed keep the person who adopts them busy for a lifetime. Aristotle admits that finding the *meson* in our actions is challenging. Extreme reactions are much easier than carefully modulated ones. In *Nicomachean Ethics* book

2 he uses a comparison from geometry. It is "a hard task to be good, for it is hard to find the middle point in anything: for instance, not everybody can find the centre of a circle, but only someone who knows geometry." You may need to think about finding the appropriate, middle response in any situation, and practice implementing it, like a child learning how to find the center of a circle or the length of the hypotenuse. Here Aristotle offers further illustrations. "Anybody can become angry—that is easy, and so it is to give and spend money; but to be angry with or give money to the right person, and the right extent, and at the right time, and for the right purpose, and in the right way—this is not within everybody's power and is not easy."

Aristotle offers some extra tips on how to identify and—more important—stick consistently to the virtuous mean in any particular circumstance. The first is that it is important to remember that even something generally regarded as a virtue can indeed turn into a problem if taken to an extreme. If we receive great praise for a standard virtue, remember the Delphic injunction, "nothing in excess." He uses the example of the myth of Niobe, who lost every one of her fourteen beloved children because she was just a little too proud of them. It is also possible to love your parents too much: he cites the example of a man named Satyrus who was so distraught when his father died that he committed suicide.

The second tip is that one of the two vices correlative to a virtue is always worse than the other. For example, Aristotle thinks that it is better to be excessively open-handed than stingy, although best of all to be appropriately generous. It is better to be self-deprecating than boastful, although best of all is an accurate assessment of your achievements and honest but not attention-seeking acknowledgment of them. He uses a graphic example from the *Odyssey*, familiar to all his students, to help his reader remember the principle. A good principle "in aiming at the mean is to avoid that extreme which is the more opposed to the mean, as Calypso advises: 'Steer the ship clear of yonder spray and surge.'" Aristotle slightly misremembers the passage in the *Odyssey* (12.219), which is actually spoken by Odysseus as he reports to his pilot the advice given to him by the other nymph with whom he had a liaison, Circe. She had warned him that the whirlpool Charybdis was *more* dangerous than the nearby serpentine monster Scylla. Charybdis would overwhelm his ship, and his entire crew would perish. Scylla would take a few of his men (in the event she eats six), but some of them would survive. Scylla, like being overly generous or falsely modest, is the lesser of two evils.

The third tip is to work out the mistakes in terms of virtue and vice to which you personally are most vulnerable. We are all different here: a fine colleague of mine never bullies anyone less powerful than him, but has been known to be unnecessarily aggressive "up the hill" toward people who have more power. The pleasure and pain we experience will help us here: if we know we are going wrong and not finding the "middle" way, the direction in which we are erring is usually the one which gives us intense pleasure. Adulterous sex, for example, is likely to be much more pleasurable than renouncing sex altogether, which would be to go to the other extreme. The *meson* is to stick to monogamous sex, which may give you less pleasure than adulterous sex but make you happier in the long run.

Aristotle is at his most lucid and sincere on universal experiences like this. Once we have identified the direction in which we are deviating from the *meson*, a question which the pleasure we experience can help us answer, "we must drag ourselves away in the opposite direction, for by steering wide of our besetting error we shall make a middle course. This is the method adopted by carpenters to straighten warped timber." Steersmen unsure of the middle course deliberately steer toward the lesser of two dangers; carpenters pay attention to the *direction* in which a piece of wood *naturally bends* in order to correct the problem.

The fourth tip involves help with that difficult challenge of "dragging ourselves away in the opposite direction." This is the trick I call "banishing Helen." In a resonant passage of the *Iliad*, the elders of Troy catch a glimpse of the lovely Helen walking along the walls, and acknowledge her outstanding beauty (3.156–60): "We can hardly blame the Trojans and Achaeans with their fine greaves for suffering protracted miseries for such a woman. She is amazingly like the immortal goddesses to look at." Like many modern psychotherapists, Aristotle encourages us to look our objects of desire squarely in the face. Denying how much you want to have that extramarital affair or that fifth glass of wine is not going to help you refuse either. But the elders continue, "But even so, however beautiful she is, let her depart upon the ships, and not stay here, not be left here to be a blight on us and our children after us." The elders knew that Helen's presence in Troy, however much pleasure it brought the Trojans, was the cause of the war and was threatening their *long-term* well-being. The right decision, which was most conducive to their permanent happiness, was to send her back to the Greeks and end the war.

Acknowledging what gives you greatest pleasure, and then asking how it may prevent you from rationally pursuing happiness, can help you negotiate the moderate path in being a good person and thus a happy one. Aristotle recommends actually quoting these Homeric lines to yourself every time you feel the need to give in to fulfill an urge for a pleasure that is not doing you any good. Finding out what the Helen of Troy is in your own life can be of the greatest advantage: if you do manage to banish her, your own personal city of Troy can flourish rather than end up burning in ruins.

Chapter 6

———— ∞ ————

INTENTIONS

"We praise and blame all men with regard to their purpose rather than with regard to their actions," writes Aristotle. Sometimes a person's underlying *intention*, rather than what has actually taken place, must be considered above all.

In more morally complex situations, if your intentions are benevolent, it is occasionally legitimate to use questionable means to achieve your virtuous ends. The need to do bad things in order to achieve a good goal depends on how coerced you are. Under coercion, most parents would lie, steal, or use violence if their intention was to save their children from harm or suffering. Aristotle fully understands this, "because men may do bad acts under compulsion." Compulsion can take many forms, at its most extreme entailing someone threatening one of your loved ones with persecution or death.

Aristotle uses two simple examples. First, striking a blow is an outrage if the intention was to insult the man struck or give pleasure to the person striking the blow. But striking a blow is not culpable at all, if the intention is self-defense. Second, taking something without its owner's knowledge may be an act of theft, if it is done with the intention of keeping it and thus harming the owner. But if the intention when you take someone else's car is to rush a heart-attack victim to hospital, and to return the car later, it obviously does not count as theft. You were compelled, by the principle that saving a life is a good thing.

Aristotle's "advanced ethics" lessons present three moral dilemmas where intention can often be the only true guide to action. First, you can do a wrong thing by *omission*. Second that *telling the truth* is both in principle and in general practice the best option. Third, that general values of conduct and fairness or *equality* all need to be tempered with more case-specific flexible *equity*. Aristotle emphasizes the individual, autonomous self and its freedom to choose to act virtuously even when everyone else is behaving badly. Such ideas must partly have emerged in response to the relentless infighting he witnessed at the sumptuous Macedonian court at Pella both in his childhood and between 343–336 BCE, when he was Alexander's tutor. Power struggles, murder, extortion, coercion, secrecy, deception and paranoia marked every relationship. But Aristotle somehow succeeded in maintaining his integrity.

Perhaps the most difficult moral choice is between intervening and not acting at all. You are worried that the child next door is being beaten: do you contact the child-welfare officials in your area or keep quiet in case you are mistaken? One of your colleagues is embezzling company money: do you tell your superiors or keep out of the situation, fearful of being labeled a snitch? The dilemma was memorably portrayed in Jonathan Kaplan's movie *The Accused* (1988), the first film to explore the unfair treatment sometimes received by women who have been raped and try to seek legal redress. Four college students rape a working-class woman in a bar. One of them has a friend who is present and does nothing to prevent the rape, although he is appalled as he looks on. But he does redeem himself by making a 911 call and notifying the police. His testimony plays an important role in the legal proceedings.

Aristotle is the first moral philosopher to have realized that we can commit injustices by *omission* as well as by *commission*. The most succinct expression of it comes in *Nicomachean Ethics* book 3: "Where we are free to act we are also free to refrain from acting, and where we are able to say 'No' we are also able to say 'Yes'; if therefore we are responsible for doing a thing when to do it is right, we are also responsible for not doing it when not to do it is wrong."

There are greater risks involved today than in Aristotle's time. Although there was an ancient Greek concept of the interfering busybody, who inappropriately stuck their nose into everybody's personal affairs, private people who kept themselves to themselves were actually regarded with suspicion. Where we might praise quiet citizens who never stick their heads above the parapet, the ancient Greeks regarded seclusion as selfish and irresponsible and an abrogation of social responsibility to the rest of your community. But even our vocabulary for initiating moral action, or intervening where we see injustice being done, often has negative overtones. Leadership is often portrayed as exhibitionism or careerism. There are no verbs in English meaning "interfere" in a positive way, with the single exception of the relatively neutral "intervene": there is, however, a wide variety of verbs which make intervention seem culpable (meddle, intrude, stick your oar in). This issue is even more difficult for women, in whom keeping a low public profile, preferably behind closed household doors, has historically been praised far more than involvement in matters of community or public concern.

When we were children, we all had to make choices between intervening and effectively colluding by remaining silent when we saw "unpopular" children bullied in the playground. Similar situations confront us all in everyday adult life. Do you make your voice heard when you see parents hit or scream at their children? Do you tolerate it when strong people cynically queue-jump ahead of frail pensioners? When fit young adults fail to offer their seat on the Underground to a woman who is eight months pregnant?

It can be difficult to intervene, because the standard defensive reaction if you do intervene is to call you a judgmental busybody or a puritanical self-appointed moral policeman. The question is whether you care more about what people who commit these everyday offenses against fairness and decency think of you, or about their victims. Aristotle was right to treat moral omission as seriously as commission, and that on our deathbeds it will not be things we have done that we regret. It will be the things we have not done.

This vital ethical principle is rarely invoked these days, except in medical ethics on the question of the morality of withholding medical treatment and "letting" a patient die. Here "omission" can be laudable, if it helps an individual who is mortally sick to die with less suffering. But far too much of our moral code these days, especially as it relates to public figures, revolves around asking if people have ever slipped up or made mistakes. Politicians are scrutinized for what they have done wrong, but rarely for what *they have not done* to improve the situation of the people they are proposing to govern. We do not ask enough what politicians, business leaders, chancellors of universities and funding councils have *failed* to do, the initiatives they have failed to launch, and how they have thus abrogated the duties of leadership. Ancient tradition had it that every day Alexander the Great felt he had not achieved something constructive, proactively, from his powerful position as king, he would lament ruefully, "I have not reigned today." He must have learned about ethical omission from his tutor Aristotle.

Philosophers since Aristotle have centered their discussions of omission on certain notorious hypothetical cases. They include the person who can swim but does not intervene to help someone drowning; the rich who would never authorize violent suppression of the mutinous poor but allow them to starve to death; the parent of a child who does not report the child's other parent to the authorities when the other parent is abusing the child. Doing wrong by omission, for an

Aristotelian, covers failure to take full responsibility as well. It is easiest to understand "culpable failure proactively to take responsibility" by looking at the way that the law frames crimes of omission, on which the jurisdictions of different countries take up varying positions.

Although willful non-disclosure of taxable income and assets can be a crime, as can willful non-disclosure of information pertaining to terrorism-related activities, British law has historically been exceptionally reluctant to recognize liability for a failure to act. The legal situation reflects the prevalent British feeling that we should celebrate private life and civic quietism. The ideal that "an Englishman's home is his castle" still dogs attempts to reform the law and police practice in cases of marital rape, disciplining of children and "domestic violence" (a horrid phrase which implies that the violence is of a qualitatively different nature than violence which one citizen inflicts on another in the street or a pub). But even in the UK, there are a few categories of situations in which a failure to act has been criminalized.

Close relationships bring recognized duties to act on behalf of a relative. You can as a parent be prosecuted for failing to feed or otherwise look after your child if she or he is harmed or dies; close family members who live together have been prosecuted successfully for manslaughter through gross negligence when failing to procure necessary medical treatment for their injured kin. A contract between people can bring with it criminal liability for failure to fulfill contractual obligations: if you are hired specifically to act as a lifeguard at a swimming pool and fail to try to save a drowning person's life because you are having a cigarette outside the pool during your own shift, for example. Creating a dangerous situation and putting other people at risk can also give rise to prosecution: leaving a house fire you have started, even accidentally, knowing that there are people in the house, and not alerting the fire brigade, would easily qualify.

Yet even in such apparently clear and extreme situations the distinction between casual (even if gross) and intentional negligence can be hazy, as Aristotle knew well. If an employer at a bank or a landlord does not alert the police to information relating to financial activities or accommodation of terrorists, are they *willfully* concealing evidence or just too busy to bother? How can we decide when a mother who deprives her child of food with the result that he dies is *intending* to kill him, or "merely" guilty of gross negligence, especially if her competence as provider is compromised by addiction, low intelligence, or psychological disease? Aristotle would certainly insist that ascertaining the level of *intent* was crucial. Yet he would, I suspect, also regard British law in respect of omission sadly deficient. It is still, for example, by no means clear whether adults *other* than the parents of a child, if aware that the child is (or might be) the victim of abuse, are liable for failure to disclose the information.

It is fortunate that most of us will never be faced with such extreme situations, but there are dozens of whistle-blowers who have lost their jobs, or at least chances of advancement, because they decided to make public, in the public's interest, information which discredited people or practices in their employing organization. Cardiologist Dr. Raj Mattu in 2014 eventually won his legal victory for unfair dismissal. He had been suspended for eight years, before being sacked in 2010, because he had exposed evidence that financial cuts imposed by a hospital in Coventry were putting patients in mortal danger through overcrowding. The lengths to which his National Health Service managers went to silence him were extraordinary. Private detectives were hired to dig up any information that might discredit him, and millions of pounds were spent on taking legal action against him. He suffered damage to his career, income, reputation and consequently his health and private life. He took responsibility for acting, as Aristotle put it, "when not to act was wrong." He was brave and admirable. Not all of us are cut from that kind of cloth; we may also have financial dependents who make risking our jobs for our principles too uncomfortable to be possible. In such cases we have to make a decision about which of our obligations effectively "trumps" the other.

But what about people who have less to lose? Aristotle is adamant that certain kinds of good deed require contacts, financial security or political power. Therefore, if you are fortunate enough to enjoy such props to your safety and security, failing to act in a good cause is far more culpable. When you appraise the super-rich, media celebrities, politicians, aristocrats or simply individuals senior to you at work, do not just ask whether they have succeeded in keeping out of trouble. Ask which charities they have supported, what stands they have made for what causes—how they have *leveraged* their huge social advantages. There are plenty of famous and secure people who have never spoken up in defense of the poor, or oppressed, or the environment. Thinking critically about omission as well as commission can enrich all our assessments of people who want our admiration and approval.

Aristotle's emphasis on the intentions behind action extends to his position on means and ends. The argument that there are situations in which a desirable outcome can only be secured by a reprehensible act takes us into some of the grayest moral areas in philosophy. It is the argument used to justify many military actions, for example the bombing of Hiroshima and Nagasaki: the tens of thousands of deaths these bombs caused are supposed to have prevented far more deaths if it had been necessary to launch a full-scale land invasion of Japanese territory. The problem is that nobody can ever know what might have happened if nuclear bombs had not been used. President Truman's chief of staff, Fleet Admiral William Daniel Leahy, came to the conclusion that "the use of this barbarous weapon at Hiroshima and Nagasaki was of no material assistance in our war against Japan. The Japanese were already defeated and ready to surrender because of the effective sea blockade and the successful bombing with conventional weapons."[9]

There was another unfortunate outcome: the use of nuclear weapons effectively kick-started the Cold War arms race. But Aristotle would have assessed the decision to drop the bombs by focusing not on the result but on the underlying intention. Was this a military decision, or a political one? Many critics of the bombing of Japanese cities of no military importance and full of civilians have argued that while Truman may well have been persuaded that he was acting to diminish overall death and suffering, the overriding intentions of his Washington advisers were to road-test the new technology (even they were shocked by the unanticipated number of deaths by radiation) and to send a warning to Joseph Stalin and the Soviet Union. It is possible that Truman needed to be more suspicious about his advisers' intentions.

Another extreme case of using intention as the yardstick in considering the justifiability of questionable means was dramatized in Philippe Claudel's affecting 2008 movie *I've Loved You So Long*. Juliette (Kristin Scott Thomas) serves fifteen years in prison for murdering her six-year-old son. Slowly, the audience learns that it was a mercy killing: Juliette had been a doctor, and used a lethal injection when her son was immobilized by a mortal illness which would cause him agonizing pain if he were left to die naturally. But Juliette had not used this information at the trial, apparently feeling that she "deserved" a long prison sentence, regardless of her altruistic intention. The discovery of her intention comes in time to help her current situation, however; her brother-in-law, who had been most reluctant to allow her contact with his daughters, eventually welcomes her presence as their aunt.

When it comes to telling the truth, every one of us confronts the means/ends dilemma on a nearly everyday basis. Lying is stressful, affecting even our physiology with changes that make lie-detector technology possible. This underlies the widespread intuitive sense, across cultures, that while there are a few types of occasions when lying is excusable, telling lies is not in the best self-interest. It is only rarely conducive to happiness, either in yourself or in those with whom you interact. This intuitive hunch finds theoretical support in Aristotelian ethics. Aristotle's discussions of truth and lies are sophisticated. He does not think that there is such a thing as a transcendent truth, in the way Plato did, nor that the truth had a metaphysical status or was an inherent good in itself. But he *did* believe that Living Well required the working out and consistent implementation of a coherent policy on truth-telling and duplicity.

Aristotle has a striking concept of people who are "true to themselves," *authekastos*, more literally "each one as himself." The true-to-themselves have consistent characters, are self-reliant, act in the same way toward everybody, and are not overly concerned with the opinion others hold of them. In this they are like the ideal "great-souled," "who is open about the people whom he likes and dislikes" and "cares more for truth than for people's opinions." It is easier to sleep at night knowing that there are in existence no e-mails, tweets or Facebook posts of which you would be ashamed in front of anybody. Offering the same, true version of events to everyone places so much less strain on the memory than trying to remember who was told which lie. It is good sense to resolve never to say or write anything to anybody that you would not be prepared to have made public if necessary. A colleague of mine criticized our boss to another colleague in the pub. The colleague listened, and then threatened to go to the boss and report what she had said. She was able to advise that he go ahead because she had already used much stronger language to the boss's face.

A person attempting to Live Well, according to Aristotle, will tell the truth when something significant is at stake, such as in a court case, compared to more informal understandings with friends and family. If you lie in these important circumstances, the lie is probably an instrument you are using in order to commit some real injustice. Injustice, for Aristotle, is inextricable from unfairness. An example would be if a builder lies in order to swindle the person hiring him out of money by insisting on being paid by the time it takes to do the job, rather than at a flat rate, and then saying that the job will take four weeks when he knows it will take eight. On the other hand, the person who hires him may tell lies to the taxation authority in order to avoid paying tax on the money she is paying to the builder. In both cases the lies are worse misdemeanors than lies: they are crucial elements in the committing of a serious injustice. These lies are parts of acts that do actual harm not only to other individuals but to the community as a whole.

Truth-telling as a way of life, and when little is at stake, interests Aristotle just as much. He studied in some detail people who use falsehood to boast about themselves (self-advertisement was a conspicuous element of ancient Greek masculinity, and the degree to which it is appropriate to brag about, or exaggerate, one's own achievements is much discussed in the *Iliad*). Boasting, even if it involves telling lies, may not do much harm if it is simply a display put on for bystanders and slight acquaintances over a pint of beer in a pub. It *can* have serious repercussions, however: nobody wants to have surgery performed upon them by a person who has falsely claimed to be a qualified surgeon. But Aristotle is fascinated by the apparently trivial fibs told by the inveterate self-promoter: "The man who pretends to have more reputable qualities than he possesses, for the sake of nothing much, seems despicable, for otherwise he would not take pleasure in lies; but he seems needlessly foolish rather than bad."

Claiming to have a lower handicap at golf, or be higher up in the management hierarchy at work, are blameworthy lies, says Aristotle, but not serious crimes. A third group of boasting liars, however, are thoroughly reprehensible. These are people who do it *with the intention of amassing money*, or the means by which to amass money. This is not just a matter of being an inveterately immodest person liable to mild exaggeration. It is a *deliberate choice*. Sometimes people do this, Aristotle is aware, simply because the power to manipulate others in serious financial affairs gives them a kick ("they take pleasure in the lie itself")— we might today call them "pathological" liars. For others, the only motive is greed or love of gain. They *lie* when they tell the old lady they are swindling that they have come to check her electricity meter, and then *commit the crime* when they make off with her silver candlesticks.

But does Aristotle believe the truth is inherently good, for its own sake? He does *not* assert that there is *never* a situation in which the person committed to Living Well might not need to employ falsehood. He is far more practical than this: telling the truth accords with enlightened self-interest. He dwells on the idea, for example, that a person who is truthful on an everyday basis, because their character is of that kind, is more likely to be trustworthy when it really matters. "For a lover of truth, being truthful even when nothing is at stake, will be even more truthful when something is at stake; he will avoid falsehood where it is disgraceful [i.e. because something is at stake], having avoided it even for its own sake." If you get into the habit of telling the truth, you are far more likely to tell the truth when the stakes, for yourself or others, are high. If you get the reputation for being a truth-teller, there will be pay-offs later. Other people will trust your word when it counts.

Yet, since intention must always be factored into our assessment of any action, there are several kinds of situations in which deliberately lying may be not only excusable, but necessary. The Italian movie *Life Is Beautiful* (1997, directed by and starring Roberto Benigni), explores the sustained lies which a Jewish father, Guido, tells his small son, Giosuè, in a concentration camp in order to maximize the boy's chances of survival. Guido says that they are playing a game in which Giosuè needs to perform tasks which will win them points. The tasks include not asking for food, crying or saying he wants to see his mother. Avoidance of attracting the guards' attention wins extra points. This fiction protects the boy from much suffering and in due course saves his life.

Children learn to lie for what they perceive to be their own self-advantage at between three and four years old; the trick here is to teach them that context is everything. Lying to people who have their best interests at heart will *not* benefit them. But lying to people who want to damage, control or deprive them may. My own biggest lie, which Aristotle would have found perfectly excusable, was in my children's defense against the Immunization Program of Illinois State Board of Education. I had researched in detail the official requirements, and had ensured that our children had received every single required injection before entering the USA for a semester-long visit. I had all the medical documentation to prove it. But on the day when we turned up at the Schools Admissions Office, the nurse in charge said that our British immunizations were invalid because Illinois decreed that slightly different gaps of time should elapse between serial injections than those that had been recommended in England. We were told that the children either had to have all the injections again (which was surely medically hazardous) or that they would be excluded from school for our entire three months in Illinois. When rational argument failed to persuade her, I faked a sudden religious conversion to a sect that outlawed medical intervention. I did not know enough about the Jehovah's Witnesses to sound convincing, but the name Ulrich Zwingli bizarrely entered my head (I do not think poor Zwingli's brand of radical Swiss Protestantism really had any views on immunization, but this did not seem to matter at the time). My husband saw what I was doing and announced that he, too, was now a convinced Zwingli-ite and thus abhorred any human intervention in the working out of God's will in our physical bodies. Somewhere in Illinois there is a document signed by us both affirming these utterly fictitious religious scruples. The nurse was annoyed, but had no choice, and allowed our children into the school forthwith.

The point here is one of means and ends. Of course the said medical officer did not *intend* to make my children have unnecessary double doses of immunization jabs, nor to deprive them of education for three months. But she did *not* use her discretion and she allowed bureaucratic myopia to prevent her even from studying the medical documents I had brought from Britain. She refused even to consider ways of being flexible about a rule which had been made without any pre-emptive thinking about international children coming to be educated in Illinois.

That nurse's inflexibility in the face of a rule applied with absolute uniformity in the Illinois public education system showed her adhering to a principle of equality but not of equity. Equity is little understood and discussed today outside specialist circles of legal philosophers, but it is essential to justice. Aristotle's seminal discussion of equity comes in his treatment of justice in the *Nicomachean Ethics*. He says that "equity, though just, is not legal justice, but a rectification of legal justice." It does not replace legal justice but enhances and complements it. He argues that laws have to make general statements, but "there are cases which it is not possible to cover in a general statement." The messy reality of human ethical choices simply cannot be properly dealt with by pre-emptive legal strikes. Laws are made by thinking about what is appropriate to the majority of cases, which necessarily creates, in a minority of situations, the possibility of injustice being done. Equity is needed because life is complicated, and responses to people who do wrong need to be modified according to the particulars of the situation.

People do wrong for all kinds of reasons, Aristotle acknowledges. Sometimes it is deliberate and wholly culpable, but sometimes there are important factors which need to be taken into consideration. It may be the underlying intention. Juliette in *I've Loved You So Long*, discussed earlier, was denying her judge and jury the right to invoke equity in her sentencing by not telling them the true reason she had killed her child. Psychologically, this was because she was "too hard on herself," and effectively denied *herself* equity, believing that the fixed penalty for child-murder was somehow appropriate in her own exceptional case. Other justifications for mercy in sentencing would be the wrongdoer's poverty, old age, low intelligence, inadequate education, vulnerability to passionate desires and emotions, state of health, degree of repentance, and likelihood to reoffend. To explain what he means by equity, Aristotle introduces one of his most brilliant analogies. Application of pre-existing rules in a way that is tempered by equity is like measuring a stone with a ruler which is not rigid but made of a material that can bend. The masons of Lesbos, he says, measure curving stones with flexible rulers made of lead. They apply the same preordained units of measurement, but result in a far more accurate reading because they can bend around the stone—"yield" to its curves, just as a good judge will mold the laws based on general principles to the minutiae of a particular moral situation.

Aristotle's flexible-lead tape measure is of huge relevance today, when the assumption too often prevails that rules, laws, policies and even family traditions need to be upheld with unwavering uniformity. The inevitable result is that true fairness is replaced by an insistence that one size *must* fit all, regardless of the injustice and other negative consequences that are entailed.

In Aristotle's day, traditional religion held that penalties should be inflexible. The primeval word for justice was *dike*, the law as administered by the top god, Zeus: in tragedy, it is *dike* which means that Orestes *must* kill his mother because she killed his father, regardless of any complexities in the circumstances. A speaker in a tragedy by Sophocles insists that divinity "knows neither equity nor favour, but is only concerned with strict and simple justice [*dikē*]." The clearest examples in our modern society of problematic and inflexible rules are automatic or mandatory prison sentences, which do not allow judges any room for thinking about mitigating circumstances and adjusting the penalty according to the principles of equity. This in turn occasionally leads to juries rebelling and refusing to convict the accused even when they know that they did commit the crime.

In a case in England a few years ago, a jury found a man innocent of murder even though he admitted to killing a man who had murdered his daughter and lived in a neighboring street. The point was that errors in policing and the loss of physical evidence meant that it had been impossible to convict the child killer and sentence him to life imprisonment, and so the bereaved father felt compelled to "take the law into his own hands." Such jurors are exercising their collective reasonableness because they are alert to the room for injustice which is created when universal regulations are applied in particular individual cases. They then act equitably, using their discretion and adjusting their decision in a way which prevents an injustice which the makers of the law on murder did not anticipate and which they did not intend: the incarceration of a bereaved father let down by incompetent policing. Equity is an ingredient of total justice, and inseparable from it.

The root semantic concept in Aristotle's word for equity, *epieikeia*, is *eikos*, which means what is plausible or appropriate. The penalty should fit the crime, rather than the crime being made to fit the penalty, as in the case of the victims of the legendary Procrustes, who stretched or amputated his victims' limbs to make their bodies fit his "one size fits all" bed. But by the time of Aristotle, the Greeks often connected *epieikeia* with another word, the verb meaning to "give in" or "yield" to something or someone. That is, equity was generally associated with introducing leniency, or "bending" by being merciful to a felon on account of mitigating circumstances. An important case in the history of legal equity where Aristotle's ideas were invoked, however, concerned the problem caused because the law as it stood did not make things *difficult* enough for the felon.

In 1880, Francis B. Palmer made a will leaving most of his estate to his grandson Elmer. Francis' daughter was to look after the money until her son Elmer came of age. At sixteen, worried that his grandfather might change the will, Elmer poisoned him. Although Elmer could be prosecuted for murder, there was no statute in existence in the relevant state (New York) to prevent him from receiving his legacy in due course. His mother challenged the imposition of the will in the Civil Court in 1889, and by a majority verdict, supported by an appeal to Aristotle's principle of equity, she won her case.

The most important argument against equity, of course, is that we can't necessarily rely on the integrity and discretion of the person who is applying it. If laws have been made with the intention of promoting equality, we need to be very careful indeed about when we allow them to be applied flexibly. This has never been put better than by the seventeenth-century parliamentarian and historian John Selden, who said that equity "is a roguish thing" and "according to the conscience of him that is chancellor." He pointed out that we do not use the size of the current chancellor's foot to measure lengths because chancellors' feet vary in size: "one chancellor has a long foot, another a short foot, a third an indifferent foot; 'tis the same thing in the chancellor's conscience." But Aristotle would respond by saying that we can't miss out on all the advantages of true justice just because some people are not capable of rising to the moral challenges equity poses. He concludes his discussion by stressing that equity, like the capacity to deliberate, is a distinctively human quality. It is one which the arbitrary gods of classical mythology can neither understand nor appreciate, and indeed would find ridiculous.

The powerful instrument of equity can certainly help us today if we find ourselves on jury service, working as magistrates, teachers, examiners, or in any position where we make decisions about rewarding merit, punishing wrongdoers or assessing competence. For parents, especially those faced with the competing claims and needs of more than one child, equity has an important domestic application. We may believe that if we have two children we should bequeath exactly half of our estate to each of them, but if one is severely handicapped and needs special lifelong care, and we intend to look after both children adequately, we will probably think that a truly equitable settlement will take into account our children's different circumstances. Feminist philosophers have recently developed this idea, derived from Aristotelian equity, of "maternal thinking" on a sociopolitical as well as domestic level. Different citizens *need* to be cared for and catered for in different ways, and true fairness will not be achieved in a society which allots every citizen precisely the same resources: to each according to their needs.

There are few easy choices in life, but adding equity to our intentions when it comes to both justice and equality can help us immeasurably to do our best as we struggle to find a walkable path through the ethical jungle of everyday human life.

Chapter 7

———— ∞ ————

LOVE

Happiness has always depended on personal relationships. Love may not be the only thing that makes the human "world go round," but it is certainly one of the most important. Whom to love, and how to love them, are decisions with which we are all faced at some point in our lives. Although we have few options until adulthood about the members of our immediate family, even schoolchildren make choices about which of their peers to befriend in the classroom or playground. Close friends become enormously important in the early teens, as we learn about forming intimate bonds outside the home. Then comes the excitement of discovering sexuality and romance and the first "love" relationships as designated by the English phrase "to be *in love with*" someone.

But forging loving relationships is only one part of the story; knowing when to end a close friendship, or at least demote it from intimate to merely sociable, concerns everyone sooner or later. Few of us reach middle age without falling out with someone we love, even a parent, child or sibling. Lifelong friends can suddenly prove disloyal or exploitative. A large proportion of marriages and cohabiting arrangements end in divorce or the equivalent. So how are we to maximize our chances of finding happiness through our close relationships with others?

Although Aristotle recognizes the power of sex, his long and detailed discussion of love (*philia*) and relationships feels so surprisingly modern because he does not treat sexual relationships as inherently exceptional or qualitatively different from other love bonds. Relationships involving sex are just one subset of the category of *philoi*, a term often far too weakly translated as "friends." The same basic principles apply to both sexual (i.e. marriage or similar arrangements) and nonsexual friendships. All relationships with people we love require effort, but the rewards are inestimable.

Aristotle regarded love as essential to human life. Many of us fantasize about affection of all kinds happening mystically and spontaneously, but Aristotle knew that it is a matter of hard work. He begins his account of human society with the primary and, he says, "most natural" partnership—the marital unit. This is an extremely intense form of friendship. It exists between you and the individual person you marry or choose to live with permanently. He envisages a heterosexual husband and wife, brought together for mutual support, with complementary spheres of competence. They also need one another if the human race is to reproduce itself, and "neither the female can effect this without the male, nor the male without the female; this is why the union of the sexes has of necessity arisen." He nowhere discusses same-sex unions, although he certainly never condemns them, either. He does endorse the speech made by Aristophanes in Plato's *Symposium*, where humans are divided into three kinds of erotically fused couples: woman/man, woman/woman, and man/man. Aristotle's point is not that any of them is intrinsically wrong, but that *excessive* amorous love of any kind outside the household can be socially destabilizing. He also tells, approvingly, the romantic story of the gay couple Philolaus (a statesman) and Diocles (an Olympic sprinting champion). After many tribulations, these lovers lie serenely at rest in adjacent graves near Thebes.

Given these two passages, there is little doubt that Aristotle would today have been open to persuasion about homosexual domestic partnerships. He is convinced that primary partnerships are about far more than sex and procreation. He says that, among animals far less sophisticated than humans, such primary attachments exist only for reproduction and "last only so long as the parents are occupied in producing their brood." In some more complex animals, more like humans, the partnership "has assumed a more complex form; for in their case we see more examples of mutual help, goodwill, and cooperation." But this complexity is most marked in humans, where the cooperation of a couple goes far beyond a physical relationship, however delightful, since it aims "not merely at existence, but at a happy existence."

There are few hard-and-fast rules in Aristotelian ethics, but he does regard adultery as unacceptable. The reason for this is that cheating on your spouse or partner erodes trust, which is in turn the basis of any satisfactory friendship. Like theft and murder, he insists, adultery is universally abhorrent: "right or wrong in the cases of these does not depend on the circumstances—for instance, whether one commits adultery with the right woman, at the right time, and in the right manner. Just doing any of them is wrong." He offers a great deal of indirect advice on marriage/lifelong partnership, since everything he says about intimate friendships applies equally to marriage. Marriage, for Aristotle, is only (although significantly) distinguished from other friendships in its increased intensity and shared investment in raising mutual offspring. This also applies to close kin bonds between parent and child and siblings: the difference between such bonds and friendships beyond the family is solely a quantitative difference of degree and intensity.

It is revealing to think about Aristotle's own life here. He lost his parents when only in his early teens. He spent many years of his life unmarried, both before and after the death of his first wife, Pythias, by whom he had a daughter, also named Pythias. Later in life, after years of widowhood, he once again found happiness with a woman named Herpyllis from his old home town of Stageira. He did not marry her, which suggests she may have been a slave or of low, non-citizen class. But he did father her son, Nicomachus, to whom he addressed or dedicated his *Nicomachean Ethics.* Aristotle also adopted his nephew Nicanor, his sister's child. His last will and testament shows how much thought he put into protecting the interests of Herpyllis and his three children. But he cultivated a circle of faithful friends with energetic commitment, especially Hermias, the ruler of the kingdom of Assos in northwest Turkey with whom he spent two years after he left the Academy, and his colleague Theophrastus, who helped him set up the Lyceum. When he writes about familial relationships and loving friendship, the insightful detail suggests that Aristotle is writing from personal experience, both of successful bonds and of deep disappointments.

In these days of Facebook we throw the term "friend" around with an ease which debases the concept. Ambitious people accept as "friends" in social media people they never intend to meet but who they want to follow them as "fans." It is therefore inspiring to go back and read the praise of true, loving friendship with which Aristotle opens *Nicomachean Ethics* book 8:

> Friendship is one of the most indispensable requirements of life. For no one would choose to live without friends but in possession of everything else that is good. Friends are of help to the young by protecting them from mistakes; to the elderly by looking after them and making up for their failing powers of action; to those in the prime of life, to help them in doing good things.

Our whole lives benefit from people who love us, which, for Aristotle, means people who have our best interests, not theirs, at heart. This generous kind of love is grounded in nature: "the affection of parent for offspring and of offspring for parent seems to be a natural instinct, not only in man but also in birds and in most animals; as also is friendship between members of the same species." This is important, because the Cynic philosopher, Diogenes, a contemporary with whom Aristotle often agrees, insisted that bonds between humans were *deviations* from nature, not to be found in the animal world. But Aristotle, who studied animals intensively and became the recognized founding father of the discipline of zoology, responded that love bonds *were* natural. The only difference is that intra-species goodwill, which can be seen in the relationships between dogs, and between birds, for example, "is *especially* strong in the human race; this is the reason why we praise those who love their fellow men. Even when travelling abroad one can observe that a natural affinity and friendship exist between man and man universally." We have all enjoyed spine-tingling moments of identification. Mine have been with other women, for example, the Somali woman in Athens who, in spite of our lack of a shared language, helped me with a pram on a crowded bus, and laughed with delight at my baby's social overtures to her.

Aristotle's study of friendship is unprecedented in Greek culture. It is far more sophisticated than almost any other theory of friendship subsequently produced. This is because he thinks that there are three fundamental categories of friendship. It is useful to consider where each friend falls in this system. This procedure can help you jettison exploitative friends, get over broken friendships when they end, make better choices of friends and work harder to maintain the ones with the most promise. It will also make you regret even more the premature deaths of true friends after you have both invested effort in the relationship. As Derek Walcott put it in his eloquent poem, "Sea Canes":

Half my friends are dead.

I will make you new ones, said earth.
No, give me them back, as they were, instead,
with faults and all, I cried.

Aristotle agreed. He says that the death of close, long-standing friends is indeed one of the hardest things which humans must confront. But recognizing the magnitude of what you have lost can make you appreciate better what you have and help you invest wisely in serious new friendships in the future.

Some friendships—perhaps the majority—are simply useful to us. Animals can also make friendships based on utility, such as between a human and a domestic animal. Friendship can exist between two animals, even of different species: Aristotle reminds us that sandpipers help crocodiles by cleaning their teeth, while crocodile teeth thus provide a source of food for sandpipers. There is nothing wrong with a utility friendship. You scratch my back and I'll scratch yours, or give your child a lift to school when you're ill. You and your friend both get something out of the relationship which is beneficial. It is a form of social barter.

With neighbors, friendliness may be useful in the same way to both of you. You may keep an eye on each other's property when one goes away. You may feed each other's pets. You may take in deliveries for your absent neighbor, and vice versa. You may share important local news or information which affects you both. Trust is important, and if you have found your "utility friend" to be unreliable, you are justified in withdrawing the benefits which you have been accustomed to confer. If the neighbor lets your hamster starve, you do not hurt their cats, but you never again offer to look after them.

Many utility friendships are based on similarity. It is useful to nurture friendly relationships with peers (fellow pupils, students, workmates, other new parents) whose needs, resources and position in the world resemble your own. Because you are peers, the relationship is usually also based on equality: neither party has much more power than the other. What you hope to get out of the relationship is of approximately equal worth. Aristotle includes under this heading the contacts we have abroad, who may help us when we visit or have deal-ings with their country, and whom we help if they have come to ours. Friendships of utility are fundamentally pragmatic arrangements, and do not even require spending much time in the friend's physical pres-ence. He noticed that they frequently occur among older people, who need more help with practical aspects of life than the young or people in their prime, but often do not even enjoy their utility friends' company, "and therefore have no use for friendly intercourse unless they are mutually advantageous."

Other utility friendships, however, exist between two dissimilar people, and Aristotle is interested in the pressures on friendship which come with asymmetry. You may engage in a "utility" friendship with people you have hired to help you look after your children, and mutual fondness may develop. But the things you offer the carer (usually money) are different from what they are offering you (childcare). As an academic, I engage in "utility" friendships with my undergraduate students, while they study with me. These friendships often mirror the parent–child relationship, since I am older and am assisting in an aspect of their maturation. But there is also a financial aspect involved, since the students' desire to attend my lectures ultimately pays part of my salary. Although there is a transaction underpinning the utility friendship, mutual affection can still often develop based on this trust. But we cannot expect support which goes beyond the mutually agreed trans-action. Many utility friendships are ruined when one party unilaterally decides to take it to another level, and is disappointed when the utility friend will not sleep with them, lend them money, or drive them to a rehabilitation center.

Aristotle is correct that utility friends may not get to know each other well; the friendship often comes to an end, without any distress, when the similarity between your lives comes to an end: you leave a school, college, workplace, or a mother-and-toddler group. Aristotle cites travelers who hook up for a part of a journey "for some advantage, namely to procure some of their necessary supplies," but subsequently separate without trauma. Much of our lives as social beings is taken up by useful friendships. But they entail basic rules as well, the most important of which is avoiding negative gossip or backbiting about others in the peer group. This can be done simply by changing the subject when negative remarks are made. There are several ways to wreck utility friendships: expecting too much from the other party, forcing intimacy where it has not been offered, or "over-sharing," unburdening yourself inappropriately about your private life.

Aristotle's next category is the friendship based on pleasure. These survive longest when the two friends derive similar things from the relationship. Aristotle provides the example of two witty people who enjoy meeting because they make each other laugh. You may have several friends with whom you indulge your passion for theater or musicals or horse racing, and others with whom you enjoy a glass of wine; this does not mean that you can ask them to assist you in any other dimension of life, nor that you have any further obligation to them. Young people often mistake the intense enjoyment which they experience as a sign that the person is of equivalent moral strength and loyalty. But many utterly charming people who can thoroughly enhance your life as a pleasure friend can never be more than that. Aristotle is surely correct when he points out that the age group most susceptible to pleasure friendships is the young:

> With the young the motive of friendship appears to be pleasure, since the young guide their lives by emotion, and for the most part pursue what is pleasant to themselves, and the object of the moment. And the things that please them change as their age alters; hence they both form friendships and drop them

quickly, since their affections alter with what gives them pleasure.

Transient love affairs, which Aristotle regards simply as a subspecies of pleasure friendship, are also most common among young people. They are good at initiating pleasure friendships because they are sociable and easily motivated by emotional impulses. There is often an asymmetry in the pleasure of each party. "The enjoyment taken in receiving amorous attention is not the same as the pleasure derived from gazing at a face one loves."

The problem here is that if the friendship is predicated on appreciation of physical beauty, then it will cease along with the beauty. (We all know wives, and even husbands, who have been abandoned when they lose their looks.) But there is hope for this sort of relationship, *provided* that it has evolved into a more symmetrical one based on reciprocal appreciation of each other's character. This does happen, admits Aristotle, but only when both parties are of equivalent moral worth. Find someone to marry who likes you for your permanent qualities, and seek the same yourself. It is amazing how few couples have held even one honest conversation about their visions of the future together before they embark on a serious relationship. There is little point, if your aims include raising children, in choosing as a life partner someone whose aims do not. If you are extremely career-focused, then things will not function with a spouse who can't accommodate your spending a great deal of time and energy at work.

This is why arranged marriages often work, since the commitment and joint projects are part of the formal agreement entered into. The 2015 winner of the popular television series *The Great British Bake Off*, Nadiya Hussain, has spoken about how she slowly fell in love with her husband, to whom she had been married, by an arrangement between their parents, when she was only nineteen. She only realized that she was "in love" with him after they had produced two children and she realized how compatible they were. She saw his behavior at close quarters and his permanent moral qualities when he became a father. The same goes for the intense love shared by writers C. S. Lewis and Joy Davidman in Richard Attenborough's biographical movie *Shadowlands* (1993). Originally they married for convenience so that Davidman, an American, could reside in Britain, but through interaction realized how many interests and values they shared and how their relationship was enriching their lives.

Both utility friendships and pleasure friendships are positive and life-enhancing. Although Aristotle does admit that bad people can make friendships of these kinds, since criminals can lie for each other in court and enjoy immoral recreational pursuits together, secondary friendships need cultivating *within their own limits*. You need to fulfill your side of whatever bargain has been agreed if the utility friendship is to flourish. The same principle applies with relationships based on pleasure: if someone has enjoyed spending time with you because you share a taste for dark comedy, then weeping all over her and expecting support during a depression will not encourage her to continue as a friend. (Indeed, Aristotle warns that allowing yourself to present a morose or surly character to the world will make it difficult for you to attract friends at all; "good temper and sociability appear to be the chief causes of friendship.")

Aristotle concludes his discussion of utility and pleasure friendships by saying that they are vulnerable to early closure: "friendships of this kind are easily broken off, in the event of the parties themselves changing, for if no longer pleasant or useful to each other, they cease to love each other. And utility is not a permanent quality; it differs at different times. Hence when the motive of the friendship has passed away, the friendship itself is dissolved, having existed merely as a means to that end." But the closure need not be at all painful, to either party, *provided that* nobody has deceived themselves into thinking that the relationship was profound.

Most friendship problems arise from confusing secondary friendships with the permanent, primary, committed sort of relationships. Aristotle puts it succinctly: "differences between friends most frequently arise when the nature of their friendship is not what they think it is." For the third, and by far the highest quality, friendship is the mutual love which occurs between members of happy families, and between intimate non-kin who make efforts. In Aristotle's view: "we consider a friend to be one of the greatest of all good things, and friendlessness and solitude a very terrible thing, because the whole of life and voluntary interactions are with loved ones."

A primary friendship between people who are both trying to Live Well forms an insurance against malicious rumors. As Aristotle says, a person "is slow to believe anybody's word about a friend whom he has himself tried and tested for many years, and with them there is the mutual confidence, the incapacity ever to do each other wrong, and all the other characteristics that are required in true friendship. Whereas the other forms of friendship are liable to be dissolved by calumny and suspicion." I am certain that Aristotle had experience of good friends defending him either against people who envied his brilliance or those who tried to imply after he had founded the Lyceum in Athens in 336 BCE that he was somehow disloyal to Athens and collaborating with Macedon.

Unlike the other two categories, primary friendships take time. The length of the friendship is a guarantee of its stability. Aristotle contrasts choosing which friend to keep with choosing which coat. When a coat gets worn out, the new one becomes preferable. Not so with friends. The longer you have known a friend, the more you can be sure that they are a good person. So even if you think your new friend is good, it is wise to prefer the older one, because the new one's commitment has not been tested. The immunity of trust to being ruptured by the behavior of either party can only be tested over time. Aristotle, with a twinkle in his eye, quotes a traditional poet, Theognis: "You can't know the mind of a man or a woman until you have tested them out as you test out cattle." Elsewhere he quotes the traditional Greek proverb about friendship: to call a man a friend, he needs to have consumed a substantial quantity of salt in your company, salt being the indispensable accompaniment to sociable meals.

Trust can't be built in a day, although it can be demolished in one. Friends who are disloyal, or let you down when you need them most, or do you wrong, do not deserve to remain primary friends. I have learned to give close friends one second chance, but only one. It may be that things went wrong because something hadn't been explained. But if, after a full discussion, they slip up again in the same way, it means that it is a result of a permanent aspect of their character rather than a misunderstanding. This may not necessitate, of course, that you cut them out of your life altogether. I still have two friends whom I can't now fully trust because they twice did not stick up for me when I needed them to, in the way I have often done for them. They have been retained but relegated to the "utility" or "pleasure" friend category. Aristotle had such "relegated" friends, because he says they need special treatment:

> Are we then to behave towards a former friend in exactly the
> same way as if he had never been our friend at all? Perhaps
> we ought to remember our past intimacy, and just as we think
> it right to show more kindness to friends than to strangers,
> so likewise some attention should be paid, for the sake of old
> times, to those who were our friends in the past, that is, if the
> rupture was not caused by extreme wickedness on their part.

Nostalgia for old intense affection can make a difference even when it is over.

Nobody can manage many primary friendships, insists Aristotle. "For perfect friendship you must get to know someone thoroughly, and become intimate with them, which is a very difficult thing to do." If you have too many primary friends, practical conflicts of loyalty arise: "it is difficult to share intimately in the joys and sorrows of many people; for one may very likely be called upon to rejoice with one and to mourn with another at the same time." Choose wisely a very few primary friends—probably fewer than the fingers on one hand—and carefully cultivate them. This includes spouse selection and, sadly, deciding who among even your blood relatives really deserves your efforts. The care entails sharing in the pain as well as their successes, and initiating cycles of good deeds toward one another. It also, advises Aristotle, requires regular contact and sustained conversation.

In these days of Skype and e-mail, it is of course much easier than it was in Aristotle's day to keep in regular contact with those we love when we are not close to them physically. Those invaluable close relationships require frequent contact. I used to not ring my husband and children often enough when I went abroad. The results were not good; now I try to check in with each of them every day.

You can spot a bad person, says Aristotle, because they will routinely choose material gain over a friend's welfare. There was a proverb in ancient Greek, "Between friends all property is in common." But immoral people use your friendship for what they can gain from it materially, rather than for the sake of friendship itself. You become, he says "an appendage" to the material advantages you can offer. Such friends, it goes without saying, are "fair weather" friends who will dump you the minute you fall on hard times and can't pay for all the drinks any more.

In one perceptive passage, Aristotle fascinatingly anticipates our

modern notion of psychological projection. Immoral people can make
shallow and transient friendships based on pleasure (two bad men can
enjoy playing poker together). But they are incapable of primary friendships of any kind because they can't trust anyone. The reason for their
inability to trust anyone else is the important point: they measure other
people by their own standards. Because they are motivated by selfishness or envy or a desire to win for its own sake, they can't even imagine
what it feels like to be inside another moral consciousness motivated
by a desire for universal happiness.

The person who really loves you as a primary friend will happily
tolerate it if you do not even know that they have done you a good
turn. This is because their goal is *not to* prove anything to you, nor
get something back in exchange, but simply *your* own maximum happiness. Good parents feel this kind of altruistic love for their children.
In fact, Aristotle thinks it is proper that "fathers love their children
more than they are loved by them (mothers more so than fathers) and
these in their turn love their children more than their parents." He
believes that the intensity of mother love is even greater than that
which fathers have for children "for people estimate work by its difficulty, and in the production of a child the mother suffers more pain."

As an extreme example of selfless love, Aristotle offers mothers
who allow their children to be adopted because they believe it is in the
child's best interest. He cites a tragedy in which Andromache, in order
to save her son Astyanax's life when he was threatened with being cast
from the walls of Troy by the Greeks, tried to smuggle him out of the
city in the hope that some other woman would adopt him. This would
have meant being deprived of him herself. Moreover, since Astyanax
was so tiny, he would never have learned about the personal sacrifice
she had made on his behalf: he might even have blamed her as the
unknown mother who, he believed, had abandoned him. Primary friends
are like good mothers in another sense: they feel genuine pain when

you suffer, and wish they could take on the pain themselves in order to relieve you. Aristotle the zoologist adds here, "and birds that share each other's pain." More than 90 percent of birds are monogamous, compared with only 3 percent of mammals, as Aristotle may have known, having observed individual birds' long-standing attachments.

Some people may find it disturbing that Aristotle does not recognize a distinction between the quality of the primary friendship which you have with a family member and one you have with non-kin. In practice most of us, most of the time, recognize a distinction between our relationships with family and with friends. It is tough but necessary to learn that people do not necessarily offer you the right type of commitment, loyalty and desire for your well-being just because you are related to them. It can feel dangerous, but it *is* worth thinking rationally through each of your familial relationships (other than with your own children, whom you have a special responsibility to love unconditionally since you chose to create them) and assessing them according to Aristotelian criteria. There may well be members even of a close nuclear family who would place their own material advantage above your well-being, damage you, or betray you, or fail to help you when you need it. Blood is not always thicker than water: acquired friends can love you far better than the group you are connected with by your DNA or by socialization and upbringing if you are fostered or adopted. Here the concept of the utility friendship can help. Aristotle would have you relegate to the status of secondary friend a cousin or sibling who has never shown any sign of reciprocating your good actions toward them. You can exchange seasonal greetings and wedding invitations, to be sure, but little more, without any need for feeling guilty.

There is great detail and nuance in the thought Aristotle put into maintaining primary friendships. He sounds as though he speaks from experience when he says that friends from childhood often do not "grow up" at the same speed. Different development can make it impossible for the former friends to get anything from the relationship any more. Or if we are intimate with someone who seems to undergo a character change, and develop an immoral streak, should we end the friendship? "Leaky" friends are generally incurable and can never be more than liabilities. But given my own rule about second (but not third) chances, I am pleased to find that Aristotle would give some primary friends one more opportunity at friendship, if the fault is curable, "for so long as they are capable of reform we are even more bound to help them morally than we should be to assist them financially, since character is a more valuable thing than wealth and has more to do with friendship."

Chapter 8

—⌘—

COMMUNITY

We are all members of communities which extend beyond our families and close friends. Our happiness depends partly on whether we are at ease with our fellow citizens in our nations and the citizens of other nations across the planet. It can be difficult to work out our responsibilities as members of groups, especially in times of political turbulence or when we do not agree with the policies of the government. Another problem is a feeling of helplessness in the face of large-scale international troubles, such as the environmental crisis, a feeling that often leads understandably to a desire for a retreat into private life and escapist recreation.

Aristotle understood this. He himself lived in times and places where it was actually dangerous to oppose the ruling powers. In Macedon, Philip II ran affairs as a ruthless autocrat; in Athens, even though it was a democracy, Aristotle was always an outsider, a resident alien, without the rights of a full Athenian citizen. He must have felt tempted to turn his back on political issues altogether and retire completely to his large personal library. And yet he did not. He continued to teach his students (several of whom were destined to be leaders), and give lectures to the ordinary Athenian public at the Lyceum. Above all he continued to write, with exceptional insightfulness, about politics and the relationship of citizens to their wider human communities and even to the natural and animal worlds.

The effective creation of happiness, for Aristotle, cannot be done alone. Humans may enjoy brief periods of solitude, but they are biologically social animals. They flourish optimally when they live in association with other humans and animals and engage in reciprocal good deeds. In ancient Greece, the deities symbolizing reciprocity were the Three Graces, sisters called "Beauty," "Joy" and "Flourishing." They were often depicted in art holding hands in a circle, because three marks the moment when a simple two-way relationship breaks out into a complex set of transactions, which form the nucleus of society. This mirrors the flow of mutual assistance around human communities in a "virtuous circle." Aristotle approves of the custom of placing a shrine of the graces prominently in a public place "to remind people to return a kindness; for that is a special characteristic of grace, since it is a duty not only to repay a service done to you, but at another time to take the initiative in doing a service yourself." It is insufficient, in virtue ethics, merely to respond to friendly overtures: you need to be a self-starter, to initiate and actively foster cooperation yourself.

The texts in which Aristotle discusses how human beings best live together are his *Nicomachean Ethics* and his *Politics.* He uses the analogy of diluting sugar in water in different concentrations to illustrate the strength of the affection felt toward different members of our own family and toward friends and fellow citizens. "The mutual rights of parents and children are not the same as those between siblings; the obligations of members of a club or social group are not identical to those of fellow citizens; and similarly with the other forms of friendship." Doing harm to someone else is increasingly serious in proportion to the closeness of the bond: it is more shocking to defraud a friend of money than a mere fellow citizen; or to refuse to help a brother but not a stranger.

In Aristotle's political theory, our relationships with fellow citizens are a special subcategory of utility friendship, since they exist for mutual advantage and cease when mutual self-interest ceases. City-states malfunction when there are no friendly partnerships in operation between the individuals who constitute the state. A trenchant account of the potential degradation of all relationships in a malfunctioning state was published in *Agamemnon's Daughter* by Ismail Kadare (2003). This novel uses the sacrifice of the heroine in Euripides' tragedy *Iphigenia in Aulis* (by which, as it happens, Aristotle was also fascinated) as a paradigm for the effect in the early 1980s of the dehumanizing regime in Albania and the moral degeneracy that afflicts any population ruled by an unaccountable government. Kadare shows how everyone is in danger of losing their moral compass when terror is the dominant psychological register:

> Each day we felt the cogs and wheels of collective guilt pushing us further down. We were obliged to take a stand, make accusations, and fling mud at people—at ourselves in the first place, then at everyone else. It was a truly diabolical mechanism, because once you've debased yourself, it's easy to sully everything around you. Every day, every hour that passed stripped more flesh from moral values.

Aristotle's ideal state is just the opposite: it is a *magnification* of the primary relationships. Good government of a city-state, aiming at the happiness of citizens, requires a foundation of friendships between citizens and will promote them.

This foundation of civic friendship is called by Aristotle "civic concord," which describes an unfluctuating attitude toward the other individuals constituting your state. The attitude comprises both good-will and a commitment to reciprocal responsibility. Its aim is to secure what is expedient for everybody in a morally conscientious way. There will always be citizens, unfortunately, who cannot sign up to the project of civic concord any more than they can make serious friendships in their personal lives, "since they try to get more than their share of advantages, and take less than their share of work and public burdens." Aristotle is clear that citizens who love only themselves, and take more than their fair share of their community's assets, are rightly censured. Moreover, "a man cannot expect to make money out of the community and to receive its respect as well; people do not try to make money out of their friends." But where the bulk of citizens treat each other as friends, the state as a whole can pursue happiness.

The utility partnership between citizens takes place on a larger canvas than utility friendships in your workplace or school. Yet Aristotle's emphasis on fellow citizenship as a species of friendship underlies his sense that there was a size beyond which happy city-states would not grow. He speaks with amazed disapproval of Babylon, so large that "when it was captured a considerable part of the city was not aware of it three days later." Overpopulation also leads to poverty; one lawgiver at Corinth he mentions argued that the best policy is to maintain the same numbers across time. Aristotle believes that there is a natural limit to the size of a civic community which functions well, just like a ship. A ship needs to be neither too small (no wider than an arm) nor too long (a quarter of a mile), because in neither case will it function effectively. Even in the fourth century BCE, he seems more concerned about overpopulation than its opposite. He also uses the "ship of state" metaphor to illustrate civic concord. Fellow citizens are partners in a community, as are sailors. "And although sailors differ from each other in function—one is an oarsman, another helmsman, another lookout man, and another has some other similar special designation," and so their individual competencies are peculiar to each, they are also aiming at a common goal, "security in navigation is the business of them all." Similarly, in a happy state, although citizens have different occupations, they share the common goal of their community's welfare.

Aristotle thinks about constitutions via the health of the individual relationships underpinning the political community. He offers a measured comparison of the four different types of constitution in ancient Greece—democracy, tyranny, aristocracy and monarchy (occasionally supplemented by a fifth, a super-monarchy incorporating several different races ruled by the "king of all," the *pambasileus*, perhaps invented to describe the Macedonian imperial project). This comparative discussion has had an incalculable influence on political thought and indeed political practice: the very vocabulary of European political theory was born at the moment when Aristotle's *Politics* was first translated into modern languages, and has been appropriated by advocates of all of these constitutional models. A month after the execution of Charles I in January 1649, John Milton's *The Tenure of Kings and Magistrates*, which justifies regicide where the king has made himself answerable only to God, uses Aristotle's definition of a monarch in the *Politics*.

Aristotle's harshest criticisms are directed at tyrannies, which he says discourage any activities among citizens that foster self-esteem and self-confidence. These activities, tellingly, include the work of philosophers such as Plato and Aristotle, "the formation of study-circles and other conferences for debate." Most of us today would not happily tolerate living under any form of constitution which suppressed self-education, or debate, or indeed any constitution other than a democracy. Today, more than half the world lives in electoral democracies. Yet by Aristotle's ethical criteria, many of these electoral democracies accept thoroughly bad behavior on a grand scale: most estimates put the proportion of humans living today in countries which respect basic human rights and the rule of law at less than 40 percent. Aristotle's response to regimes which use torture in an attempt to elicit information is this: stop it because it doesn't work. As he stated, coolly, in his *Rhetoric*, "those being subjected to torture are as likely to give false evidence as true, some being ready to endure everything rather than tell the truth, while others are equally ready to make false charges against others, in the hope of being sooner released from torture."

He knows about the many problems associated with democracy. In a passage which speaks loud across the centuries, he acknowledges that regulation of property ownership causes discontent: "for if both in the enjoyment of the produce and in the work of production they end up not equal but unequal, complaints are bound to arise between those who enjoy or take much but work little and those who take less but work more." He soberly concludes that these are hard problems to solve: "In general to live together and share all our human affairs is difficult, and especially to share such things as these." Yet he chose to live in Athens for more than three decades of his adult life, even as a resident alien without citizen's rights, and therefore can't have found the democratic system inimical.

He speaks with less disapproval of democracy than of any other system. In his *Rhetoric* he defines the goals of different constitutions in a way which makes democracy appear preferable: the goal of democracy is liberty, as opposed to wealth (the goal of oligarchy), high culture and obedience to law (the goal of aristocracy), and self-protection (the goal of tyranny). He points out that the constitution with the most "scope for friendship and justice between ruler and subjects" is democracy, "where the citizens being equal have many things in common." The constitution which is most hostile to friendship and justice between citizens is, unsurprisingly, tyranny.

Aristotle also thinks that although democracies can degenerate, the mass electorate empowered in a democracy *potentially* comes to far better decisions than the small number of rulers involved in the other types of constitution. He compares a decision taken by the masses to the type of public feast to which many different citizens contribute different dishes. This will inevitably be better than a dinner provided by any single host: when citizens come together to judge legal cases or deliberate, "just as the multitude becomes a single man with many feet and many hands and many senses, so also it becomes one personality as regards the moral and intellectual faculties. This is why the general public is a better judge of the works of music and those of the poets, because different men can judge a different part of the performance, and all of them all of it." We might today learn from Aristotle's recommendation that in the ideal democracy, all citizens are enabled and encouraged to participate in government, through the institution of short terms of office and financial support to take leave for something like jury duty. Aristotle also points out that a large number of citizens is more difficult to corrupt than an individual, just as it is harder to pollute "a large stream of water" than a thin trickle. An individual's judgment can be distorted by anger or some other strong emotion, but it is unlikely that all the citizens in a democracy will feel angry simultaneously.

At least half the planet's population does not take relative political stability for granted. Aristotle is a utopian because he imagines the possibility that everyone alive will be able to realize their potential and make full use of all their faculties (the distinctive "Aristotelian principle" according to American political philosopher John Rawls). He even imagines a futuristic world when technological advances would make human labor (and therefore, in his own historical context, slavery) unnecessary. He remembers the mythical craftsmen Daedalus and Hephaestus, who constructed robots which could move and work to order, obviating the need for human servants: "for if every tool could perform its own work when ordered, or by seeing what to do in advance, like the statues of Daedalus in the story, or the tripods of Hephaestus which the poet says 'enter the divine company automatically'—if shuttles could weave like this, and plectrums strum harps of their own accord, master craftsmen would have no need of assistants and masters no

need of slaves." It is almost as if he anticipated modern developments
in artificial intelligence.

Aristotle's utopian political theory is flexible. You can be a capitalist
or socialist, a businesswoman or a charity worker, vote for (almost) any
political party, and still be a consistent Aristotelian. Because Aristotle
emphasizes that social structures are only stable if they accommodate
human nature, he has sometimes been a pinup for conservatives: he is
praised in Benjamin Wiker's *Ten Books Every Conservative Must Read*
(2010). Aristotelian capitalists, however, need to be of the kind who
will not tolerate poverty among their fellow citizens. Aristotle knew
that humans come into conflict when commodities are scarce. But he
acknowledges the basic laws still underlying modern capitalism. He is
the first ancient Greek author to explain the meaning of a "monopoly,"
use that particular word, and provide examples. His point is to refute
people who say that philosophy is useless, by proving that philosophers
are capable of running successful businesses—it's just that they prefer
to concentrate on higher things. Thales, the founder of natural science
in the sixth century BCE, was criticized by people who said that
philosophy and the life of intellectual inquiry were useless. But he was
able to use his scientific knowledge to predict one winter that next
summer's crop of olives was going to be abundant. He had the foresight
to rent all the olive presses in his area, acquiring a complete monopoly
on them, and then charged high fees for subletting them. He made a
fortune, Aristotle tells us, "so proving that it is easy for philosophers
to be rich if they choose, but this is not what they care about."

In his insistence on grounding political theory in humanity's basic
needs, Aristotle conceived by far the most advanced economic ideas
ever to have appeared in his time; this was the main reason why Karl
Marx admired Aristotle so much and why he has had as consistent a
following among political leftists as among conservatives. Yet
Aristotelian socialists need to acknowledge that extending compulsory

public ownership to domestic accommodation does not work. Where there is no clarity about who is responsible for a state asset, Aristotle believes that nobody takes responsibility for it at all. He has also noticed that the greater number of people involved in the possession of any kind of property, the less care any one individual takes of it. People look after things because they enjoy the sense of private ownership and because the things have value for them; both these qualities are diluted if shared with others. Aristotle thinks that "everybody loves a thing more if it has cost him trouble: for instance, those who have made money love money more than those who have inherited it." Acquiring assets of any kind through hard work produces a stronger attachment than receiving them effortlessly.

The Aristotelian socialist will be pleased to find him condemning extreme poverty as a cause of conflict and crime, and taking seriously the radical view of a contemporary leveler called Phaleas of Chalcedon, who saw inequality in property as the universal cause of civil strife. Phaleas recommended that all citizens should own an identical amount of property. Although Aristotle does not agree with such an extreme equalization, he cites with apparent approval the recommendation in Plato's *Laws* that no citizen should be allowed to own an estate more than five times the size of the smallest one. (This, of course, is a degree of inequality radically lower than that tolerated under modern western capitalism. On 7 June 2016, Sir Martin Sorrell, chief executive of the advertising group WPP, publicly defended his proposed £70.4 million annual pay package. That is not five times as much as a warehouse worker, but 5,000 times as much.) Aristotle accepts that inequality in wealth is associated with problems including divisive litigation and revolting obsequiousness toward the super-rich.

Yet Aristotle also saw that economic uniformity might threaten both the diversity of households which enriches state culture, and the crucial distinction between membership of a family and membership

of a state: a state consisting of entirely identical elements will be less
happy than one tolerating a limited degree of inequality, just as if in
music "one turned a harmony into unison or a rhythm into a single
foot." The Aristotelian socialist needs to accept that there is a distinction between bad behavior and bad constitutions.

Although Aristotle's moral philosophy can be practiced (within
limits) by people espousing both right- and left-wing political views,
it would be impossible for a climate-change denier to find much encouragement in Aristotle. As a natural scientist who believed in meticulous
research based on repeated acts of empirical observation of what the
world presents to him (*ta phainomena*) and rigorous examination of
hypotheses, if Aristotle could visit our world today, he would be alarmed
at the weight of the evidence of human-caused environmental damage
he saw around him. His detailed studies in his scientific works on the
physical world, and our place as living, breathing, embodied human
creatures within it, are also *preconditions* of his moral philosophy.

By seeing humans as animals, if advanced ones, Aristotle effected
a transformation in the ethical relationship between us and our material
environment that still has unlimited significance for us today. As we
become aware of the full extent of the damage we have inflicted as a
species on the planet we share with so many other living things, we
can see that his scientific ideas are indeed fundamental to our project
to obtain human fulfillment. Aristotle would have been appalled at the
mess we have made of the world by a failure to take our responsibility
to it and its non-human residents seriously. Moreover, his commitment
to living planned lives in a deliberated way, taking long-term and total
responsibility for our physical survival as well as our mental happiness,
would, scientists and classicists agree, make him an environmental
campaigner today.

Ecology regularly uses Aristotle's theories because they stress
causality in the physical world, and because his focus on the integrity

and interaction of everything in the world is compatible with complex systems theory.[10] Ecologists point to Aristotle's beautiful description of the oneness and interconnectedness of nature (*physis*) in his *Metaphysics*:

> All things [in the universe] are ordered together somehow, but not all alike—both fishes and fowls and plants; and the world is not such that one thing has nothing to do with another, but they are connected. For all are ordered together to one end . . . all share the good of the whole.[11]

Plants, animals and human beings exist, as Aristotle sees it, in concentric circles of interdependence: "Nature proceeds little by little from things lifeless to animal life in such a way that it is impossible to determine the exact line of demarcation." He grasped the concept that climate can change over time and how environmental changes can threaten the human race: in his *Meteorology* he speaks of the aging of the earth and the changes of land and sea in relation to one another. Whole races (*ethnoi*) have been destroyed before they have been able to record what was happening to them. Over time, he says, the land around Mycenae has become dry and barren.

Equally relevant to environmentalism is Aristotle's moral conception of economics. He says that business activity can be divided into two categories. The first is natural, and part of Living Well, since people need things to live comfortably in their households. But this kind of business activity has inherent limits, since there is a point at which humans have sufficient goods to exist. But the other type of business activity, which he sees as fundamentally unnatural, is bound by no limits whatsoever: he could be describing unbridled industrial capitalism.[12] Only humans have moral agency, and therefore only humans, as co-inhabitants of the natural world on Planet Earth with an astounding number of plants and animals, have the unique responsibility to look after that planet. But humans also have the capacity, because of their unique mental endowment, to cause terrible damage: as Aristotle said, drawing a chillingly true distinction, a bad man can do 10,000 times more harm than an animal. Because humans have invented weapons, and can use them for evil ends, immoral people become "the most unholy and savage of animals."

Aristotle's works on animals also display confidence in the judgment and observations of uneducated people, related to his conviction that the "smart mob" constituted by democracy makes the best collective decisions. He reports what he learned about the women islanders of Cos who farm silk from the giant peacock moth (*Saturnia pyri*), and its development through caterpillar and cocoon stages, when the women "unwind and reel off the cocoons of these creatures, and afterward weave a fabric with the threads thus unwound; a Coan woman of the name of Pamphila, daughter of Plateus, is said to have been the first inventor of the fabric." He talked to hunters who told him how they enchant deer through playing music to them, and that there is a colloquial term for the first short horns produced by young stags comparing them with clothes pegs.

His detailed discussions of the hearing capacity of fish, and their sense of taste, only came into being through prolonged conversations with fishermen about the way they exploited noise, silence and tasty bait to maximize their catches. He talked at the two Athenian harbors of Phaleron and Piraeus about differences in species of anchovy. He learned demotic nicknames which the fishermen give to shellfish depending on their physical appearance or other attributes, like "onion" and "stinkard." This would have appalled Plato. The head of the Academy, with his august theory of the "forms," would surely have scoffed at his student's eloquent insistence that scientists should listen to "ordinary" individuals dealing with plants and animals on an everyday, working basis, whether as hunters, farmers or fishermen: "those who have lived in a more intimate communion with the phenomena of nature are better able to lay down such principles as can be connected together and cover a wide field."

The most important lesson we can learn from Aristotelian science is about the human race's relationship with the rest of nature. Aristotle begins his discussion of changes in the color of fur and plumage in living things with hair-graying patterns in the human animal. Where "the hair over the temples is the first to turn grey, and the hair in the front grows grey sooner than the hair at the back; and the hair on the pubis is the last to change colour." From this statement he proceeds to animals, most of which, like humans, "only change colour as a result of age." Cranes are one exception; diet, seasonal molting or environmental factors such as the nature of the river water in which sheep are bathed can cause color changes in other species.

Man shares his gregarious nature with some other animals, such as bees, wasps, ants and cranes, explains Aristotle. But, being a complicated animal, man does also enjoy solitude, at least in limited amounts. Like humans, some animals live under recognizable forms of government: bees have rulers, for example. Some animals are nomadic, while others settle, even build permanent houses, and train their young to use their homes properly, in the same way as humans. He is especially enthralled here by the swallow:

> In the same way as men do, the bird mixes mud and chaff together; if it runs short of mud, it souses its body in water and rolls about in the dry dust with wet feathers; furthermore, just as man does, it makes a bed of straw, putting hard material below for a foundation, and adapting all to suit its own size. Both parents cooperate in the rearing of the young; each of the parents will detect, with practised eye, the young one that

has had a helping, and will take care it is not helped twice over; at first the parents will rid the nest of excrement, but, when the young are grown, they will teach their young to shift their position and let their excrement fall over the side of the nest.

An animal lover, he delights in the observations in his zoological works. Many sentences suggest that if he were alive today, like Sir David Attenborough he would be making wonderful TV nature documentaries. It is difficult to dislike a man who writes of a certain species of wren that "is hardly larger than a locust, has a crest of bright red gold, and is in every way a beautiful and graceful little bird."

Aristotle advances sophisticated theories about birds' migrations across the Black Sea and the Mediterranean, which must have required meticulous observation. In some ways, he thinks birds are particularly close to *Homo sapiens*: we share with them not only that we walk upright on two legs, but also "the faculty of uttering articulate sounds." He concludes by musing on the respective vocal gifts distributed across the animal world:

some animals emit sound while others are mute, and some are endowed with voice: of these latter some have articulate speech, while others are inarticulate; some are given to continual chirping and twittering, some are prone to silence; some are musical, and some unmusical; but all animals without exception exercise their power of singing or chattering chiefly in connexion with the intercourse of the sexes.

He seems to have interviewed some bird-catchers with expertise in different types of bird intelligence and with a lively turn of phrase: he describes the long-eared owl as "a great rogue of a bird, and is a capital mimic; a bird-catcher will dance before it and, while the bird is mimicking his gestures, the accomplice comes behind and catches it." He participated in an experimental drinking session with a talkative Indian parrot: "by the way, after drinking wine, the parrot becomes more saucy than ever."

In Aristotle's day, the human population was small in relation to even the known world, and Aristotle's contemporaries were uncertain as to the limits of the territory beyond what they had already explored and had regular contact with. Although food was sometimes scarce, there was little consciousness that anything provided by nature— timber, fish stocks, songbirds, mountain lions, new coastlines to colonize—might ever entirely run out. Aristotle offers a prophetic glimpse when he describes shellfish, and discovers that in the lagoon on Lesbos a particular species of scallop—the red scallop—has actually been rendered extinct. It has been killed off completely, partly by droughts but also "partly by the dredging-machine used in their capture." Humans have contributed to the extermination of an entire community of a previously living thing. This is probably the earliest reference in world literature to overfishing, now an internationally recognized environmental emergency. He also cites the destruction which can be caused by human interference with naturally occurring animal populations, motivated by financial greed, and refers us to "the man of Carpathos." The Carpathian tried to make money out of hare breeding, and introduced the first pair onto the island. Carpathos was soon overrun with hares, which devastated its crops, vegetable beds and plant ecology.

Aristotle is aware of the destructive potential of farming to interfere in nature. He even suggests that kitchen vegetables flourish better if left to the elements than if they are irrigated artificially. He certainly condemns some human practices in the farming of animals as contrary to nature and pernicious. Some animal breeders used to make the young males of certain species breed with their own mothers. This mother–son inbreeding was attempted either because the owners could not afford to hire a stud or because the animals they possessed were regarded as particularly fine specimens with specific attributes they wanted to perpetuate.

This practice is not unknown among breeders of pedigree dogs today, although it is rightly regarded as genetically risky and abusive; line breeding, where animals mate with distant cousins, is infinitely preferable. Aristotle is in no doubt that animals do not naturally want to mate with their mothers, and has collected examples of animal resistance to enforced "Oedipalism": "The male camel declines intercourse with its mother; if his keeper tries compulsion, he evinces disinclination. On one occasion, when intercourse was being declined by the young male, the keeper covered over the mother and put the young male to her; but, when after the intercourse the wrapping had been removed, though the operation was completed and could not be revoked, still by and by he bit his keeper to death."

Aristotle studied horse-rearing at close quarters. In another example, he reports that a young stallion forced to impregnate his own mother directed his violent response against himself, like a tragic hero:

The king of Scythia had a highly bred mare, and all her foals were splendid; that wishing to mate the best of the young males with the mother, he had him brought to the stall for the purpose; that the young horse declined; that, after the mother's head had been concealed in a wrapper he, in ignorance, had intercourse; and that, when immediately afterwards the wrapper was removed and the head of the mare was rendered visible, the young horse ran way and hurled himself down a precipice.

And the different methods of raising and feeding horses seem to worry Aristotle. Horses should be allowed to roam freely at pasture, since then they remain free of disease apart from an affliction of the hoof which is in any case self-rectifying. But stables are breeding-grounds for malnutrition and all forms of infection: "stall-reared horses are subject to very numerous forms of disease: one which attacks the hind-legs" (possibly equine degenerative myeloencephalopathy, the result of a vitamin deficiency, or equine infectious anemia or equine herpesvirus-1).

And although Aristotle knew nothing of selfish genes or natural selection, he is certainly aware of a relationship between each region's climate, landscape, and the type of animals to be found there. In lands in or to the north of Greece like "Illyria, Thrace, and Epirus the ass is small, and in Gaul and in Scythia the ass is not found at all owing to the coldness of the climate of these countries. In Arabia the lizard is more than a cubit in length, and the mouse is much larger than our fieldmouse." Equally, he can have known nothing about species resonance. Yet he tells us of an occasion in 395 BCE when all the ravens disappeared from southern Greece at the time when a battle much further north resulted in a particularly high death toll. Ravens are opportunistic carrion birds. Aristotle calmly infers from this, that even across vast distances, "it would appear that these birds have some means of intercommunicating with one another."

In his *History of Animals*, Aristotle presents his remarkable classification of all animals on the face of the earth, which is simultaneously an exposition of what it means to be a human, since humans are but animals with a few distinctive characteristics. There are, however, a few areas in which animals are definitely superior. There are things which animals can do and humans can't: when describing animals with visible outer ears, he claims that man is the only one "which cannot move this organ." There are, in fact, some people—admittedly a small minority—who can wiggle their ears, but clearly Aristotle was not one of them. Aristotle also knows that, in some animals, most of the senses are far more highly developed than in man: "of the senses man has the sense of touch more refined than any animal, and so also, but in less degree, the sense of taste; in the development of the other senses he is surpassed by a great number of animals."

Aristotle recommends kindness to animals, as does Xenophon the Athenian, author of works on horses and dogs *The Cavalry Commander* and *Hunting with Dogs,* and a student of Socrates. Just as in humans, where he knows that poverty is a direct case of social conflict, Aristotle insists that aggression in animals is linked to scarcity of resources, especially food. He has recommendations on how to deal with male elephants at mating season, and says that "abundance of food tends to tame them." Indeed, he argues that it is hunger which causes difficulties between men and wild beasts:

> One may go so far as to say that if there were no lack or stint of food, then those animals that are now afraid of man or are wild by nature would be tame and familiar with him, and in the same way with one another. This is shown by the way animals are treated in Egypt, for the result of food being constantly supplied to them is that even the fiercest creatures live peaceably together. In some places crocodiles are tame to their priestly keeper from being fed by him.

He is, however, aware, that human zoological knowledge makes it easier to exploit animals. He discusses how pigs are fattened in Thrace. He reports that the horns of young cattle are so soft that they can be trained to grow into any shape if they are coated with wax and molded artistically. And he knows of a surprising method for culling dangerous snakes. They "have an insatiate appetite for wine; consequently, at times men hunt for snakes by pouring wine into saucers and putting them into the interstices of walls, and the creatures are caught when inebriated."

Most of all, he revels in interaction and *cooperation* between humans and animals. He records the history of Athens' most famous mule, who reportedly lived to the age of eighty at the time when the Parthenon was being built (that is, in the 430s BCE). Because of its great age, the mule was "retired" and no longer required to work. But it turned up every day to help drag burdens, side by side with the others, and to encourage them. "In consequence a public decree was passed forbidding any baker driving the creature away from his bread-tray." Aristotle also has a strong inkling of the superior intelligence of the dolphin, which many scientists now believe really is only rivaled in intellectual capacity by *Homo sapiens*: he tells of a shoal of dolphins which entered a harbor in Caria (southwest Turkey) and remained there until a fisherman set free a dolphin from their community which he had caught in his net.

Along with the dolphin, the animal on which Aristotle spends the most loving descriptive attention is another of the most social and intelligent: the elephant. He is impressed by the elephant's trunk:

> it has a nose with such properties and size that it can use it in the same way as a hand. For it eats and drinks by lifting up its food with the aid of this body part into its mouth, and with the same organ it lifts up articles to the driver on its back; it can pluck up trees by the roots with it, and when walking through water it uses it to spout the water up. This organ can be either crooked or coiled at the tip, but it can't flex like a joint, for it is composed of gristle.

But it is the elephant's brainpower and temperament that he admires above all: "Of all wild animals the most easily tamed and the gentlest is the elephant. It can be taught a number of tricks, the drift and meaning of which it understands; as, for instance, it can be taught to kneel in the presence of the king. It is very sensitive, and possessed of an intelligence superior to that of other animals."

There are several other reports he collected of constructive interaction between humans and animals. He regarded female red deer as highly intelligent, because he noticed that they bring their fawns close to the sides of public roads; the wild animals who prey on young deer are deterred from attacking them there through fear of the humans passing by. He tells of the cooperation between wolves and fishermen in the northeastern Black Sea region, by the Sea of Azov; provided the fishermen divide their spoils with the wolves, all is well. But if they do not give them fish, the wolves "tear their nets in pieces as they lie drying on the shore." The presence of a particular kind of fish he calls the *anthias* is a sign that there are "no dangerous creatures in the vicinity, and sponge-divers dive in safety." The divers, he tells us, are so grateful to the *anthias* that they have renamed it the "sacred fish."

Aristotle recognized that humans, as animals, must prioritize the struggle to survive physically—to get enough food and water and shelter not to die next week—before they can enjoy the life lived self-consciously, aiming at individual and collective happiness. He is struck by the resilience humans can show in the face of the ceaseless struggle to obtain a livelihood. He personally imagines that having no time to enjoy the world of the mind would be almost intolerable. He would have been the first to stress that anyone reading this book is already privileged by having sufficient leisure left over after financing and preparing her family's meals to think about less basic imperatives.

Aristotle's distinction between surviving biologically and living a deliberated life directed toward happiness can therefore help you sympathize with the homeless and the hungry, refugees and exiles, the disabled and the mortally ill, and with abused animals. So there is no point in feeling guilty about having sufficient time to think about becoming the Best Possible You. The most ethically developed person is the most likely to want to help the disadvantaged and the damaged. Be grateful that you are in this fortunate position and get on with Project Happiness.

Chapter 9

⸻ ❧ ⸻

LEISURE

Aristotle devoted several pages of both his *Ethics* and *Politics* to the topic of leisure. He is cited in all serious studies of the sociology, philosophy and psychology of leisure, from Thomas Aquinas in the thirteenth century to Josef Pieper's influential *Leisure: The Basis of Culture* (1948). His radical ideas about leisure have implications for our own times, especially his insistence that leisure is more important than work and that people misuse it if they are not educated in constructive pastimes. He notes that Sparta never flourishes in times of peace because its constitution, while training the Spartans well for combat, "has not educated them to be able to live in idleness." Boredom is the enemy not only of peace but of happiness.

Aristotle's views of the purpose of leisure departed radically from those held by all his predecessors and contemporaries. The popular idea of leisure time in ancient Greece, where most people, free and enslaved, worked tremendously hard, was that it was best spent on physical pleasure and ephemeral amusements. Just as in the nineteenth century, when the Norwegian-American economist Thorstein Veblen invented the ideas of the "leisure class" and "conspicuous consumption," the ancient working population envied the rich both their more extensive free time and the amusements they filled it with: Aristotle says that most people suppose "that diversions are a component part of happiness, because princes and potentates devote their leisure to them." But this belief is misguided, says Aristotle, because such amusements "are often more harmful than beneficial, causing men to neglect their health and their estates." They have little to do with real happiness at all.

Our word "leisure" actually comes from the Latin verb *licere* (to be allowed): leisure is the time when you are free from the requirement to work and are "allowed" to choose how you spend it. The Greek word used by Aristotle, *schole*, originally meant time which you could call your own, or in which you could please yourself. In due course one meaning of *schole* acquired academic connotations, and gave rise to our word "school," because the philosophers saw that leisure was (among other things) a precondition of intellectual activity for its own sake. But Aristotle's far-reaching concept of leisure encompasses far more than time available for study and debate. On the one hand it includes necessary relaxation after work, bodily rest and recuperation, the fulfillment of natural bodily appetites for food and sex, and amusement or pleasurable entertainment to obviate boredom. But it also includes every other form of activity in which humans engage after fulfilling the laborious tasks necessary to secure the means of survival (shelter, nutrition and self-defense). Leisure, Aristotle insisted, if used rightly is the ideal human state. A few people are fortunate enough to do what they like to do best—fulfill their unique potential—and get paid for it. They earn a living by doing what they would choose to do anyway if they had a private income and round-the-clock leisure. But financial necessity means that most people spend a good deal of their working lives wishing they were not at work. For Aristotle, work and recovery from work are never ends in themselves: they are the merely the means to the further leisure activity in which our full potential for happiness can be realized.

As a civilization we are obsessed with work. Aristotle's privileging of planned and constructive leisure over work or simple relaxation runs counter to our idea that we are defined by our jobs and professions.

When we ask someone what they "do," we mean what they do to make a living, not whether they spend their leisure hours singing in a choir or visiting medieval castles. The very idea of having enough leisure to worry about how to use it well would prompt scornful laughter from many working people, who believe that it is the sort of problem on which time is wasted by airy-fairy ivory-tower intellectuals far removed from the pragmatic reality of everyday life. Yet it is *only* in our leisure hours that Aristotle believes our full human potential can be realized. The objective of work is usually to sustain our lives biologically, an objective we share with other animals. But the objective of leisure can and should be to sustain other aspects of our lives which make us uniquely human: our souls, our minds, our personal and civic relationships. Leisure is therefore wasted if we do not use it purposively.

He would have been repelled by the modern concept of the "work ethic," which, as Max Weber showed in *The Protestant Ethic and the Spirit of Capitalism* (1905), first arose as a result of the Reformation and the Industrial Revolution. People began to believe that the problems of poverty and securing enough provisions for survival could be solved, but only by complete dedication to work. Labor might one day be rendered unnecessary by machines, but only after many centuries of extra-intensive labor. Work consequently acquired a much higher status, or at least work geared toward maximizing output of material goods. This had several ramifications. Work stopped being a means to an end—supporting life—and became an end in itself. The idea of "nonproductive" work, work in spheres not strictly necessary for our biological survival, became perceived as less intrinsically valuable than industrial work. As the economist Adam Smith put it in *Wealth of Nations* (1776), "unproductive labour" includes not only monarchs but "churchmen, lawyers, physicians, men of letters of all kinds, players, buffoons, musicians, opera-singers, opera-dancers, etc." Pressure to maximize output meant that working hours stopped being seasonal and became dictated by mechanical timekeeping. They were also massively extended, leading at the peak of the Industrial Revolution to the unending drudgery of the residents of Coketown, as portrayed in Charles Dickens' *Hard Times* (1854), and to the horrors of twelve-hour working days and child labor.

In the same year, Henry Thoreau published *Walden*, which describes life in a simple log cabin in rural Massachusetts, with plenty of time for reading and reflection. It explores the psychological deprivation inflicted on capitalist society. In the crazed pursuit of superabundant commodities, humankind has forgotten the reason and purpose of life altogether, and has even begun to invent new needs in order to justify the disproportionate amount of time spent at work manufacturing unnecessary commodities. Thoreau has a profoundly Aristotelian fantasy: every village in New England will one day subsidize its own Lyceum, full of books, newspapers, learned journals and works of art, and invite the wisest men in the world to visit and enlighten the local population during their extensive leisure hours. Aristotle would have approved of Thoreau's emphasis on education as the solution to the "problem" of using leisure constructively. He was painfully aware that people in general are not socially prepared for making good choices about how to use their leisure time, even though, in his view, it is the most important part of our lives. He went so far as to argue that good use of leisure in an ideal society would be the main goal and objective of education. His outlook could scarcely be more modern.

One response to a lack of training in use of leisure is workaholism, a syndrome first identified just after the Second World War, when many people experienced difficulties settling back down into "normal" life after a state of high alert. Compulsive working round the clock harms physical and mental health. Some nations and organizations are taking serious steps to discourage it: in France, workers have won the right not to check their e-mail accounts outside their official working hours. But at the same time, children are being encouraged to develop obsessive attitudes to work by ever-increasing academic pressures and a concomitant ever-decreasing emphasis in many schools on activities which could contribute to a fulfilling "leisure life" later: learning musical instruments, arts and crafts, hobbies and exercise. Leisure and recreation, given the speed of technological change, need urgently to be discussed in our society. Longer lives offer substantially more years where we may not need to work for our keep at all. The increasingly rapid advances in artificial intelligence mean that many of the time-consuming tasks on which human society depends will be done by robots, computers and machines. This is likely to lead to a much greater proportion of any given population being employed for fewer hours a week than the human race has been accustomed to. And Aristotle's revolutionary views on leisure will become of increasing relevance the less we are actually at work.

More free time will make self-education more achievable. Increased leisure, along with cost-free resources on the Internet, make a world-class education available to anyone with an Internet connection. Access to knowledge used to be dependent on access to a library, the context in which Matt Damon's working-class character in the movie *Good Will Hunting* (1997) tells an arrogant Harvard student, "You dropped 150 grand on a fuckin' education you could have got for a dollar fifty in late charges at the public library." But even libraries have been superseded. Some universities, including MIT, offer open-access courses entirely free of charge. Others, such as Harvard Business School, publish top-level blogs by brilliant scholars. Filmed lectures and podcasts on every conceivable topic are available through TED, YouTube and iTunes. But for many of us, fully occupied during the working day, directly educational activities are the last thing we want during relaxation time. The answer is to combine pleasure and personal development through careful choice of recreational entertainment.

Harry Allen Overstreet, the inspirational chair of the philosophy department at CUNY from 1911 to 1936 and the author of several bestselling books on self-help and social psychology, understood that recreation is a serious business: "Recreation is not a secondary concern for a democracy. It is a primary concern, for the kind of recreation a people make for themselves determines the kind of people they become and the kind of society they build." Overstreet had trained as a classical philosopher and this famous quotation sums up Aristotle's position on the potential of leisure to enable human flourishing or its opposite. What you choose to read or watch or listen to in your leisure time directly affects your development as a moral being—how you continuously *create* yourself, as the etymology of *recreate* suggests. This means, according to Aristotle, that your choice of recreational activity directly affects your happiness.

Aristotle himself was an enthusiastic walker, who valued bodily health and pleasure highly. He certainly would have encouraged pastimes which involved exercise, creative pursuits, music and the enjoyment of fine food and drink. But the only leisure interest to which he devoted serious philosophical thought was literature, and in particular dramatic literature, which is the central topic of his *Poetics*. It is actually remarkable that he should do this, because his teacher Plato had objected so strongly to the arts that they are banned from his ideal city-state in the *Republic*. Why would Aristotle, a serious thinker whose objective was understanding the world in a way that would produce the best possible human community, spend so much time thinking about the fictional stories enacted in the popular theater? The only explanation is that he was personally convinced that such entertainment had the potential massively to enhance the emotional and moral life of both individual spectators and the community as a whole.

Aristotle clearly loved theater, music and the visual arts. All his works abound in references to singers, choruses, harp players, dancers, poems and poets, statues and handicrafts. But he also had first-hand evidence of the arts' social benefits. When he moved to Athens at the age of forty-eight to found his Lyceum, he built it much nearer than Plato's Academy to the Athenian Theatre of Dionysus on the south side of the Athenian Acropolis. Athens was still the acknowledged center of dramatic entertainment and activity. Anyone from any city in the Greek world who wanted to make their mark in the theater world automatically headed for Athens, just as aspiring movie-makers head for Hollywood today. We can imagine Aristotle walking at dawn with Theophrastus and their students, along with many other Athenian citizens and residents, to attend the tragedies and comedies in the city-center sanctuaries and theaters of Dionysus, and excitedly analyzing them as he strode back home to the Academy at nightfall. Athenian drama was designed not only to enthrall its spectators but to train them in the cognitive, moral and political skills they needed to run a healthy city.

Every now and then a public row erupts over the limits of what it is appropriate and decent to ask people to watch or hear in a TV program, movie or stage play. Violence, bad language, sexual explicitness and nudity have been (and in many jurisdictions all over the world still are) subject to direct or indirect censorship. *Monty Python's Life of Brian* (1979) caused a scandal and was accused by some Christians of being blasphemous; a film containing Tony Harrison's performance of his brilliant, expletive-rich poem *v.* on Channel 4 in 1987 was deplored by the conservative *Daily Mail* and other self-appointed guardians of public morals; the extended and brutal rape scene in Jonathan Kaplan's movie *The Accused* (1988) was criticized by some feminists as pandering to men's sadistic fantasies. More recently, parents have been warned about their children's psychological desensitization to violence by computer games, especially those in which players take the role of "first-person shooter." But what is not often realized is that this debate stretches far back into antiquity, and was first thrashed out philosophically in Plato's Academy between Plato and his most brilliant student, Aristotle. Aristotle argued that we do not unthinkingly imitate what we see in artworks: if they are made responsibly, we think about what we see, and decide, among other things, whether it is desirable to imitate it *or not.*

Aristotle was the first philosopher to argue that the arts could be wonderfully educative. He argued passionately that the producers of drama and music in a democracy hold such great responsibility that they should be publicly appointed officials, and of secondary importance only to priests. They should take precedence even over publicly appointed ambassadors and heralds. Aristotle also makes frequent use of examples from myths, famous theater works and epic poems in his works on diverse other topics as well as ethics. His discussion of excess and deficiency in human characters owes much to the stereotypes he had watched in contemporary comedy. We can be sure that if he were alive today he would have been an avid consumer of television programs, novels and movies, and would have used them to illustrate moral points. He was the first thinker ever to work out arguments for the edificatory potential of stories and enacted entertainments, and many recent and contemporary philosophers have simply elaborated his ideas when they apply them to movies.

Walter Benjamin, for example, saw that the arts, and above all film, can enhance our moral, social and political lives. Iris Murdoch, Martha Nussbaum and Paul W. Kahn have argued that philosophical ideas, especially ethics, find their best, most nuanced and intelligible exposition not in academic treatises but in the particular cases portrayed in the arts, because they are examples of practical application and therefore emotionally compelling.[13]

It is much easier to access good art today than it was in Aristotle's day, when plays were only performed at certain festivals months apart.

The Internet has made it easier than ever before to access and choose movies, plays, books and TV programs to which we expose ourselves and our children. High-quality entertainment, with some planning, can contribute to our happiness and growing wisdom every day of our lives. Movies, because they can be enjoyed inexpensively at home and even in the hospital beds, are a truly democratic art form. A close friend of mine, who was dying of multiple sclerosis, found great comfort and gratification in his huge collection of DVDs even when he could scarcely move any part of his body.

In chapter 2 of his *Poetics*, Aristotle asks the ultimate question—why do humans, unlike other animals, have the arts at all? First, we are born with a greater instinct than other animals for imitation. Children learn their very first ways of being from imitating what other humans do. And second, humans of all ages and occupations *enjoy* imitative arts. We get *pleasure* from looking at pictures or enactments of reality. By and large, nature uses pleasure to guide all animals toward what is good for them: nourishment or reproducing their species. And in the human, an advanced and social animal, the pleasure we get from looking at pictures, or watching plays, can help us *learn about the world*. The arts can serve as a vast encyclopedia of human experience, enabling us to learn about things, however difficult the subject matter, which we might never experience directly in reality.

Aristotle also noticed that we can not only bear *but actually like* looking at realistic artistic likenesses of things which would give us pain, rather than pleasure, to look at in reality. The examples he gives are repellent creatures and human corpses. We may react badly when we see a real spider or jellyfish, but Aristotle knew, because he dissected and carefully drew diagrams of them, that a picture of, for example, a cuttlefish, can allow a student of zoology to learn a great deal about that species even if she or he has never even seen this kind of marine invertebrate.

His other example—corpses—is fascinating. It is unlikely that Aristotle had ever been present at the dissection of a human cadaver. But we know that there are plenty of dead bodies in ancient art and literature. Much of the Homeric *Iliad* revolves around the corpses of handsome warriors slain on the battlefield such as Patroclus and Hector. Greek tragedy even asks its audiences to look physically for extended periods at the corpses of individuals murdered by close family members—the children of Jason and Medea, dangling from their mother's chariot at the end of Euripides' *Medea*, or the bleeding corpse of his suicidal son Haemon which Creon carries, weeping, onto the stage at the end of Sophocles' *Antigone*. Aristotle argues that art allows us to think about dead bodies, even those of people killed in horrific circumstances, and learn about something even as frightening as death in a pleasurable way.

This revolutionary insight helps explain why we read novels, or go to the art gallery, cinema or theater, to immerse ourselves in worlds characterized by violence and suffering of an intensity and on a scale we would find absolutely unbearable in reality. We can educate ourselves about the suffering caused by the fascist bombing of Spanish towns from Picasso's *Guernica* (1937). We can identify with the plight of African American men in New York in the 1930s from Ralph Waldo Ellison's novel *Invisible Man* (1952). We can learn about the experience of women incarcerated in Federal prisons from Jenji Kohan's hit television series *Orange is the New Black* (2013). Moreover, this form of education, as Aristotle insists, "gives pleasure not only to philosophers but also in the same way to everyone else," even if to a lesser degree. When it comes to the arts and to the acquisition of knowledge, he is an unimpeachable democrat.

So Aristotle's prescription for all the arts is simple. Any play, poem, painting or sculpture which is going to be at all successful needs to offer the viewer/reader/listener either pleasure or something useful.

Nobody will go to see a film if it is neither pleasant to watch nor remotely informative. But a *good* piece of art needs, he insists, to be *both*. This precious argument provides the critic of any artwork with a gold standard for evaluating its worth. The question "Did I enjoy it?" is important. But if the answer to the question "Did I learn anything from it?" is negative, there must be a question mark over its claim to high quality.

Commissioning producers and financiers of theater and cinema should take more seriously education as well as entertainment. The London theaters are currently full of frothy, feel-good comedies and the cinemas with endless remakes, recycled plots, prequels, sequels and spin-offs involving comic-book superheroes or gun-toting secret agents foiling alleged terrorist plots. Intensely noisy action sequences or elaborate digital visual sequences often take up far more of the film than dialog of any kind. Bradley Cooper was nominated for an Oscar in 2014 for Best Actor for his performance in *American Sniper* when David Oyelowo wasn't nominated for his extraordinary realization of the role of Martin Luther King Jr. in *Selma*. It's not that *American Sniper* isn't enjoyable. The people are pretty, the acting adequate and there are a few nods to the emotional issues faced by soldiers. But where you can learn a great deal about the civil rights movement from *Selma*, as well as thoroughly enjoying it, you won't *learn* anything from *American Sniper* except a little about how to handle a McMillan TAC-338 rifle.

Learning history through fiction can thoroughly enhance your life. If the novel, play or movie has been well put together, you will learn without making any effort at all, awash in a sea of pleasure. Imaginative scenarios in the company of authors, directors and screenwriters who possess a reputation for scrupulous historical research can be as illuminating as any historical handbook. Mary Renault's beautiful evocations of ancient Greek history, especially her novel *The Mask of Apollo* (1966), set in Aristotle's own fourth century BCE, fed my passion for classics as a teenager. Since much of history is a series of acts of barbarism one group of humans has perpetrated upon another, learning about it through artistic media which bring gratification as well as horror obviously makes sense. Everyone will compile their own list: mine is headed by William Golding's *The Inheritors* (1955), which dramatizes encounters between Neanderthal man and *Homo sapiens*, Xavier Herbert's Australian epic *Capricornia* (1938), Salman Rushdie's *Shame* (1983), which finally made Pakistani politics comprehensible to me, and Margaret Walker's *Jubilee* (1966), one of the greatest novels of the American Civil War and Reconstruction, but from the perspective of the underclasses.

And one of the beauties of the worked-out Aristotelian ethical view of the world is that it makes analyzing other people's lives, in a non-judgmental way, much more interesting too. Considering which qualities of character and behavior lead to happiness or misery in other people, and how they make difficult decisions, or deal with random misfortune, can be entertaining, enlightening and present you with models for imitation or avoidance. Real life provides a constant panoply of ethical case studies for observation and analysis. Real history also becomes most exciting when thought about from an ethical angle—why did Leonidas take his few hundred Spartans off to near-certain death at Thermopylae when the Persians invaded Greece? It turned out to be an effective propaganda exercise in raising the morale of Greeks everywhere and encouraging resistance to Persian imperialism. But the qualities of character, deliberative process, interests he was protecting (he after all only took with him older warriors who had fathered living sons) and ultimate motives—all these bear infinite analysis. History offers us a gymnasium for developing our ethical muscles. And so does fiction.

Aristotle valued the freedom of fictional stories, which brought important ethical situations into reality. Writers operating in the realm of "what might happen" or (in the case of fiction set in the historical past) "what might have happened" need to think very hard about ethics and how events may plausibly unroll, as Aristotle puts it, "according to the law of probability or necessity." This led Aristotle, in chapter 9 of the *Poetics*, to the inevitable but revolutionary conclusion that a fictional genre (he is thinking specifically about tragedy) "is a more philosophical and a higher thing than history: for poetry tends to express the universal, history the particular." Aristotle is fascinated by the idea that a fictional genre, like tragedy set in the mythical past, has a greater scope than a factual one for exploring "how a person of a certain type on occasion speaks or acts, according to the law of probability or necessity."

By Aristotle's day there must have been over 2,000 tragedies written, and the wide range of references in his *Poetics* shows that he had seen or read a substantial number of them himself. He digested them and provided an intense training in how to appreciate fictional stories from a moral perspective identical with that formulated in his ethical treatises and absolutely grounded in the experience of being human. This is what makes his analysis timeless. He asks why bad things happen to humans (effectively discounting all the religious reasons which the tragic texts offer), and reducing the causes, more or less, to two: human error and random accident. The human being, as intelligent moral agent in a world where some factors can't be understood by intelligence or controlled by moral agency, is at the undisputed center of Aristotle's theory of the arts. He is fascinated by the complete *lack* of providential justice in the world.

This is why his favorite play when it comes to expounding his artistic theory is Sophocles' *Oedipus Tyrannus*, which lays most stress on the absolute unfairness of fate, luck or chance in human life. Oedipus ends up making the horrific discovery that he has married his own mother Jocasta, and had four children by her, after killing his own father Laius (unaware of his identity) in what was basically a road-rage incident which had spun out of control. It is a stark instance of someone suffering undeservedly, because this awful destiny had been determined for any son of Laius and Jocasta allowed to survive infancy. Oedipus was headed for a terrible future before he was even conceived.

Sophocles places Oedipus' zero responsibility for the crimes of parricide and incest, neither of which he committed knowingly, side by side with his excellent intellect. He won the throne of Thebes and its beautiful queen by saving the citizens from destruction when it was threatened by the obnoxious sphinx years before. But he is himself, of course, the root cause of their suffering. His crimes have brought the pollution upon the city. The paradox posed by this tragedy is that someone of a lesser intelligence and drive might never have discovered his true identity; without Oedipus' coruscating intellect, Jocasta and Oedipus might have lived to ripe old ages blissfully unaware of their true relationship. Instead, they discover it by inferential reasoning, Jocasta a few minutes before her husband. The "recognition" in this play—that Oedipus is the same person as the baby whom Jocasta ordered to be exposed on the mountain to die—is undergone by both spouses and is agonizingly drawn out. Jocasta goes to their marital bedroom and hangs herself. Oedipus follows her, unpins the brooches from her swinging corpse and stabs his eyes out. His brother-in-law Creon takes over power in the city and forcibly separates him from two of his children—his sisters/daughters Antigone and Ismene. During one revolution of the sun, the mighty and adored Tyrant of Thebes has been discovered to be its true hereditary monarch, and lost his status, his family, and his faculty of sight.

The realistic picture Sophocles paints is of a man on the edge of self-control as he desperately seeks solutions to an insoluble problem. The spectator constantly needs to distinguish between the features of Oedipus' personality which have contributed to his experiences and career, and the bad luck over which he never had any control. No wonder Aristotle relished this as a case study in ethics. The relationship between the plot, the character, the thought processes and the speeches in which they are communicated is minutely planned and executed. And these four elements of tragedy—plot (*muthos*), character (*ethos*), mental activity (*dianoia*) and language (*lexis*)—are indeed the four, in that order, he identifies as the crucial elements of the genre. This principle still applies, just as truly, to any other form of quality fiction.

Oedipus is a model tragic hero for Aristotle because he is of the type best suited to eliciting in us pity and fear, which Aristotle regards as the appropriate emotional responses to tragedy. As the deposed autocrat of Thebes staggers from the stage, the blood pouring from his eye sockets, there is no possibility that we do not share in his pain. And because there was nothing whatsoever he could have done, we fear that such a terrible fate might await us, too. In the dazzling chapter 13 of the *Poetics*, Aristotle explains that the hero has to be of the right moral nature for these emotions to be properly aroused. We need to see a man undergoing a drastic change in his life, and the most tragic is a change which takes him from a state of happiness and success to one of misery and failure through some kind of mistake (*hamartia*).

Aristotle insists that the only way we can *assess* character is by watching people actually in the process of doing and saying things. The *hamartia* of a hero is not a permanent psychological flaw or tendency. It is something they do or say, or omit to do or say when they should. It is, for Aristotle, like the rest of good tragedy, *human ethics in action*. It is this human-centered moral and psychological focus which is what gives quality fiction—dramatic, cinematic or novelistic— its importance: it has the unique capacity to help us learn about ourselves, dark subjects and the world even as we delight in pleasurable recreation.

One of the words most inextricably associated in the popular imagination with Aristotle is his theory of tragic *catharsis*. Watching tragedy involves the emotions of pity and fear, and through arousing them produces "the catharsis of emotions of that kind." Aristotle was the son of an eminent medical practitioner and will have witnessed and perhaps assisted in medical procedures; because he traveled or lived in several different parts of Greece, he will have been able to compare diverse local approaches to healing and therapy.

In *Politics*, Aristotle speaks of the role of music, as experienced in certain religious rites, in the treatment of emotional people through "a certain catharsis and alleviation accompanied by pleasure." This discussion constitutes crucial evidence for the acknowledged power possessed by some special sacred melodies in helping ancient Greeks handle extreme emotions. If, when he mentioned tragic *catharsis* in the *Poetics*, Aristotle had the parallel of the "sacred melodies" in mind, then we need to imagine tragic drama as arousing pre-existing strong emotions in its participants, in a homeopathic process, and not only pleasing those participants but also making them better able to cope with such emotions when the theatrical experience is over.

Several links between theater and medicine are perceptible in the ancient world. There are large numbers of medical metaphors in the poetry of Greek tragedy. Sophocles was said to have introduced the cult of the healing hero Asclepius into his own household. Sanctuaries of Asclepius were often built adjacent to theaters, for example at Epidauros, Corinth and Butrint (in what is now Albania). At the risk of drawing anachronistic parallels, Aristotle could be describing an experience comparable to that familiar today, of watching a film in the category known as "weepies" or "tear-jerkers," involving highly emotive scenes accompanied by a powerful musical score, and permitting oneself to "enjoy" a good cry at the sufferings of the onscreen characters. In Britain, at least, groups of friends, usually women, even organize parties with large boxes of tissues in order to enjoy a "weepie" together, and I can personally attest that the experience can bring about a sense of cleansing and alleviation of psychic pain, accompanied by pleasure.

The *Poetics* teaches us how to read literature, watch drama and think about art ethically in a way which, if we have decided to try the Aristotelian road to happiness, enriches our everyday lives. For aspiring writers, it still offers invaluable advice, especially about the fourfold formula of plot, character, mental processes and language. The most important secrets are held in those incomparable chapters 6, 9 and 13, but the creative artist will find much other stimulus elsewhere. Aristotle's ideas of the single, unified action underlying any perfect plot can help prevent meandering storylines which lose the attention of the audience. In his day, apparently, some dramatists believed that a play could be well enough unified simply by focusing on the life and experiences of a single hero, such as Theseus or Heracles. Aristotle knows that this can easily become a loose, episodic, plotless narrative, and we know he is right: how many "biopics" struggle to create any real sense of continuity from a single person's life, let alone connection between their chronologically ordered sequence of scenes?

Theater is not the only leisure activity which Aristotle discusses, although it is the one to which, in his surviving works at any rate, he devotes his most extended discussion. But he does not offer specific instructions on how to harness our leisure time to constructive self-fulfillment. It cannot be standardized. Each one of us is different and must make this judgment call about the purposive use of our leisure for ourselves. But I am sure he would have included all aspects of self-education, and we know from a writer called Heraclides of Crete that the lectures given by philosophers at Athens, such as Aristotle, were well attended by the general public in their leisure hours. But his emphasis on the cultivation of relationships as crucial to happiness suggests that who you spend your leisure time with can be just as important as how you spend it. His inspiring model of community grounded in reciprocal good deeds and civic concord implies that leisure activities such as volunteering, political activity or socializing locally are inherently constructive. The important point to take away is that leisure is not a secondary matter. Making full use of it requires even more thought and effort than our working lives. For it is at leisure that we will find our true selves and our greatest happiness.

Chapter 10

---⊗⊗⊗---

MORTALITY

Thinking about happiness inevitably involves thinking about death. Regardless of our views on religion, the gods, and the afterlife, we all live in the certain knowledge that we and those we love are going to die. Our bodily existence as we currently experience it will be terminated. While emphasizing that thinking about our deaths was a necessary process in living well and in being happy, Aristotle stared this truth full in the face: "death is the most terrible of all things, for it is the end." How can we, like him, both face this painful knowledge and use it to promote our chances of achieving happiness while we are still alive?

Hominids have always been terrified of death. Fifty thousand years ago, Neanderthals practiced surprisingly complex rituals for the deceased, adorning them with flowers and red ochre before burying them carefully in shallow graves. The earliest recorded human story in *The Epic of Gilgamesh* concerns its hero's quest to learn the secret of immortality. Contemplation of death automatically raises the great unanswerable questions about the mysteries of existence and the unseen forces motoring the perceptible world, questions which we first ask as children. Why am I here? Where did I come from? Who or what is in charge of the universe? Are there gods? Do they care about me and my behavior? Should I worship them? What happens to me after I die?

Is suicide permissible? When people I love die, can I still have any
communication with them?

The prominence of these questions ebbs and flows in our minds
relative to our immersion in day-to-day concerns. When we are setting
out in life, discovering and fulfilling our potential, working hard,
making friends and romantic relationships, having children, taking
decisions and enjoying recreation, they may seem remote and almost
infinitely deferrable. But there are other times, which often come swiftly
and without warning, when they become burning issues—when we or
our loved ones are ill or seriously injured, diagnosed with dangerous
or terminal diseases, imminently dying, suicidal, or bereaved. They
also become pressing when our children or those depending on us want
answers or need to be comforted in times of loss or deep suffering.
Extreme trauma through an accident or near-death experience can also
produce a need to come to a better understanding of our relationship
with mortality and religious beliefs, as in the character played by Jeff
Bridges in Peter Weir's movie *Fearless* (1993), who comes to question
everything he has taken for granted about life and death after surviving
a plane crash.

Even if, for religious or spiritual reasons, you believe in the possibility of some kind of afterlife, much of what Aristotle has to say about
death and dying can be of benefit to you and your loved ones during
your current lifetime. His teacher Plato also had a great deal to say
about the role of death in human life, even though he regarded death
as making only a superficial alteration in the physical world of appear-
ances. For Plato, human souls are immortal and repeatedly reincarnated
in the physical world. His unchangeable and perfect world of transcen-
dence to which they repeatedly return was identified by early Christians
with God the Creator. Aristotle knew that many of his readers might
believe in an afterlife. There are some hints that his ethics could
accommodate his listeners' belief in the immortality of the soul in the

fragments of a speech he wrote to comfort the bereaved, who were not trained philosophers, when a Cypriot called Eudemus had died in battle. But Aristotle himself undoubtedly saw death as final, as most atheists and agnostics do today. You may *wish* for immortality, he insists in the *Nicomachean Ethics*, but you may not *choose* it, since it is impossible.

Any other view would have been incompatible with his scientific understanding of the world as outlined in his book resonantly titled *On Coming to Be and Passing Away*. Things in our physical world including human animals are in a permanent process of coming into being or generation, growth, alteration, decay and cessation. Death happens because the heat which is inborn in any living organism is destroyed. Life continues in an animal for the period of time that the innate warmth lasts. It is this heat which, he says, "so to speak 'fires' the consciousness." When the heat is extinguished at death, the composite organism consisting of the warm body and the consciousness or "soul" begins to disintegrate. As he writes in *On the Soul*, it can no longer experience feelings or intellectual activity which can be said to belong to the individual "person."

Many philosophers subsequently have agreed with Aristotle's view that the individual human's consciousness ceases to operate at death, as if a lightbulb were turned off or an electric plug pulled out of its socket. This bleak prospect has therefore been a major philosophical preoccupation across time. Counselors and psychotherapists supporting people who are dying or facing bereavement tend to stress *acceptance* of death—"going out quietly"—as the ultimate goal. But there is actually no such prescription in Aristotle, who regarded it as the greatest of evils facing humankind. The honest truth about Aristotle's philosophy is this: the better you have practiced his ethics, and therefore the happier you have become, the more it looks, at least at first sight, that you have to lose when you die. If you have succeeded in making highly successful relationships, the thought of the interpersonal contact with your loved one ending can bring extreme but unbearable clarity to the delight your love of them brings, a clarity which may make any philosophical or theological comfort we are offered about death seem useless. Robert Graves observes this in his searing poem "Pure Death":

> We looked, we loved, and therewith instantly
> Death became terrible to you and me.
> By love we disenthralled our natural terror
> From every comfortable philosopher
> Or tall, grey doctor of divinity:
> Death stood at last in his true rank and order.

Aristotle, who loved his family and friends intensely, did think a good deal about death. Had he learned of the attitude to death advocated by the Chinese philosopher Confucius two centuries before him, he would have had a mixed reaction. He would approved of Confucius' emphasis on leading a morally good life in the here and now, rather than speculating about ghosts or the afterlife. But he would have criticized Confucius for avoiding all discussions of death. For there are ways in which Aristotelian ethics can ameliorate death's destructiveness, and thus provide some consolation. But for an intellectually honest and curious man like Aristotle, *denial* of death, or closing his eyes to it, was out of the question. Nor is there any indication in his philosophy that quiet *acceptance* or *acquiescence* in the face of death is compulsory. There is a pervasive sense that *acknowledgment* of our mortality and confrontation with its full implications can be used effectively to help us to live *and* die well. But that does not mean that we are not permitted, as Dylan Thomas urged his father, to "rage against the dying of the light." Such rage is well explored in Isabel Coixet's 2008 movie *Elegy*, adapted from Philip Roth's novel *The Dying Animal*, which centers on a famous public intellectual who simply fails to come to terms with aging and imminent death.

Philosophical views on death subsequent to Aristotle have been extremely varied, but since he is the first thinker to have faced unblinkingly the full implications of the cessation of consciousness, most of them ultimately can be traced back to him. At one extreme they see anger as the only appropriate response to mortality and take a position similar to Thomas' injunction not to "go gentle into that good night." Yugoslavian-American philosopher Thomas Nagel, for example, has argued that life makes us familiar with the good things it has to offer, so losing them in death, at whatever age, involves deprivation, whether of selfhood, sensations or experiences.[14] Elias Canetti, a Bulgarian-German Jewish writer who lived much of his life in Britain and won the Nobel Prize in Literature in 1981, was convinced that we should not aim to accept death, but to see it as useless and malign, "the basic ill of all existence, the unresolved and the incomprehensible." He despised all religious attempts to make sense of death, and claimed that to accept death with equanimity is even equivalent to accepting murder.[15] The Spanish philosopher and classical scholar Unamuno saw humans as locked in a permanent, insoluble and tragic conflict between their emotional, feeling selves, which long for permanent existence, and their rational selves, which know that organic life must end. But unlike Nagel and Canetti, Unamuno does draw an Aristotelian inference—that it *is* important to try to live virtuously—from this acknowledgment that death is deprivation, akin to murder, a tragedy: "Man is perishing. That may be, and if it is nothingness that awaits us let us so act that it will be an unjust fate."[16] The very injustice of death is a reason for trying to live good lives so that death seems all the more unmerited when it comes.

The sense that death is unjust received its most vivid expression in Blaise Pascal's *Pensées* (1670):

Let us imagine a number of men in chains, and all condemned
to death, where some are killed each day in the sight of the
others, and those who remain see their own fate in that of
their fellows, and wait their turn, looking at each other sorrow-
fully and without hope. It is an image of the condition of men.[17]

Pascal's chain gang, like the Spanish prison cell shared with the other
condemned in Sartre's short story "The Wall," the dentist's waiting
room in the poetry of Elizabeth Bishop, the valley of the shadow of
death of Psalm 23 or the fallen tree in Samuel Beckett's *Waiting for
Godot*, is a metaphor for the lives of mortals. But Aristotle's rebuttal
of Pascal would have been robust: we are not in chains and we are not
forced to spend our whole time watching our fellows die. We have free
will, agency, and a potential for great happiness acquired through living
in the right way and in loving relationships. We can hope to live in
pleasant homes, work toward goals, experience constructive work and
recreation, enjoy pleasurable sensations, wonder at the variety and
beauty of the natural world, and think for the larger proportion of our
waking lives about other things than death. There are philosophers
whose obsession with death borders on fetishism and would seem
excessive to Aristotle, including Heidegger, Camus, Sartre and Foucault.
As with everything in the moral world, a mean between deficiency and
excess holds true for our grappling with the prospect of death.

"Looking to the end" an appropriate amount of the time can help
us do what Aristotle most wants—live in the best and most enjoyable
way. Montaigne, who had something of a love/hate relationship with
Aristotle, may have gone too far in thinking about his end virtually
all the time: "I unbind myself on all sides; my farewells are already
half made to everyone except myself. Never did a man prepare to leave
the world more utterly and completely, nor detach himself from it more
universally, than I propose to do." But in thinking about his own death,

Montaigne made a discovery: it restored him to full vitality—made him feel much more *alive*: "When I dance, I dance; when I sleep, I sleep."[18] Nietzsche, similarly, saw that confronting our mortality and rejecting hopes of an afterlife make it necessary for us to assume full, adult responsibility for the state of our reality, which in turn requires us to live better and with greater vigor.

Moral self-sufficiency or self-reliance (*autarkeia*) involves an individual's independence and requires him or her to be "true to themselves." Acknowledging that only you can face up to the prospect of your own death—you cannot find a surrogate to undergo it for you—is part of being true to your own *self*. Heidegger, an often obscure and opaque philosopher whose thoughts on the nature of existence are not usually paired with those of Aristotle, made death central to his oddly similar concept of the authentic human subject—the "I" that signifies a unique self—in *Being and Time*. Heidegger saw all humans as torn between conforming to the rules and normative values of society and their strong perception that they are an individual and solitary subject, a separate and authentic "I." Doing what society expects anesthetizes us against our sense of being unique and singular selves, whose singularity consists precisely of our unavoidable loneliness when we die. So in order to be authentic and true to our singular selves while we are alive we *must* "look to the end" and contemplate our deaths. Heidegger says that "all being-with-others will fail us" when the "issue" is death, and our sense of being a unique entity will cease with our consciousness. Yet, paradoxically, that knowledge can return us to our worlds of work and relationships as much more energetic and committed moral agents.[19] The sense of what death destroys can make us much more creative, too: as Michelangelo said, "No thought exists in me which death has not carved with his chisel."

In discussing whether a man who is dead can be called happy, Aristotle reveals one strangely comforting attribute of death: when you die, some things change, but (rather surprisingly) the one thing that does not change at all is the "person" who dies. Your unique self becomes clearer, more defined, precisely because in death your personhood loses its capacity to alter. In the human record and other people's memories, your "self" as a unique person is made complete in ceasing to be susceptible to change when you die.[20] When there is a death in the family, the unique person who died continues to exert a presence, often a more powerful one because in death the extent and quality of their contribution can appear more distinct. If you have three siblings and one dies, you will always be one of four siblings. Wordsworth articulates this deeply in his poem "We are Seven" in which a little girl insists that "we are seven" even though two of her six siblings "in the church-yard lie." The death of children, because of the sense of unfulfilled potential, always seems the most unjust. Two excellent films which explore the degree of pain but also the variety of possible responses are Atom Egoyan's *The Sweet Hereafter* (1997), which explores the compulsion to find someone to blame, and Kenneth Lonergan's searing, beautifully acted *Manchester by the Sea* (2016).

Aristotle sees all living organisms as having come into conscious-ness, and in the right circumstances grown to achieve their full potential, before gradually declining and passing away. This means that each life has its own storyline, or "arc," like a character in a well-written novel. It has its own narrative unity over time, as Aristotle said in his *Poetics* a good play or epic poem needs to have. He also used the analogy of the dramatic plot when insisting that the early sufferings of an indi-vidual character are of more or less importance to assessing his "total" happiness than what happens after his death. The individual who has embraced Aristotelian ethics will have comprehended at an intellectual level the idea that he has a life of his own, a unified period during which he exists in the world as a single entity, the shape of which, if he takes responsibility and acts as a self-sufficient agent, he can direct himself. He can be the author of his own story and promote its unity, coherence and completeness. Humans do think in terms of storyline, and "looking to the end" can help us to prepare for a less dissatisfying final chapter. This way of looking at life can bring enormous comfort. And Aristotle knew how we are emotionally pleased by organized closure. Psychologists today believe that desire for closure is hardwired in the human brain, and that it may have a biological basis, which helps us deal, as we age, with the years of decline and prospect of death.[21]

Aristotelian ethics encourage us to plan our lives in terms of the endeavors we want to undertake in order to fulfill our human potential. These days there is a fashion for people who are dying to make lists of all the things they want to get done first. The 2007 movie *The Bucket List*, directed by Rob Reiner, shows two dying men making a list of all their unfulfilled desires and setting about fulfilling them. These ambitions include skydiving, flying over the North Pole, and visiting Mount Everest. The movie is motivational and has helped many people when they are diagnosed with terminal illnesses. So has Akira Kurosawa's *Ikiru* (1952), partly inspired by Tolstoy's *The Death of Ivan Ilyich*, in which a Tokyo bureaucrat who feels he has failed to achieve anything that gives his life meaning is diagnosed with terminal cancer. His response is to spend his last weeks successfully lobbying for a new playground to be opened for the city's children.

But Aristotelian ambitions concern much more sustained and interconnected projects, of which most of us have a whole constellation. A project can be a child we raise, a friendship we cherish, a business we start up, a house or garden we make beautiful, a charity we support, a school we govern, a type of dog we breed, a hobby we pursue, mountains we climb, a political cause, a book we write, or a collection of antiques. Our personhood unites these projects. The Aristotelian nurtures all her projects on a continuing basis, linking her past, present and future. Thinking about death can enhance the possibility of her

projects turning out successfully. Each one of the projects will be affected
differently by her death. Some of them will cease when she dies, but
some will not. This is where serious thought, and where necessary
action, become essential.

Discuss your own death with close family and friends. These
projects—loving relationships—do not cease when we die. Thankfully,
hardly any of us will face the negation of *all* their life's projects which
even the Aristotelian would find almost impossible to bear. Aristotle's
example of the man whose capacity for happiness was utterly destroyed
is Priam, who saw all his sons die and the city he had ruled so long,
so well, burned to the ground. But most of us do not face the misfortunes of Priam. Some of your loved ones will survive and they remain
your loved ones regardless of your own consciousness ceasing. Looking
after their interests includes not only facing emotional consequences,
but making known your wishes concerning end-of-life medical treatment, your minor possessions not catered for in your will, your funeral
ceremony, and how your remains should be handled. I have a colleague,
a widow, who is in unnecessary distress because she never asked her
husband where he wanted his ashes scattered. Since she does not know
where to scatter them, she remains emotionally unable to collect them
from the crematorium. Thinking about death can even help you find
the energy and discipline to complete projects, like dealing with the
paperwork to set up a charity, writing a novel, or aiming to climb
Mount Kilimanjaro. Delegation can help with the continuation of some
projects: it is important to be clear, if we have worked hard to make a
beautiful home, or successful business, or an antiques collection, whether
we want it preserved after our deaths and who should inherit it.

Aristotle himself took Dying Well as seriously as he had taken
Living Well. He did not discuss how to face death in detail in his
philosophical works, but accounts of his own death and his actual will,
which survives, function as an example to us all.

Aristotle died in exile from Athens in 322 BCE. His denial that the gods interested themselves in human affairs, and his scientific approach to the world, made him vulnerable to prosecution on religious grounds. Once Alexander was dead, his enemies in Athens seized their opportunity and charged him with impiety just as Socrates had been prosecuted eight decades previously. But Aristotle did not court execution as Socrates had done. Socrates had the opportunity to escape from Athens and stay alive, but preferred to remain and martyr himself. Aristotle, on the other hand, even though he was by this time suffering from a serious stomach complaint, probably cancer, was not the kind of man to give up on life. He took refuge at the estate, with a garden and a guest cottage, belonging to his mother's family in Chalcis on the island of Euboea. His companion Herpyllis, mother of his son Nicomachus, accompanied him. He died there in 322 BCE. He must have been anxious, and he must have missed the life of the Lyceum and the friendship of Theophrastus, whom he left in charge, desperately.

But the move to Chalcis provided Aristotle with a beautiful place to prepare for the death which his medical knowledge probably led him to expect. He derived emotional sustenance from reading classical literature: one moving fragment, written toward the end of his life, says that he enjoys the old myths increasingly "the older and more isolated I become." Chalcis was and still is a healthful, breezy seaside town. It is cheering to think that in his final illness, he will have taken his last walks along the long sunny promenade, perhaps with Herpyllis and his children, to discuss how best to face the prospect of his death and their future without him. Grief when a much-loved person dies is the worst emotional pain most humans undergo, and it is worth preparing for. Aristotle took comfort in reading the old classics of Greek literature, with their portrayal of the deaths of heroes: we can watch intelligent films about dying. Darren Aronofsky's *The Fountain* (2006) reveals what it is like for a dying woman who wants her husband

to spend all her remaining time enjoying each other's company, while
he cannot cope with the impending loss, and is obsessively distracted,
trying to research a potential cure for her. For the aftermath of bereavement, there is an extraordinarily sensitive reading in Philippe Falardeau's
dazzling Québécois *Monsieur Lazhar* (2011), which explores the grief
both of some children whose teacher dies and of the substitute teacher,
a political refugee whose wife and young family were murdered in his
homeland.

In Aristotle's will, the reflection which has gone into thinking
through different potential futures, depending on who would die first
among the survivors he loved or felt responsibility for, is worthy indeed
of the most competent of deliberators. He had two biological children,
Nicomachus and his daughter Pythias, and he had also adopted his
nephew Nicanor. Knowing that he was about to die in circumstances
of political tension, and personally facing hostility from some Athenians,
he named as chief executor the most powerful man available at the
time, Antipater, his long-standing Macedonian supporter, and by then
the governor of Greece. Aristotle meant business. This choice ensured
that nobody could flout the terms of the will except at their peril.

One detail near the beginning of the will implies that Aristotle
wrote or revised the text shortly before he died, suggesting that he
knew he was mortally ill. His nephew and adoptive son Nicanor, the
child born to Aristotle's sister Arimneste and her husband Proxenus,
was to be the second named executor, but he was apparently abroad.
Until Nicanor returned, Aristotle asked that a team of four friends,
plus Theophrastus, the (presumably very busy) new head of the Lyceum,
"if he is willing and it is possible for him" to take responsibility for
looking after "the children and Herpyllis and their inheritance."

Aristotle clearly respected his adopted son Nicanor. He made him
guardian of both his own children. But since Nicanor was Aristotle's
nephew, and much younger, Aristotle recognized that the relationship

with Aristotle's biological children would be "as if both father and brother." Nicanor was to take special care of Pythias, "and to see to everything else in a manner worthy both of himself and us." Women without a father were vulnerable to exploitation and needed a benevolent man to represent them in legal and financial affairs. Aristotle therefore wanted Nicanor to marry Pythias and take over responsibility for her and their mutual offspring. Such was his concern for Pythias that Aristotle even named a second trustworthy potential husband in case Nicanor were to die: Theophrastus.

Perhaps the most enigmatic figure in Aristotle's personal life was his long-standing lover Herpyllis, a woman from his old home town of Stageira. The reason he did not marry her is probably that she was of lower social status, perhaps a slave or freedwoman. I suspect that he was also concerned for the psychological security of his daughter Pythias: conflict between step-parents and stepchildren was much feared in the ancient world. The one promise the dying heroine of Euripides' *Alcestis* extracts from her husband is that he will never remarry and thus inflict a possibly hostile stepmother on their children. Pythias may also have been pleased with the instruction in Aristotle's will that her own dead mother's bones were to be disinterred and buried beside those of her father.

Yet, even as Aristotle's concubine, Herpyllis bore him the son Nicomachus for whom he made such vigilant provision. Aristotle also carefully inserts the touching little phrase that Herpyllis "has been good to me." This signals that his executors are to carry out assiduously his detailed and affectionate instructions concerning her:

> If she wishes to marry, to give her to someone worthy of me.
> In addition to the other gifts that she has received previously
> they should give her a talent of silver, from the estate, and
> three female slaves, if she wishes, and the female slave that

she has at present, and the slave Pyrrhaeus. And if she wishes to live in Chalcis, she is to have the guest cottage by the garden. If she wishes to live at Stageira, she is to have my father's house. Whichever of the two she chooses, the executors are to equip it with furniture that seems to them suitable and that Herpyllis approves.

Had the mother of Aristotle's son pleaded with him not to let generals and philosophers choose her internal decor?

The provision Aristotle makes for his slaves, although not unheard of for a fourth-century man of property, still suggests that he had developed warm personal ties with them. They were all to be freed immediately on his death, or at a specified later date (such as his daughter's marriage). Some were to be given generous legacies in addition. Aristotle ensured that not one of the slaves who attended him was to be sold (this would risk them becoming vulnerable to a far less kind master): "The executors are not to sell any of the slaves who looked after me, but to employ them. When they reach the appropriate age, they should set them free as they deserve."

Like all ancient Greeks, Aristotle was interested in the means by which humans could achieve some kind of immortality if the influence of what they did lasted beyond their deaths. The most obvious way was through having children and grandchildren to carry on your genetic code and your family line. Authors since Homer had also spoken with pride about the immortality which having your heroic feats or even misfortunes recorded in a famous song bestowed, so that your name and exploits would still be heard after many generations. Portrait statues, paintings, inscribed gravestones, tombs and mausoleums were commissioned by those who could afford them to keep the public memory of themselves and their loved ones alive. Philosophers, especially Plato, had suggested that producing new *ideas* resembled giving birth, for important concepts exist to change minds and lives long after the people who formulated them are dead.

Aristotle was fascinated by all these expedients humans had invented to circumvent biological death. Although he did not personally believe that humans had sentient life after death, he was careful not to trample on people's instinctive need for rituals which they believed connected them with their dear departed. He accepted that to insist that the friendship bonds which held together Greek society were completely dissolved by death would be, as he put it, literally "unfriendly" (*aphilon*). He wrote a poem in praise of his dead friend Hermias, the ruler of the kingdom of Assos where Aristotle spent his late thirties. He appointed his most trustworthy friend and disciple, Theophrastus, to succeed him at the Lyceum and left the world knowing that dozens more young philosophers would perpetuate and develop his intellectual discoveries. But he added one extraordinarily helpful instrument to the toolkit of dealing with death or bereavement: the systematic development of your powers of conscious recollection.

People who are dead do live on in the memories of those who loved them and those who were affected by them. An Aristotelian will use her memories in a disciplined and methodical way to help her cope with her own aging process and with the loss of loved ones. Aristotle was the first thinker we know of to distinguish between memory and deliberate recollection, and to see how important the latter is: the human being, alone among animals, has the power of deliberate recall. Socrates, who promulgated a theory of reincarnation, had developed the idea that learning things actually constitutes a form of recollection, a recollection of things we have already learned in a previous life. But Aristotle had no time for the idea that our minds have been born into other bodies in previous eras. He was interested in how the minds *we have right now* were hardwired by nature to develop in particular ways, and then how each individual experience, along with the exercise of imagination and memory, has contributed to their maturation.

Aristotle wrote a whole treatise *On Memory and Recollection* in which he explores this amazing human faculty. It is an enthralling read because of the intimacy which makes you relate to how it felt to be inside his own head. He describes the irritation caused by catchy tunes and sayings—"ear-worms"—which you can't "get out of your head"; even though we may try "to give up the habit and do not mean to yield to it, we find ourselves continually singing or saying the familiar sounds." He is perfectly aware of the mind's ability to block or repress memory and of what is now called "recovered memory syndrome": "it is evident that it is possible to remember things which are not recalled at the moment, but which one has perceived or suffered all along." Perhaps Aristotle had himself at some time recovered memories of trauma he had suffered in childhood but had forgotten for many years. He made an effort to experience and describe in minute detail what happened when he was contemplating the mental pictures which his consciousness generated. Mental pictures mean that he is engaged either in imagining something hypothetical, or anticipating something that will take place in the future, or randomly remembering past experiences or deliberately recollecting them: "it is impossible even to think without a mental picture."

Aristotle's most extended discussion of the imagination is in another dialog, *On the Soul*. But in *On Memory and Recollection*, the important issue for Aristotle is that there is a big difference between remembering something randomly—although that can be valuable—and deliberately recollecting. Some other animals clearly have memory. Aristotle has watched animals "learn" through experience; a dog knows the way on a familiar walk because she has been on that walk before. But a dog can't sit quietly and intentionally think about what it was like to be a puppy, or where she traveled with her owner last summer, or her mother's appearance.

Yet, for all the seriousness of his discussion of recollection, Aristotle brings a smile to my lips when he distinguishes between recollection and random memory: "Men who have good memories are not the same as those who are good at recollecting, in fact, generally speaking, the slow-witted have better memories, but the quick-witted and those who learn easily are better at recollecting." One can *learn* to be good at recollection. But Aristotle's observation that the slow-witted have better memories suggests to me that, like many professors today whose brains are usually involved in thinking about intellectual material of one kind and another, some ancient Greek "absentminded professors" had dreadful memories when it came to remembering shopping lists or other aspects of everyday experience.

Memory and recollection have different relationships with the senses. Memory, says Aristotle, is connected with our sense-faculties. Marcel Proust came up with the term "involuntary memory," *mémoire involontaire*, in *À la recherche du temps perdu* (1913–22), when eating tea-soaked madeleines "jogged" his memory and reminded him of eating that kind of cake with his aunt as a child. But more than two millennia before Proust, Aristotle had carefully distinguished between the "jogged," involuntary memory which our senses prod us into experiencing (*mneme*), and the information about our pasts which we can retrieve deliberately by "voluntary" acts of recollection (*anamnesis*). The latter is an exclusively human gift. It is a conscious capacity of our intellects rather than an unconscious one of our senses.

In a beautiful image, Aristotle describes how the "Proustian" memory is created: our minds, through the sense perceptions, are liking sealing wax which receives an impression from an external stimulus, the signet ring. He thought hard about people whose memories function poorly—the very old, the very young, the mentally impaired. He explains this by saying that the part of their minds affected by sense perceptions is not susceptible to the "signet ring"; it is not like viscous sealing wax which will imminently dry and retain the ring's impression. It resembles running water in the case of children or hard old walls in the case of the elderly or mentally impaired. But unlike memories instigated by sensory stimulus, deliberate recollection is a uniquely and distinctively human capacity: "the process is a kind of search." It is a power that, if developed and exercised, can benefit our pursuit of happiness. It is related to our other distinctively human capacity, for deliberation about action, which is integral to Doing the Right Thing and to the fulfillment of our potential. On a more universal human level, the very study of history and the ideas of people like Aristotle in the past, is a kind of collective human process of disciplined recollection that is indispensable to our understanding of the human project and is a guide to our future.

I suspect that Aristotle's father, Dr. Nicomachus of Stageira, had a particular interest in mental illness. Aristotle often shows his awareness of the different kinds of abnormal consciousness which we would call the various psychiatric disorders. He writes with exceptional insight about how people suffering from delusions confuse different kinds of mental picture—actual memories of the past with scenarios invented by their imaginations. He describes the case of one Antipheron of Oreus, a "madman" who spoke of his "mental pictures as if they had actually taken place" and as if he "actually remembered them." Aristotle also speaks of the distress caused by defective memories to people of depressive or melancholic tendency. His conviction that memory has a close relationship, through the senses, with our bodies, and that in some sense our experience of mental pictures of any kind is a physical activity, can sound remarkably close to the findings of modern neuroscience. In particular, he describes depressives who feel bitter annoyance, "when, in spite of great concentration, they cannot remember." Had Aristotle's father used a form of psychotherapy that asked patients to remember past trauma, and experienced the frustration of individuals who had completely "blocked" the memories of the events in question?

Aristotle was also fascinated by the power of images outside the mind to prompt and stimulate recollection. There was a bust of Socrates in the Lyceum which he used as a teaching aid. His biographers said that he himself commissioned statues of his wife Pythias and friend Hermias after their deaths, and wrote poems about them. They also said that he had a portrait of his mother painted. In the *Poetics* he describes the pleasure which people gain from "recognizing" someone in a picture and being able to say who they are, and how this can be an educational as well as pleasurable experience. In *On Memory and Recollection*, he investigates our "internal" pictures of people we know. He thinks that they function both as something to look at in repose—as having a real life of their own—but also "as a likeness, an aid to memory." The example he gives is a dark-haired student of his by the name of Coriscus. His mental picture of Coriscus can act just like a portrait—allowing Aristotle to look at and think about Coriscus even though he has not seen him recently. The power to enjoy Coriscus' internal presence in your mind, even to look at him, whenever you want to, is something only the human capacity for recollection enables us to do. If Coriscus appears in our mind's eye it may be involuntary— we may not have summoned that particular picture deliberately—and it may indeed be less a memory than an image which has been triggered by another sensation or another memory. In any case, both the actual portrait of Coriscus and the mental picture of Coriscus to which Aristotle had voluntary as well as involuntary access meant that he could think about his student even in his absence. Aristotelian psychology, along with the biographical tradition of his careful memorialization of loved ones, suggests a helpful strategy when facing death and bereavement.

I wrote much of this chapter when my own mother was dying, after a long and fulfilled life, at the age of ninety. I found great comfort in thinking about what Aristotle's writings suggest he would have said to me. Although my grief was considerable, consciously using his ethical system enabled me to feel much more at ease with the whole sad situation, and thus to appear calm and cheerful at a time when others needed me to be. It also underlined to me how important it is to live life in the best way possible, for life is very precious indeed. In particular, I found that using my own power to recall helped me deal with one especially painful period at my mother's bedside. Her warm responses—weak hand-patting, an occasional smile from between all the tubes—suggest it helped her too.

I consciously set about remembering, in as much detail as possible, moments of happiness I had felt in her company as a child. Old photos and talking to other members of the family can help considerably, but the really rich memories are triggered by Aristotle's "deliberate recollection." Systematically going in my consciousness through the years of my earlier life, and the houses we lived in, the seaside holidays in Yorkshire and Scotland, the three primary schools I attended—all brought extraordinarily vivid memories of my mother, in her prime, flooding back. The day when I was three and we danced around a small record player in her bedroom because she had bought a vinyl single of the Beatles' "She Loves You." The total delight I had felt as she held me tight and went down a waterslide in an open-air pool on a summer's day (she managed to mouth through her oxygen mask that she thought this must have been at Dunbar). How she bought Pears soap especially for me, because I loved looking at things through its caramel transparency. How we played Poohsticks for hours on a bridge over a stream in the Yorkshire Dales and she showed me how to make sure my own piece of bracken went fastest by aiming it at a swift rivulet. Sitting by the television set, squealing with delight, when she sat with me to "Watch with Mother." How the single best day in a kitchen of my life involved her, bowls of cookie dough, and a brand new set of pastry cutters she bought me in the shape of chicks, angels and Easter bunnies. How I secretly reveled in being in the hospital at about eight years old, after an emergency appendectomy, despite the acute pain. This was because she visited me every day, all on her own, while my siblings were at school. For once I didn't have to compete with them for her undivided attention. As she was dying, I wrote these and other newly tracked-down recollections shortly after I went so consciously in search of them in my vaults of memory. They are going to bring me reliable comfort on the motherless road that now lies ahead.

Bereavement is different for people without the promise of afterlife held out by religion. Aristotle did not believe in an afterlife. But although he was accused of impiety, in fact he was not an atheist at all. He was not even an agnostic as it is understood today. He just did not believe that distant divine entities had any interest in human affairs. His rejection of Platonism and his firm grounding of ethics in nature meant that a religious view of human behavior became redundant. Aristotelians do not base the quest for understanding of the nature and goals of Living Well in a religious or metaphysical view. They base it in a naturalistic one instead. But that by no means excludes the possibilities that there are divine beings or that some aspects at least of the practice of religion might be of benefit to humankind.

Aristotle noticed that the different ethnic groups of the world all "speak of the gods as ruled by a king, because they themselves too are some of them actually now so ruled and in other cases used to be in the olden days; and as men imagine the gods in human form, so also they suppose their manner of life to be like their own." It is only the limits of the human imagination, he believes, that means gods are envisaged anthropomorphically. Aristotle also knows that tyrants can use religion to increase their power over their subjects; the gods of myth have been invented "to influence the vulgar and as a constitutional and utilitarian expedient." Aristotle's own god or gods, on the other hand, are completely remote from us; the gap is so great that we can't expect a relationship with them, either as friends or autocratic rulers.

In his work on physics and metaphysics, as well as occasionally the *Nicomachean Ethics*, he indicates that he thought contemplating the material universe might bring us much closer to "God." At least, it is more likely to bring us closer to God than simply imagining the celestial entities as (a) looking like humans but (b) actually being superhuman monarchs who interact with their human "subjects," which is how most people in his world understood divinity. He seems to have believed that the heavenly bodies were "more divine" than humans. Sometimes he calls the sun, stars, and planets "the divine bodies that move through the heaven," "the visible divine things" or "the heaven and the most divine of visible things." Since his whole philosophical system recognized the centrality of movement and change, he thought that God, however remote, must be one of the "first principles" or original sources of the movement which sets the rest of the universe in motion. So God is a "mover," but one "unmoved" and unchangeable by humans or indeed by any other stimulus, force, or entity.

In asking what God consists of or what God does, Aristotle applies his customary process of elimination, and in a tongue-in-cheek passage asks what God does *not* do. Unlike humans, who at their best live according to the virtues, God is beyond any kind of ethics at all. God does not spend time on business transactions, displaying virtue through the way he writes contracts and return deposits. God does not have to demonstrate courage by facing physical danger. If we were to praise God for controlling evil desires, we would actually be insulting him by implying that he even had such desires to control. Nor does God have anyone on the celestial plane to whom to give money, thus displaying generosity. Aristotle drives the absurdity of imagining gods in human form by conjuring—only to dismiss—the notion of divine coinage and currency. And it would be a cop out, he jokes, to claim that they are eternal but always asleep "like Endymion."

All this leads up to Aristotle's conclusion that God must be connected with activity which is in accordance with the activity of the highest of all the virtues, and we as humans are at our best, being most "virtuous" and therefore at our happiest, when we are exercising our intellect actively. It is during the time we spend thinking actively about the world, and theorizing about it—the *theoretic* or thinking life—that we as humans approach closest to divinity. Aristotle was clearly often told that it is dangerous to equate human intellectual activity with God, for he goes out of his way to warn his reader against "people who advise us that a man should have man's thoughts and a mortal the thoughts of mortality." Humans, at least for the brief periods when they are engaged in intellectual contemplation of something that interests them, and thus are completely happy, are getting the opportunity, temporarily, to do what Aristotle's God does all the time.

The most famous passage on "God" in all of Aristotle appears in the twelfth book of his *Metaphysics*. This is conventionally known to philosophers as *Metaphysics Lambda*. It is an extremely dense and diffi-cult text, but the gist is clear. "God" is actualized thought, or *thought in action*, which we humans can temporarily enjoy. It is the same as pure happiness or pleasure. Thinking on the highest level, with our finest faculties, temporarily turns us into "God" or at least allows us to participate in the divine. Actualized thought is what makes us alive, and this is the same as "God." But whereas we are temporary beings with a biological lifespan, "God" is life most good and eternal. "We hold, then, that God is a living being, eternal, most good; and therefore life and a continuous eternal existence belong to God; for that is what God is."

This argument may sound more mystical than most of the down-to-earth Aristotelian common sense and practical wisdom which has been explored in this book. And yet, at a deep level, the argument that "God" is eternal thought or understanding uncannily adumbrates the suggestions of some of the most advanced intellects of our own day. In particular, in his bestseller *A Brief History of Time* (1998), Stephen Hawking sounded eerily Aristotelian when he concluded that "if we discover a complete theory, it should in time be understandable by everyone, not just by a few scientists. Then we shall all, philosophers, scientists and just ordinary people, be able to take part in the discussion of the question of why it is that we and the universe exist. If we find the answer to that, it would be the ultimate triumph of human reason— for then we should know the mind of God."

But what is the Aristotelian, who thinks that humans participate in the divine because they can exercise reason and use their minds to understand the universe, to do when it comes to established religion? Unlike Plato, Aristotle hardly discusses piety, at least in his ethical treatises. Given the way he grounds his ethics in nature rather than theology, this is not altogether surprising. But just occasionally in his other works he briefly reveals an approval of certain conventional ways of honoring the gods in terms of the social or other benefits such rituals can confer, including group recreation. This position is helpful; even if you do not "believe in" God in any conventional sense, it can be constructive occasionally to go to church, mosque, synagogue or temple when you or your community seeks ritual consolidation or comfort.

In his *Politics*, Aristotle assumes that it is important for the city-state, the context in which humans are most likely to thrive, to take good care of the cults of the gods. He praises, for instance, "associations formed for the sake of pleasure, for example religious guilds and dining clubs, which are unions for sacrifice and social intercourse." He thinks that in a well-run city-state, people are brought together "to perform sacrifices and hold festivals in connection with them, thereby both paying honour to the gods and providing pleasant holidays for themselves. For it may be noticed that the sacrifices and festivals of ancient origin take place after harvest, being in fact harvest festivals; this is because that was the season of the year at which people had most leisure." In a distinctively Aristotelian piece of advice to women, combining his advocacy of walking and his ancestral doctor's eye with an apparent approval of at least a modicum of respect for traditional rituals, he explicitly recommends that in a well-run city-state, pregnant women will be encouraged to "take care of their bodies, not avoiding exercise nor adopting an inadequate diet"; for exercise, he suggests "a daily walk for the due worship of the deities whose office is the control of childbirth."

Uninhibited superstition is a different matter. Aristotle was likely to have agreed with his friend and fellow Peripatetic Theophrastus, who described the fears of the laughably superstitious man in a book of moral sketches entitled *Characters*. Theophrastus' typically superstitious man is terrified by contact with women who have given birth, insane people and epileptics. The primeval taboos which associated actual pollution—*miasma*—with such people seem to have struck rational philosophers at the Lyceum as hilarious and absurd. In his own works, Aristotle often refers to the superstitious, unscientific explanations uneducated people believe for phenomena which can actually be explained from nature through empirical observation. But social bonding through dining clubs under the aegis of particular gods and heroes, or a pregnant woman's healthful stroll to make offerings at a shrine of Artemis (the goddess who oversaw the biological aspects of women's lives), are a different matter. Aristotle does not seem to regard such constructive, conventional religious habits as in any way harmful.

But this is still not quite enough for me. If, as an Aristotelian, I personally have no inclination to practice regular prayers or rituals, and do not believe in their efficacy, what am I to make of the many people in the world who do? This issue has caused me anxiety, partly because most members of the family I was born into believe in God and practice one form or another of Protestant Christianity. Many of my dearest friends are Roman Catholics or devout practitioners of religions including Judaism, Islam, Sikhism and Hinduism. Many of them live virtuous lives practicing ethics similar to my own, and are helped in so doing by their religious beliefs. More people in the world in which I live believe in God than don't, and many of them believe that their god or gods directly involve themselves in human affairs. Provided that they don't force anyone else to accept their views, or theocratically try to substitute them, rather than the secular pursuit of universal happiness, as the premise of legislation and civic relationships, or quarrel with my rights to pursue happiness without gods and to disagree with them, I need to accept other people's religious beliefs without qualification and interact respectfully with them as fellow citizens. There is absolutely no evidence that Aristotle ever did otherwise.

Living without belief in a god or gods who intervene in human affairs, or indeed without hope of an afterlife, is most challenging when times are rough. Many of Aristotle's own contemporaries, including members of the Macedonian royal family, underwent initiation into top-secret mystery religions in the hope that they could thus secure immortality. For some of us, the urge to pray for supernatural assistance becomes overwhelming when we are in serious trouble of any kind. But it is strongest when we are dying ourselves or facing the death of people we love. A craving to believe in miraculous cures, or a blissful afterlife, can assail even the most rational agnostic. And there is no inherent harm in this. Nothing which brings comfort when people are suffering should be dismissed lightly. Yet facing up to the reality of human mortality can make life itself, while it lasts, infinitely richer and more vivid. There are also advantages to confronting the likelihood that our consciousness simply ceases when our body stops functioning, as the electrical current stops circulating when we remove a plug from a socket. Being dead means no further pain or suffering, as well as no further pleasure.

Life, for Aristotle, is the whole point. He devoted his own life to thinking about what being alive meant—for plants and animals, fish and birds as well as humans. He watched, full of wonder, in his famous "chick" experiment, how chicks developed from the moment when their eggs were laid to their existence several days after they hatched. He recorded the results of his observations every day in precise, rational, scientific prose which approaches pure poetry:

> About the twentieth day, if you open the egg and touch the chick, it moves inside and chirps; and it is already coming to be covered with down, when, after the twentieth day is past, the chick begins to break the shell. The head is situated over the right leg close to the flank, and the wing is placed over the head; and about this time is plain to be seen the membrane resembling an after-birth that comes next after the outermost membrane of the shell.

And that wonder and respect for life, along with his conviction that with patience and a moral effort even terrible emotional suffering can be overcome, are what made Aristotle opposed to suicide.

Early Christians, who wanted to domesticate Aristotle and reduce the explanatory power of his human-centered world view, invented a false story. They said that he had committed suicide after acknowledging the involvement of God in the physical makeup of the world—that is, that he had renounced both his human-centered ethics and his science. He had, they claimed, jumped into the straits of Euripus which separate Chalcis from the Greek mainland. He was driven by exasperation that he could not scientifically explain the high tides that swirl in the narrow channel and therefore, in his final moments, acknowledged that there was a mysterious divine power at work in the world which his intellect could not decipher. But this was propagandistic nonsense. The problem with suicide, for Aristotle, is the *intention* behind it, which is a negative one—to *escape* from "poverty, or the pangs of love, or pain." He has noticed that one category of suicidal people is constituted by serial malefactors, who kill themselves to *escape* from their pasts and the social opprobrium which has resulted: "men who have committed a number of crimes, and are hated for their wickedness, actually flee from life and make away with themselves." The person who kills himself or herself is not doing it because it is the thought-through best action in the circumstances, the decision of a competent deliberator, but out of weakness in the face of difficulty. Aristotle seems to approve of the Athenian legal situation, where suicide was not a crime, but neither was it sanctioned.

Suicide has been investigated by philosophers throughout history. Philosophers who agree with Aristotle in objecting to suicide, such as Plato and Kant, all address the issue by placing the suicidal person in the context of relationships with three entities: with themself, with society, and with God. In another passage, however, Aristotle seems to be interested solely in the individual's relationship with their community. For him, the man "who kills himself in a fit of passion" is committing a crime, voluntarily, and the injury is sustained by the community. It loses one of its members, and since we all have responsibilities toward our communities, we inflict that loss if we kill ourselves.[22] Suicide is a sort of murder if there are people who love or depend on us in any way, even other citizens. It is interesting that he qualifies this claim by the notion that the criminal suicide does so in a fit of passion. It is not at all clear that he would include a deliberated, premeditated self-killing by someone who believed they were a burden or were already dying.

Aristotle never says whether he would approve of suicide or assisted dying in the case of terminally ill individuals; if he did oppose it, some of us today would want to make the case to him for the right of mortally ill people in full control of their reasoning powers to die painlessly and with dignity. But in other cases, professionals with expertise in suicidal people stress that the impulse is often transitory and therefore unde-liberated. This makes it completely incompatible with the convinced Aristotelian's policy of doing the right thing in order to Live Well. Many people consider suicide when deeply unhappy, especially in the aftermath of a bereavement or a broken relationship. But the Aristotelian will realize that everything changes, and that the future holds potential for happiness, overwhelming the current despair. Abraham Lincoln, who wrestled with depression all his life, stayed alive and achieved his potential, despite several suicidal episodes, by focusing on this certainty of change. In 1862 he wrote these profoundly Aristotelian words to a young woman friend whose father had died:

> It is with deep grief that I learn of the death of your kind and brave father; and, especially, that it is affecting your young heart beyond what is common in such cases. In this sad world of ours, sorrow comes to all; and, to the young, it comes with bitterest agony, because it takes them unawares. The older have learned to ever expect it. I am anxious to afford some alleviation of your present distress. Perfect relief is not possible, except with time. You can not now realise that you will ever feel better. Is not this so? And yet it is a mistake. You are sure to be happy again. To know this, which is certainly true,

will make you somewhat less miserable now. I have had experience enough to know what I say; and you need only to believe
it, to feel better at once. The memory of your dear father,
instead of an agony, will yet be a sad sweet feeling in your
heart, of a purer and holier sort than you have known before.

In the certainty that our emotional state will change, if an Aristotelian
feels suicidal he will, instead, manage to decide to act in ways which
may seem more difficult in the short term.

Change is constant. Throughout his works, Aristotle uses imagery
to illustrate the idea that part of a thing, or even its overall total form,
can change and disappear, while other parts of it can survive. The same
alphabetical letters, for example, if rearranged together in different
ways, he says can compose either a tragedy or a comedy. In nature,
everything ceaselessly and without fail comes into existence and then
passes away, its constituent matter contributing toward the coming to
be of another entity. But Aristotle, importantly, acknowledges the
difference between organic reproduction and the cyclical, elemental
recreation of the water which turns cloud in the air into rain and back
in due course into cloud. Unlike rain and clouds, "men and animals do
not return upon themselves, so that the same creature comes-to-be a
second time." When you are dead you are dead. But even here there is
comfort. It was never inevitable that you should have come into being
just because your father had. You might never have been conceived.
But if you exist, there is one beautiful certainty: your father must have
"come to be" before you. Your father (like your mother) was here, as
part of the constant generational reproduction of the human race. He
was here. He lived. He contributed. That life was lived. Nothing and
nobody can ever take it away.

Finally, we can all take comfort from one of Aristotle's most beautiful sentences. He even proposes that the permanent process of coming

into being which we see in the natural world—in humans, endless reproduction down the generations—is "God's solution to the problem of creating an eternal being." God would have liked the universe to be eternal, and came as near as possible to creating an eternal universe "by making coming-to-be a perpetual process." This lends the entire history of the cosmos, including that of the human race and of each one of us as an individual, an ultimate unity and coherence: "The continuous coming-to-be of coming-to-be is the nearest approach to eternal being."

ACKNOWLEDGMENTS

This book owes a great deal to the patience and sympathetic support of my agents Peter Straus and Melanie Jackson, my expert publishers and editors Ann Godoff, Stuart Williams and Jörg Hengsen and my copy-editor David Milner. Over the years I have learned from conversations with several fine Aristotelians, classicists and philosophers, including Tom Stinton, Gregory Sifakis, Sara Monoson, Christopher Rowe, Malcolm Schofield, Heinz-Günther Nesselrath, Jill Frank, David Blank, Phillip Horky, Richard Kraut, Sol Tor, Carol Atack, Francis O'Rourke, Paul Cartledge and John Tasioulas. But the book could never have been completed without the sympathetic and continuous support of my family—my husband Richard, and daughters Georgia and Sarah Poynder. Sarah intrepidly traveled with me and Leonidas Papadopoulos to visit every place in which Aristotle ever lived; the journey was also kindly assisted by Christina Papageorgiou, Symeon Konstantinidis and John Kittmer.

GLOSSARY

anamnesis	recollection
arete (plural *"aretai"*)	excellence, virtue
autarkeia	self-sufficiency
authekastos	being true to oneself
dianoia	intellectual activity
dynamis	potentiality
endoxa	common beliefs, generally held assumptions
energeia	actualization
enthymeme	proof by reasoning
epieikeia	equity
ethos	character
euboulia	good decision-making
eudaimonia	happiness, the state of mind achieved by practicing virtue ethics
hamartia	mistake, error
hedone	pleasure
hexis	a property or quality
hypokrisis	performance, rhetorical delivery
kakia (plural *"kakiai"*)	faults, vices, bad qualities
megalopsychos	having a great soul, being magnanimous
meson	the mean between extremes
phainomena	empirical observations
phronesis	practical wisdom
physis	nature
polis	city-state
prohairesis	preference, choice
praxis	action, activity
skopos	goal
sophos	wise person, specialist, expert

symboulia	giving and taking advice
telos	objective, purpose, end, ending, death
theoria	theory, coming up with an explanation
to meson	the mean
zoon politikon	an animal who lives in a civic community; a human

FURTHER READING

These recommendations are to be read in addition to those referenced in the Notes.

INTRODUCTION

J. L. Ackrill, *Aristotle the Philosopher* (Oxford: OUP, 1981).
Mortimer I. Adler, *Aristotle for Everyone* (New York: Macmillan, 1978).
Jonathan Barnes, *Coffee with Aristotle* (London: Duncan Baird, 2008).
Joseph Williams Blakesley, *A Life of Aristotle* (London: John W. Parker, 1839).
Sarah Broadie, *Ethics with Aristotle* (New York: OUP, 1993).
Jonathan Haidt, *The Happiness Hypothesis: Putting Ancient Wisdom to the Test of Modern Science* (London: Arrow, 2006).
Terence Irwin, *Aristotle's First Principles* (Oxford: Clarendon Press, 1993).
Burgess Laughlin, *The Aristotle Adventure: A Guide to the Greek, Latin and Arabic Scholars who Transmitted Aristotle's Logic to the Renaissance* (Flagstaff: Albert Hale, 1995).
Carlo Natali, *Aristotle: His Life and School* (Princeton: Princeton University Press, 2013).
Rupert Woodfin and Judy Groves, *Introducing Aristotle: A Graphic Guide* (Cambridge: Icon Books, 2001).

CHAPTER 1: HAPPINESS

J. Ackrill, "Aristotle on Eudaimonia," *Proceedings of the British Academy* (1974), pp. 3–23.
Julia Annas, *The Morality of Happiness* (Oxford: OUP, 1993).
Sissela Bok, *Exploring Happiness: From Aristotle to Brain Science* (New Haven: Yale University Press, 2010).
Anthony Kenny, *Aristotle on the Perfect Life* (Oxford: Clarendon Press, 1995).

Richard Kraut, "Two conceptions of happiness," *Philosophical Review* 88 (1979), pp. 167–97.

G. Richardson Lear, *Happiness and the Highest Good: An Essay on Aristotle's Nicomachean Ehics* (Princeton: Princeton University Press, 2004).

Roger Sullivan, *Morality and the Good Life* (Memphis: Memphis State University Press, 1977).

Nicholas White, *A Brief History of Happiness* (Oxford: Blackwell Publishing, 2006).

CHAPTER 2: POTENTIAL

Jean de Groot, "Dunamis and the Science of Mathematics: Aristotle on Animal Motion," *Journal of the History of Philosophy* 46 (2008), pp. 43–67.

Jill Frank, "Citizens, Slaves, and Foreigners: Aristotle on Human Nature," *American Political Science Review* 98 (2004), pp. 91–103.

Jim Garrison, "Rorty, metaphysics, and the education of human potential," in Michael A. Peters and Paulo Ghiraldelli Jr. (eds.), *Richard Rorty: Education, Philosophy, and Politics* (Lanham: Rowman & Littlefield, 2001), pp. 46–66.

Edith Hall, "'Master of Those Who Know': Aristotle as Role Model for the Twenty-first Century Academician," *European Review* 25 (2017), pp. 3–19.

Elizabeth Harman, "The potentiality problem," *Philosophical Studies* 114 (2003), pp. 173–98.

Michael Jackson, "Designed by theorists: Aristotle on utopia," *Utopian Studies* 12 (2001), pp. 1–12.

Lynn M. Morgan, "The potentiality principle from Aristotle to Abortion," *Current Anthropology* 54 (2013), pp. 15–25.

Martin E. P. Seligman, *The Optimistic Child*, 2nd edition (Boston & New York: Houghton Mifflin, 2007).

Charlotte Witt, "Hylomorphism in Aristotle," *Journal of Philosophy* 84 (1987), pp. 673–9.

CHAPTER 3: DECISIONS

Robert Audi, *Practical Reasoning and Ethical Decision* (London: Routledge, 2006).

Agnes Callard, "Aristotle on Deliberation," in Ruth Chang and Kurt Sylvan (eds.), *The Routledge Handbook of Practical Reason* (London: Routledge, 2017).

Charles Chamberlain, "The Meaning of Prohairesis in Aristotle's Ethics," *Transactions & Proceedings of the American Philological Association* 114 (1984), pp. 147–57.

Norman O. Dahl, *Practical Reason, Aristotle, and Weakness of the Will* (Minneapolis: University of Minnesota Press, 1984).

D. L. Martinson, "Ethical decision-making in Public Relations: What would Aristotle say?," *Public Relations Quarterly* 45 (2000), pp. 18–21.

J. McDowell, "Deliberation and Moral Development in Aristotle's *Ethics*," in J. McDowell, S. P. Engstrom and J. Whiting (eds.), *Aristotle, Kant, and the Stoics: Rethinking Happiness and Duty* (Pittsburgh & Cambridge: CUP, 1996), pp. 19–35.

Monica Mueller, *Contrary to Thoughtlessness: Rethinking Practical Wisdom* (Lanham: Lexington Books, 2013).

C. Provis, "Virtuous decision-making for Business Ethics," *Journal of Business Ethics* 91 (2010), pp. 3–16.

Heda Segvic, "Deliberation and choice in Aristotle," in Myles Burnyeat (ed.) with an introduction by Charles Brittain, *From Protagoras to Aristotle: Essays in Ancient Moral Philosophy* (Princeton & Oxford: Princeton University Press, 2009).

CHAPTER 4: COMMUNICATION

Janet M. Atwill, *Rhetoric Reclaimed: Aristotle and the Liberal Arts Tradition* (Ithaca & London: Cornell University Press, 1998).

Paul D. Brandes, *A History of Aristotle's Rhetoric* (London: Scarecrow, 1989).

Jamie Dow, *Passions and Persuasion in Aristotle's Rhetoric* (Oxford: OUP, 2015).

Richard Leo Enos and Lois Peters Agnew (eds.), *Landmark Essays on Aristotelian Rhetoric* (London: Lawrence Erlbaum Associates, 1998).

Eugene Garver, *Aristotle's Rhetoric: An Art of Character* (Chicago & London: University of Chicago Press, 1994).

Ekaterina Haskins, "On the term 'Dunamis' in Aristotle's definition of Rhetoric," *Philosophy and Rhetoric* 46 (2013), pp. 234–40.

Amélie Oksenberg Rorty (ed.), *Essays on Aristotle's Rhetoric* (Berkeley & London: University of California Press, 1996).

Sara Rubinelli, *Ars Topica: The Classical Technique of Constructing Arguments from Aristotle to Cicero*, with an Introduction by David S. Levene (Dordrecht: Springer, 2009).

CHAPTER 5: SELF-KNOWLEDGE

Susan K. Allard-Nelson, *An Aristotelian Approach to Ethical Theory* (Lewiston & Lampeter: Edwin Mellen Press, 2004).

Timothy Chappell (ed.), *Values and Virtues: Aristotelianism in Contemporary Ethics* (Oxford: Clarendon Press, 2006).

Howard J. Curzer, *Aristotle and the Virtues* (Oxford: OUP, 2012).

Marguerite Deslauriers, "How to distinguish Aristotle's virtues," *Phronesis* 47 (2002), pp. 101–26.

Edwin M. Hartman, *Virtue in Business: Conversations with Aristotle* (Cambridge: CUP, 2013).

D. S. Hutchinson, *The Virtues of Aristotle* (London: Routledge, 2016).

Richard Kraut, *Aristotle on the Human Good* (Princeton: Princeton University Press, 1989).

Martha Nussbaum, *The Fragility of Goodness* (Cambridge: CUP, 1986).

Glen Pettigrove, "Ambitions," *Ethical Theory and Moral Practice* 10 (2007), pp. 53–68.

J. Urmson, "Aristotle's Doctrine of the Mean," *American Philosophical Quarterly* 10 (1973), pp. 223–30.

CHAPTER 6: INTENTIONS

Michael Bratman, *Intentions, Plans, and Practical Reason* (Cambridge, Mass.: Harvard University Press, 1987).

P. Crivelli, *Aristotle on Truth* (Cambridge: CUP, 2004).

Javier Echeñique, *Aristotle's Ethics and Moral Responsibility* (Cambridge: CUP, 2012).

S. Dennis Ford, *Sins of Omission: A Primer on Moral Indifference* (Minneapolis: Fortress Press, 1990).

Alfredo Marcos, *Postmodern Aristotle*, with a foreword by Geoffrey Lloyd (Newcastle upon Tyne: Cambridge Scholars, 2012).

Martha C. Nussbaum, "Equity and Mercy," *Philosophy and Public Affairs* 83 (1993), pp. 83–125.

Roger A. Shiner, "Aristotle's theory of equity," in S. Panagiotou (ed.), *Justice, Law and Method in Plato and Aristotle* (Edmonton: Academic Printing and Publishing, 1987).

John Tasioulas, "The paradox of equity," *Cambridge Law Journal* 55 (1996), pp. 456–69.

CHAPTER 7: LOVE

E. Belfiore, *"Family friendship in Aristotle's Ethics,"* *Ancient Philosophy* 21 (2001), pp. 113–32.

Robert J. Fitterer, *Love and Objectivity in Virtue Ethics* (Toronto & London: University of Toronto Press, 2008).

Barbro Fröding and Martin Peterson, "Why virtual friendship is no genuine friendship," *Ethics and Information Technology* 14 (2012), pp. 201–7.

Todd L. Goodsell and Jason B. Whiting, *"An Aristotelian theory of family,"* *Journal of Family Theory & Review* 8 (2016), pp. 484–502.

R. Hursthouse, "Aristotle for women who love too much," *Ethics: An International Journal of Social, Political, and Legal Philosophy* 117 (2007), pp. 327–34.

Juha Sihvola, "Aristotle on sex and love," in Martha C. Nussbaum and Juha Sihvola (eds.), *Sleep of Reason: Erotic Experience and Sexual Ethics in Ancient Greece and Rome* (Chicago & London: University of Chicago Press, 2002).

Lorraine Smith Pangle, *Aristotle and the Philosophy of Friendship* (Cambridge: CUP, 2003).

S. Vallor, "Flourishing on Facebook: virtue friendship & new social media," *Ethics and Information Technology* 14 (2012), pp. 185–99.

CHAPTER 8: COMMUNITY

Susan D. Collins, *Aristotle and the Rediscovery of Citizenship* (Cambridge: CUP, 2006).

Jill Frank, *A Democracy of Distinction: Aristotle and the Work of Politics* (Chicago: Chicago University Press, 2005).

Richard Kraut, *Aristotle: Political Philosophy* (Oxford: OUP, 2002).

Armand Marie Leroi, *The Lagoon: How Aristotle Invented Science* (London & New York: Bloomsbury, 2014).

David Roochnik, *Retrieving Aristotle in an Age of Crisis* (Albany: SUNY Press, 2013).

Skip Worden, "Aristotle's natural wealth: the role of limitation in thwarting misordered concupiscence," *Journal of Business Ethics* 84 (2009), pp. 209–19.

CHAPTER 9: LEISURE

Victor Castellani, "Drama and Aristotle," in James Redmond (ed.), *Drama and Philosophy* (Cambridge: CUP, 1990), pp. 21–36.

Damian Cox and Michael P. Levine, *Thinking through Film: Doing Philosophy, Watching Movies* (Chichester: Wiley-Blackwell, 2012).

Edith Hall, "Aristotle's theory of katharsis in its historical and social contexts," in Erika Fischer-Lichte and Benjamin Wihstutz (eds.), *Transformative Aesthetics* (London: Routledge, 2017), pp. 26–47.

Paul W. Kahn, *Finding Ourselves at the Movies* (New York: Columbia University Press, 2013).

Kostas Kalimtzis, *An Inquiry into the Philosophical Concept of Scholê: Leisure as a Political End* (London & New York: Bloomsbury Academic, 2017).

242

Joseph Owens, "Aristotle on Leisure," *Canadian Journal of Philosophy* 11 (1981), pp. 713–23.

J. Pieper, *Leisure, the Basis of Culture* (New York: Random House, 1963).

F. E. Solmsen, "Leisure and Play in Aristotle's Ideal State," *Rheinisches Museum für Philologie* 107 (1964), pp. 193–220.

Wanda Teays, *Seeing the Light: Exploring Ethics through Movies* (Malden, Mass.: Wiley-Blackwell, 2012).

CHAPTER 10: MORTALITY

Anton-Hermann Chroust, "*Eudemus* or On the Soul: A Lost Dialogue of Aristotle on the Immortality of the Soul," *Mnemosyne* 19 (1966), pp. 17–30.

Christopher Deacy, *Screening the Afterlife: Theology, Eschatology, and Film* (New York: Routledge, 2012).

Brian Donohue, "God and Aristotelian Ethics," *Quaestiones Disputatae* 5 (2014), pp. 65–77.

John E. Hare, *God and Morality: A Philosophical History* (Oxford: Blackwell, 2007).

Gareth B. Matthews, "Revivifying Aristotle on life," in Richard Feldman, Kris McDaniel, Jason Reibley and Michael Zimmerman (eds.), *The Good, the Right, Life and Death: Essays in Honor of Fred Feldman* (Aldershot: Ashgate, 2006).

Martha C. Nussbaum, "Aristotle on human nature and the foundations of Ethics," in J. E. J. Altham and Ross Harrison (eds.), *World, Mind, and Ethics: Essays on the Ethical Philosophy of Bernard Williams* (Cambridge: CUP, 1995), pp. 86–131.

Amélie Oksenberg Rorty, "Fearing Death," *Philosophy* 58, no. 224 (1983), pp. 175–88.

Kurt Pritzl, "Aristotle and Happiness after Death: *Nicomachean Ethics* 1. 10–11," Classical Philology 78 (1983), pp. 101–11.

Richard Sorabji, *Aristotle on Memory*, 2nd edition (London: Duckworth, 2004).

NOTES

1. Karen Horney, *Neurosis and Growth* (New York and London: W. W. Norton, 1991); Viktor Frankl, *Man's Search for Meaning* (New York: Washington Square Press, 1984); Mihaly Csikszentmihalyi, *Flow* (New York: Harper & Row, 1992); Martin E. P. Seligman, *Authentic Happiness* (London: Nicholas Brealey Publishing, 2003).
2. The *Sarvasiddhanta Samgraha*, verses 9–12.
3. Craig K. Ihara, "Why be virtuous," in A. W. H. Adkins, Joan Kalk Lawrence and Craig K. Ihara (eds.), *Human Virtue and Human Excellence* (New York: Peter Lang, 1991), pp. 237–68; Thomas Hill Green, *Prolegomena to Ethics* (1883).
4. Edith Hall, "Citizens but Second-Class: Women in Aristotle's Politics," in C. Cuttica and G. Mahlberg (eds.), *Patriarchal Moments* (London: Bloomsbury, 2015), Ch. 3.
5. See the short film at https://www.youtube.com/watch?v=-mo YjtCmV8Q
6. Robert J. Anderson, "Purpose and happiness in Aristotle: An Introduction," in R. Thomas Simone and Richard I. Sugarman (eds.), *Reclaiming the Humanities: The Roots of Self-Knowledge in the Greek and Biblical Worlds* (Lanham & London: University Press of America), pp. 113–30, at p. 113.
7. Bronnie Ware, *The Top Five Regrets of the Dying: A Life Transformed by the Dearly Departing* (London: Hay House, 2012).
8. A video of this sermon is available for viewing in the Southern Christian Leadership Conference Records held in the Emory University Archives (Program 7652): see http://findingaids.library.emory.edu/documents /sclc1083/series19/subseries19.1/
9. William D. Leahy, *I Was There* (New York: Whittlesey House, 1950), p. 441.
10. See R. Ulanowicz, "Aristotelian causalities in ecosystem development," *Oikos* 57 (1990), pp. 42–8; Laura Westra, "Aristotelian roots of ecology:

causality, complex systems theory, and integrity," in Laura Westra and Thomas M. Robinson (eds.), *The Greeks and the Environment* (Lanham: Rowman & Littlefield, 1997), pp. 83–98, and in the same volume, C. W. DeMarco, "The greening of Aristotle," pp. 99–119.

11. Richard Shearman, "Self-Love and the Virtue of Species Preservation in Aristotle," in Westra and Robinson (eds.), pp. 121–32. And especially Mohan Matthen, "The organic unity of Aristotle's world," in the same volume, pp. 133–48.

12. Özgüç Orhan, "Aristotle: Phusis, Praxis, and the Good," in Peter F. Cannavò and Joseph H. Lane Jr. (eds.), *Engaging Nature and the Political Theory Canon* (Cambridge, Mass. & London: MIT Press, 2014), pp. 45–63.

13. Iris Murdoch, *The Sovereignty of Good* (London: Routledge & Kegan Paul, 1970).

14. Thomas Nagel, *Mortal Questions* (Cambridge: CUP, 1979), pp. 1–10.

15. Elias Canetti, *The Human Province*, translated by Joachim Neugroschel (New York: Seabury Press, 1978), pp. 127–8, 141–2.

16. Miguel de Unamuno y Jugo, *The Tragic Sense of Life in Men and in Peoples*, translated by J. E. Crawford Flitch (London: Macmillan, 1921), p. 263.

17. Blaise Pascal, *Thoughts*, translated by W. F. Trotter (London: Dent, 1908), p. 199.

18. *The Complete Works of Montaigne*, translated by Donald M. Frame (Stanford: Stanford University Press, 1957), 1.20 and 3.13.

19. Jeff Malpas, "Death and the unity of a life," in Jeff Malpas and Robert C. Solomon (eds.), *Death and Philosophy* (London & New York: Routledge, 1998), pp. 120–34.

20. Ivan Soll, "On the purported insignificance of death," in Malpas and Solomon (eds.), pp. 22–38, at p. 37.

21. Kathleen Higgins, "Death and the skeleton," in Malpas and Solomon (eds.), p. 43.

22. David Novak, *Suicide and Morality* (New York: Scholars Studies Press, 1975), pp. 59–60.

INDEX

All works are by Aristotle ("A"), unless otherwise stated.